Traversing Digital Babel

Information Policy Series
Edited by Sandra Braman and Paul Jaeger

The Information Policy Series publishes research on and analysis of significant problems in the field of information policy, including decisions and practices that enable or constrain information, communication, and culture irrespective of the legal siloes in which they have traditionally been located as well as state-law-society interactions. Defining information policy as all laws, regulations, and decision-making principles that affect any form of information creation, processing, flows, and use, the series includes attention to the formal decisions, decision-making processes, and entities of government; the formal and informal decisions, decision-making processes, and entities of private and public sector agents capable of constitutive effects on the nature of society; and the cultural habits and predispositions of governmentality that support and sustain government and governance. The parametric functions of information policy at the boundaries of social, informational, and technological systems are of global importance because they provide the context for all communications, interactions, and social processes.

Virtual Economies: Design and Analysis, Vili Lehdonvirta and Edward Castronova

Traversing Digital Babel: Information, E-Government, and Exchange, Alon Peled

Traversing Digital Babel

Information, E-Government, and Exchange

Alon Peled

The MIT Press
Cambridge, Massachusetts
London, England

MIT Press books may be purchased at special quantity discounts for business or sales promotional use. For information, please email special_sales@mitpress.mit.edu.

This book was set in Stone Sans Std and Stone Serif Std by Toppan Best-set Premedia Limited, Hong Kong. Printed and bound in the United States of America.

Library of Congress Cataloging-in-Publication Data

Peled, Alon, 1962–
Traversing digital Babel : information, e-government, and exchange / Alon Peled.
    pages   cm.—(Information policy series)
Includes bibliographical references and index.
ISBN 978-0-262-02787-8
1. Government information.   2. Electronic government information.
3. Interagency coordination.   4. Intergovernmental cooperation.   5. Government information–Economic aspects.   6. Information policy.   I. Title.
    ZA5049.P45   2014
    025.04—dc23
                        2014003836

10 9 8 7 6 5 4 3 2 1

To my children
Anat, Eytan, Shira, and Matan
You light up my life
with love and joy

Contents

Acknowledgments   ix

Series Editor's Introduction   xi

Introduction: The Archaeological and Electronic Mountains   1

1   The Information Sharing Crisis that Does Not Go Away   13

2   Coerce, Consent, and Coax: Existing Information Sharing Approaches   39

3   Why Open Data Finds Agencies' Doors Closed   57

4   How Data Trade Opens Agencies' Closed Doors   75

5   Public Sector Data as a Contested Commodity   105

6   The Public Sector Information Exchange (PSIE)   125

7   Four PSIE Challenges   161

8   A Political Strategy to Promote PSIE   179

Appendix: Abbreviations   193

Notes   199

References   201

Index   249

Acknowledgments

Between 1998 and 2001, I lived next to Tel Gezer, a man-made mountain in central Israel, where twenty-eight civilizations are buried one beneath the other. Inspired by Gezer, I published an article comparing it to the computer system of the U.S. Internal Revenue Service (IRS). This amusing comparison was well received but I quickly became disappointed with my own work. I believe that a social scientist must not only explain the world but also try to improve it a little. My article did not do this—it suggested that government computers are too complex to share information. I spent the next decade thinking about how to convince government officials to improve such sharing. Consequently, this book explains why government officials fail to share information, and also proposes a new path to resolving this problem.

The Israel Science Foundation and the Hebrew University of Jerusalem supported this research. I am grateful to Professor Sandra Braman who nudged me to pursue wiser intellectual directions. I am indebted to Stuart Robbins whose wise comments guided me to improve the final version of the book. I am grateful to Michael Ziv Kenet, Jessica Genauer, Adam Hoffman, Alexander Troitsky, and Ofer Pogorelsky, my research assistants, whose help was invaluable. My parents, Arye and Sylvia, and my brother, Amir, provided me with unconditional love and support. My wife, Alisa, inspires me daily with her devotion to her students. Our four children, Anat, Eytan, Shira, and Matan, are the reason that I get up every morning and go to sleep every night with a smile on my face.

Alon Peled, Jerusalem, 2014

Series Editor's Introduction

Sandra Braman

It may seem on the surface as if the first two books in the Information Policy Series are as far apart from each other as possible. Vili Lehdonvirta and Edward Castronova's *Virtual Economies*, about how to design such economies, lies on the governance side of the domain marked by the series description and will have long-term effects on governmentality. Alon Peled's *Traversing Digital Babel*, with its proposal for a market-based solution to inter-agency information flow problems, is on the government side and addresses a classical information policy issue.

Both books, though, are taking part in the same conversation about macro-level developments affecting relationships among the state, society, and the law. These are unfolding during a period in which technological innovation—and thus changes in the kinds of information we can create and the ways in which we can use them—is a significant driving force. This conversation is about how informational power interacts with other forms of power, and how it can be used most effectively in shaping society today. It is about the relative value of transactional—or mathematical— uncertainties as a tool of governance in addition to laws and interpretation of laws, administrative rules, and implementation programs. And it is about the extent to which, and the dimensions along which, degrees of freedom will or could expand. All of these subjects of the conversation in which these two books are taking part affect, and are very affected by, information policy.

Peled's proposal to create a market in inter-agency information flows breaks ground in the matter of organizational form. In the context of government, this means state-society relations, those between the public and private sectors, and between the state and citizens. Ronald Coase's 1937 insight that a key reason for having organizations at all is that they so

Series Editor's Introduction

significantly reduce transaction costs is being rethought by many as it applies in a world increasingly populated by networked organizations. One popular path has gone in the direction of reducing the role of commoditization, in essence shrinking the economy, by creating an information commons.

Peled's suggestion goes in the opposite direction along the dimension of commoditization. His proposal to create a market *inside* of the large, multi-unit organizations of national governments intensifies treatment of information as a commodity, arguing from a largely implicit assumption that doing so best serves constitutional goals. Markets in government information in a world so politically, logistically, environmentally, and, increasingly, legally interdependent across levels of the legal structure as well as across national borders would affect relations between citizens and states in ways of profound importance to the nature of the informational state as well as to relations of states with each other, with non-state actors, and with the international system.

For these reasons and others, the ideas presented in this book are likely to trigger critique, lively debate, and experimentation. Bitcoin is the most recent of the adventures that have made abundantly clear that what happens in virtual economies doesn't stay in virtual economies. When it comes to *Traversing Digital Babel*, Eli Noam's point offered in another context applies: "Ideas matter."

Introduction: The Archaeological and Electronic Mountains

Like an archeological *tel* (an ancient man-made mountain that contains multiple civilizations buried one beneath the other), public sector agencies stack computer technologies on top of older technologies, creating a man-made electronic mountain. The cost of connecting these computer systems is exorbitant. They consist of arcane programming languages and closed mainframe designs and lack interfaces to interact with other systems.

The U.S. Internal Revenue Service (IRS) offers a prime example of an electronic mountain. Since the 1954 overhaul of the U.S. Internal Revenue Code, Congress has passed 238 additional tax laws. Because tax laws are not retroactive, IRS programmers have created and continue to maintain multiple annual tax "versions" of the entire Internal Revenue Code so that auditors can assess historical tax returns. Each annual version of this Code requires an independent layer of software that is not written to communicate with other tax versions (Davis 1997). Moreover, tax laws often have an effective duration after which they expire. So, each annual software layer inside the IRS electronic mountain must know which information elements to "borrow" from other historical layers and how to correctly use the borrowed information.

To run its most critical daily routines, the IRS relies today on more than 50 million lines of COBOL (COmmon Business Oriented Language) programming code. COBOL is a business application programming language that was introduced in the 1960s. Today, this language is viewed as obsolete, making it difficult to implement new business processes and new service delivery models, such as online, real-time processing. However, to this day, most agencies' computer systems rely on tens of millions of lines of COBOL to execute their daily routines (Greenberg 2012b; Koman 2007; Serbu 2012). The U.S. Social Security Administration (SSA) alone relies on software programs that collectively contain 60 million COBOL lines (U.S. Government Accountability Office 2012n; hereinafter cited as GAO). Changing a single data element buried inside an electronic mountain can require great expense. The U.S. Centers for Medicare & Medicaid Services (CMS) estimates that the replacement of the Social Security Number (SSN) data element on the Medicare cards of 48 million Americans with a different number (to reduce Medicare-related fraud) will cost $800 million (GAO 2012c). This cost might double if we factor in correctly additional quality assurance (QA), documentation, and rewrites of secondary modules that must accompany such a change.

History and technology have shaped the internal structure of both archeological tels and public agency electronic mountains. These man-made mountains contain layers of civilizations embedded in, respectively, either clay or computer software and organized in a genealogical vertical order. At the IRS, for example, generations of government officers and information technology (IT) experts borrowed computer components such as databases from their ancestors and added new software to meet new challenges. At both the IRS and in the tel each civilization has extended the life of the strata it is founded on by borrowing artifacts such as walls or modules, programs, and scripts from a previous civilization. Shards of ancient pottery or old computer manuals might be reused to inform later generations, evidence of each civilization's problem-solving methods over time, as illustrated by figure I.1 below.

The seemingly irreconcilable disparity between agencies' distinct and noncommunicative electronic mountains instills fatalism as government officers are taught that nothing they do can change this reality. So, how can we overcome agencies' perverse incentives to improve information sharing? Surprisingly, we find guidance in the tale of Frederick Jones Bliss, the first Holy Land explorer to excavate Tel Gezer, a man-made mountain in central Israel of ancient civilizations layered one on top of the other.

A Tale of a Tel: How Bliss Unlocked the Secrets of the Man-Made Mountain

Throughout the nineteenth century, mistrustful foreign and local populations fought over Holy Land relics. The first Protestant Holy Land explorer was beaten to death en route from Jerusalem to Beirut. Puritans

Tel Gezer

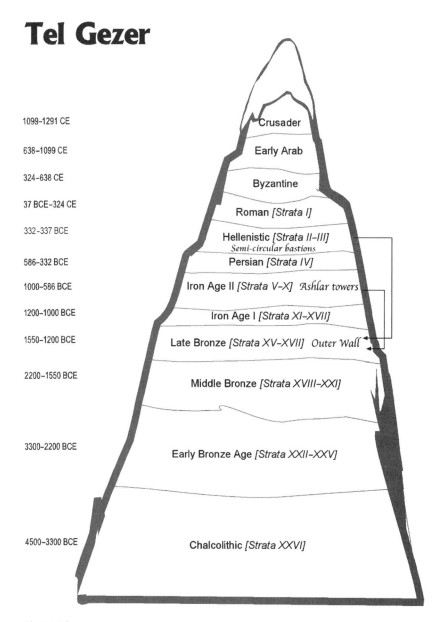

1099–1291 CE	Crusader
638–1099 CE	Early Arab
324–638 CE	Byzantine
37 BCE–324 CE	Roman *[Strata I]*
332–337 BCE	Hellenistic *[Strata II–III]* *Semi-circular bastions*
586–332 BCE	Persian *[Strata IV]*
1000–586 BCE	Iron Age II *[Strata V–X]* *Ashlar towers*
1200–1000 BCE	Iron Age I *[Strata XI–XVII]*
1550–1200 BCE	Late Bronze *[Strata XV–XVII]* *Outer Wall*
2200–1550 BCE	Middle Bronze *[Strata XVIII–XXI]*
3300–2200 BCE	Early Bronze Age *[Strata XXII–XXV]*
4500–3300 BCE	Chalcolithic *[Strata XXVI]*

Figure I.1
Tel Gezer compared to the U.S. Internal Revenue Service (IRS) computer system.
Sources: Dever 1967, Dever 1971, Dever 1973, IRS 2014, Peled 2007, Stern, Lewinson-Gilboa, and Aviram 1992.

Internal Revenue Service

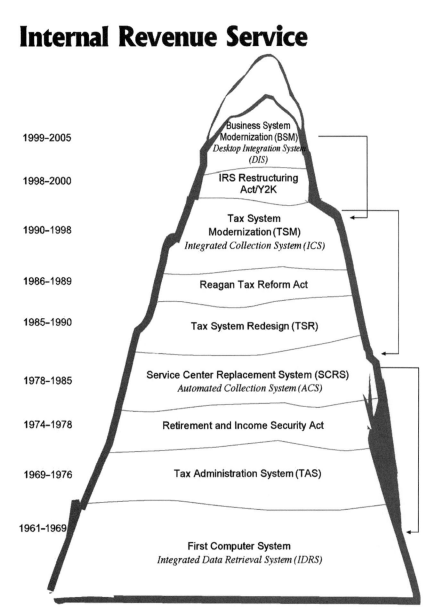

1999–2005	Business System Modernization (BSM) *Desktop Integration System (DIS)*
1998–2000	IRS Restructuring Act/Y2K
1990–1998	Tax System Modernization (TSM) *Integrated Collection System (ICS)*
1986–1989	Reagan Tax Reform Act
1985–1990	Tax System Redesign (TSR)
1978–1985	Service Center Replacement System (SCRS) *Automated Collection System (ACS)*
1974–1978	Retirement and Income Security Act
1969–1976	Tax Administration System (TAS)
1961–1969	First Computer System *Integrated Data Retrieval System (IDRS)*

Figure I.1
(*continued*)

and Unitarians in Boston and Greek and Catholic Priests in Bethlehem exchanged heated words and even shed blood in fierce competition over relics. In Safed (1875), a sheikh and his people beat British Royal Engineers and destroyed their camp. In the 1870s, Germans, the French, the British, and Ottomans fought over the priceless Moabite Stone. A local Bedouin tribe shattered the stone, reducing it to black gravel, to find the "secret value" inside (Silberman 1982).

The first excavators displayed arrogance and indifference that exacerbated mistrust and hostility from local peoples. The Jewish community of Jerusalem raged after de Saulcy (1863–1864) returned to France with sarcophagus fragments taken from the tombs of kings. Muslim worshipers in the Haram al-Sharif (Temple Mount) hurled stones on Charles Warren (who excavated Jerusalem between 1867 and 1870) and his workers because of their sledgehammers' noise.

Mistrust spread from the Levant to Europe. In 1864, French and British explorers accused each other of plagiarism. Between 1883 and 1885, a humiliated Prussian Parliament angrily debated who was responsible for appropriating seventy thousand thalers to purchase fake "Moabite pottery" for the Imperial Museum. In the same period, the British queen almost spent one million pounds to purchase the "World's Oldest Bible." The merchant trying to sell her the bible committed suicide after a French explorer declared that the fifteen sheepskin parchment strips were fake. In retrospect, however, it appears that these strips were authentic (Silberman 1982, 131–146).

In 1894, the British Palestine Exploration Fund (PEF) appointed Frederick Jones Bliss as its Chief Holy Land Excavator. Bliss was a sickly, inexperienced, and unemployed American who received the post because no one else wanted it. But Bliss was also an enthusiastic, hardworking, politically astute, humble, and self-taught archeologist. A fluent Arabic speaker, Bliss developed close friendships with his Arab foremen and displayed interest and compassion toward his local workers. He was the first explorer to hire women, usually the wives of his employees. During Ramadan, he paid his female workers yet allowed them to go home early to prepare for the holiday.

Bliss's kindness and attention to detail paid off. Local workers taught him that biblical names were still used by locals to measure distance; Bliss then correctly deduced the distance of biblical terms such as the "Hebron measure." Bliss's careful observation of his workers helped him to understand how their ancient ancestors had lived in the same location. He quickly understood water's critical importance to the region and correctly identified the direction of the ancient Jerusalem walls by tracking the city's old water system. By observing how his employees moved between villages, Bliss became the first explorer to understand the importance of the connections between tels. He therefore simultaneously dug five tels in a ten-mile area in the Southern Shephelah (including Tel Gezer.) For Bliss, the present provided clues to understanding the past.

Bliss also enjoyed a beneficial relationship with the Ottoman authorities. As an American born in Lebanon he won Ottoman officials' trust. On his own time, Bliss helped the authorities supervise the Mount of Olives clearance of Byzantine remains, and traveled to inspect the antiquities of Moab on their behalf. Grateful, they granted him permission to continue digging even when relations with Britain were strained. On one occasion, Bliss helped the Ottomans against the wishes of his employers. Ottoman officials sought to stem illegal trafficking in ancient objects by displaying them in a Jerusalem museum. Bliss surrendered 465 objects to the Ottomans and helped to display them. He explained to his British employers that it was wise to cooperate to "keep the friendship with the Turks and do nothing to shake their confidence" (Hallote 2006, 145).

Bliss's actions nurtured new trust-based relationships. Western explorers, Ottoman officials, and local workers began to share information. Bliss converted this information into scientific knowledge. He is considered the father of biblical archeology because he pieced together information gathered from people and from mute objects to create the first scientific archeological accounts. He is also remembered for extending the Petrie system in order to use ceramics to correctly date civilizations.

Regrettably, Bliss's tale ends grimly. In 1900, the PEF decided to terminate his appointment. PEF officials sought a more aggressive explorer who would fill the PEF's London coffers with shiny biblical objects to attract donors. Unfortunately for Tel Gezer and for biblical archeology, the PEF found exactly such a man to replace Bliss. Born in Dublin in 1870, Robert Alexander Stewart Macalister was a brilliant man with an impeccable resume. Whereas Bliss was a patient, humble, and cautious explorer, Macalister was impatient, arrogant, and careless. For his first Holy Land digging project he selected the large Tel Gezer site and excavated it aggressively between 1902 and 1909. His laborers toiled year-round from sunrise to sunset but Macalister complained that they were dishonest, lazy, and filthy. On one occasion, the great 1902 cholera plague killed many of his employees from the nearby Abu-Shusheh village. Macalister complained that the rapidly expanding village cemetery threatened to consume some of his digging area (Dever 1998). His Tel Gezer project bankrupted his employer, the PEF (Moscrop 2000).

Macalister had no patience for Bliss's slow scientific digging methods. He dug deep trenches and mixed the debris of civilizations (Thomas 1984), preventing future archeologists from reconstructing his work (Macalister 1912). In the mid-1960s, William Dever began to re-excavate Tel Gezer. Dever was furious to uncover the destroyed site. In 1967, he lamented that Macalister tore rich material out of historical context and published it in a way that made it useless for historical reconstruction (Dever 1967).

The tale of Bliss and Macalister contains the vision, goals, and key lessons of this book. It is a tale about how small incentives such as employment for an additional household member, paid leave to prepare for a religious holiday meal, and pro bono work to assist the Ottoman authorities can have a big impact. Bliss's humble and accommodating nature together with these incentives generated trust and nudged formerly bitter rivals to talk to each other and share information. The same logic applies to allegedly incompatible agency computer systems. If people across agencies start cooperating with each other, their systems might begin exchanging data (Robbins 2006, 2).

The Bliss and Tel Gezer story is about creating an ecosystem where living and mute objects (people and artifacts) are partnered to accomplish great things. It is a tale of humble, observant, and innovative individuals like Bliss who use the present as a clue to understand the decisions and actions of past generations, and the limitations they impose on present generations. Such individuals can employ these insights to design more robust and flexible systems on the foundations of previous systems. Regrettably, it is also a tale about how fragile these rare ecosystems are and how easy it is to destroy them.

The Book's Vision, Goals, and Organization

Throughout history, traders have searched for "royal merchandise"—a product that is abundant in one place and in demand in another. Markets and fairs evolved around trading such royal merchandise. In the process new bonds of collaboration developed among traders. This book argues that, today, information is a royal merchandise whose exchange can lead to the development of similar bonds of trust and collaboration among officials in large, complex, and multilayered governments.

Yet government officials are reluctant to share information. The 9/11 investigation committee concluded that federal agencies' inability to share information was the U.S. government's greatest failure before the terror attacks (GAO 2006a). Similarly, scholars defined the lack of information sharing among U.S. federal agencies before Hurricane Katrina (August 29, 2005) and in its aftermath as an example of an "appalling lack of coordination and stunning lack of inter-organizational goodwill" (Kapucu and Van Wart 2008, 733).

Information sharing failure haunts every government. Why do government agencies fail to share information with each other and what can be done to encourage agencies to improve information sharing? The book explains that information serves agencies: they use it to convince legislators to grant additional resources, to fortify their autonomy, and to increase their reputation as savvy organizations. Inadvertently, legislatures prompt agencies to isolate information assets from each other. New legislation often compels agencies to create new, autonomous information systems. Likewise, IT vendors hired by government to build information systems rarely advise officials to connect new information systems with older ones; these vendors gain profit from separately maintaining old systems and building new ones. So, over time, it is increasingly difficult for agencies' separate computer systems to communicate with each other.

However, agencies are complex. At times they battle for turf for the purpose of securing appropriations. At other times, they act to serve the common good. On other occasions, agencies behave as capitalists seeking to profit from their data. This book purposefully exploits the latter behavior to improve information sharing. The proposed framework provides incentives to agencies that successfully exchange information assets with other agencies. The proposal is to create an internal Public Sector Information Exchange (PSIE) through which agencies will trade information. PSIE will help each agency to discover useful information held by other agencies. This will encourage agencies to develop high-quality and accessible information assets in order to exchange them with other agencies.

Today, agencies spend millions on business intelligence (BI) technologies to identify information gems buried in their electronic mountains. Imagine a universe where governmental data moves freely across agency boundaries. Imagine a universe in which agencies willingly expose their data so other agencies can access it and link it to their own data. In this universe, agencies will harness BI techniques to detect interesting relationships between information that they own and data that they purchased from other agencies. Agencies could then use information more effectively to make better decisions, better prioritize governmental work, and provide improved service to citizens.

In this imaginary universe, agencies will discover that the secondary use of their data by other agencies becomes a new incidental and flexible source of income. Eager to exploit and increase this type of income, agencies might even invest to make it easier for outsiders to interact with their information assets. A new knowledge ecosystem will then be unleashed within government. This new ecosystem will contribute greatly to revitalizing the economy. This book argues that the most effective way to use public sector information to increase economic growth must begin inside government by improving information sharing among agencies.

The book employs multiple research techniques including the analysis of reports on information sharing failures, information sharing debates, and information sharing programs in the public sectors of the United States, Great Britain, Finland, Canada, Brazil, Australia, New Zealand, and the European Union (EU). The most detailed descriptions of information sharing failures are found in the reports of the U.S. Government Accountability Office (GAO) and the U.S. Office of Management and Budget (OMB). The book draws extensively on these reports. Countries besides the United States also suffer from costly governmental information sharing failures; yet, none of these countries has a governmental auditor mechanism such as the GAO that is permitted by law to penetrate deeply into the details of these failures. Some of the more innovative information sharing solutions are found in the public sectors of Australia, the Netherlands, and Iceland. The book uses interviews and correspondence with senior public sector officials in a dozen countries, the study of governmental audit data, longitudinal statistical analysis, analysis of Memorandum of Understanding (MoU) agreements signed among U.S. agencies, and one participatory observation study. The book consults diverse literary sources including:

historical reports on contested commodity exchanges and the first medieval exchanges in Europe, governmental investigative reports, legislative hearings, information sharing patent applications, and secondary scholarly and media reports.

The book also addresses the topic of sharing sensitive but nonclassified national security information. However, it does not address the topic of integrating and sharing classified intelligence sources. Heightened secrecy, compartmentalization, and control concerns dominate this domain (Roberts 2004, 2012). Therefore the book proposes to introduce novel information trading ideas in less secretive domains such as disaster relief, the environment, and economic growth. Readers are encouraged to consult the glossary of abbreviations in the appendix.

Chapter 1 describes public sector information sharing failures in the United States and worldwide and asks: why do agencies share information so poorly? The term *agencies* in this book refers to all public sector organizations. Chapter 2 describes three approaches (coerce, consent, and coax) that have attempted to address this question. It argues that scholars oscillate between pessimistic-descriptive narratives of information sharing failures and naïvely positive-prescriptive suggestions of how to fix these failures. Learning from experience is the only solution for such oscillations. Therefore, chapter 2 finds some hope in scholarship that explains how incentives sometimes improve information sharing based on observations of concrete data exchange experiments in the public sector.

Chapter 3 penetrates deeper into the root cause of the information sharing failure by examining the U.S. open data (OD) program. The OD approach currently enjoys extensive support among politicians, scholars, and laypeople alike. The chapter demonstrates that there is a significant gap between OD rhetoric and the concrete and empirical results of this program worldwide. Chapter 3 argues that most agencies have learned to appear as if they are cooperating with the OD program while in fact reducing their involvement to the bare minimum. Chapter 4 explains that agencies work hard to develop information assets. Therefore they do agree to trade these assets, but do not easily surrender them for free. Chapter 4 also explains why the current information sharing regime based on bilateral information exchanges is wasteful.

Electronic exchanges to buy and sell information already exist (Mayer-Schonberger and Cukier 2013, 121–122). Still, this book's novel framework of empowering governmental agencies to trade data with each other is likely to be controversial due to ethical and political challenges. Chapter 5 proposes to view public data as a contested commodity: a commodity whose exchange evokes an ethical debate. The trade histories of thirty contested commodities are examined to reveal three lessons that are applied to the idea of public data exchange and to suggest which types of data will be best suited to trade. Chapter 6 illustrates how agencies can exchange information as a contested commodity in a PSIE program. This program will be tailored to each country's needs. To illustrate this, two types of PSIE programs are introduced: an exchange model, suited for the United States, and a supply-chain model, practiced in Australia. The chapter discusses the legal, economic, and technical foundations of such programs.

Chapter 7 suggests that, before launching a PSIE program, citizens must debate and then agree to a new balance between the goal of increased governmental efficiency and protecting other political values such as privacy. In conclusion, chapter 8 suggests a *politics first* approach to convert PSIE from an abstract idea to a reality. The chapter provides advice for politicians, government officials, IT experts, and citizens on how to promote such an approach. The final section draws lessons from Bliss's archeological practices in unearthing Tel Gezer for creating a successful information sharing environment. Ultimately, Bliss's work practices teach that a successful information sharing program must be embedded in a people-first approach, based on the understanding that only incentivized people can ensure information sharing success.

1 The Information Sharing Crisis that Does Not Go Away

This chapter introduces five infamous public information sharing failures. Next, it argues that these failures are troubling because of the central role that information plays in redefining the character and functions of the public sector in the modern state. This discussion highlights agencies as Big Data owners whose appetite for data surpasses even that of private sector corporations such as Google. However, agencies fail more frequently than private sector corporations to share their datasets. The chapter provides several reasons for these frequent failures, and summarizes the primary damage stemming from public information sharing failure.

Infamous Governmental Information Sharing Failures

The Challenger Launch Explosion (1986)

On January 28, 1986, 73 seconds after liftoff, the Space Shuttle Challenger exploded. Seven astronauts including teacher Christa McAuliffe died in the accident. Having watched the horror on live TV, the public and the media demanded to know what went wrong. The Rogers Commission attributed the cause of the accident to a technical failure of the O-rings that sealed a critical joint of the solid rocket booster (SRB). The Challenger was launched on a cold day (30°F) and the temperature of the O-rings was even colder (around 20°F). The rubber O-rings lost their resiliency. A flicker of flame emerged from the leaky joint, grew, and engulfed the fuel tank. The tank ruptured and exploded. Morton Thiokol, the U.S. National Aeronautics and Space Administration (NASA) contractor, designed, manufactured, delivered, and assembled the O-rings (Tufte 1997, 38–39).

Morton Thiokol and NASA engineers debated the faulty design of the O-rings during the eight years before the Challenger accident. They had solid evidence based on SRBs retrieved from the ocean that the O-rings might fail in cold temperatures. The night before the launch, Thiokol and NASA engineers convened to discuss how the O-rings would perform in the predicted cold weather of the launch day. Thiokol's engineers recommended not launching the shuttle. This information was not shared with senior NASA managers. Scholars explained that political pressures on NASA to launch on time, groupthink culture, and information overload propelled NASA's senior managers to approve the launch (Hall 2003; Vaughan 1996).

Yet the more direct explanation for the human cause of the Challenger accident remains a failure to share information inside NASA and between Thiokol and NASA. The Rogers Commission was troubled by the propensity of NASA management to contain potentially serious problems and to attempt to resolve them internally rather than communicate them forward (Rogers Commission 1986). One dramatic moment during the Rogers Commission's hearings captured this information sharing problem:

Chairman Rogers: By way of a question, could I ask, did any of you gentlemen, prior to launch, know about the objections of Thiokol to the launch?
Mr. Smith (Kennedy Space Director): I did not.
Mr. Thomas (Launch Director): No sir.
Mr. Aldrich (Space Program Director): I did not.
Mr. Moore (Associate Administrator for Space Flight): I did not.
Chairman Rogers: So the four, certainly four of the key people who made the decision about the launch were not aware of the history that we have been unfolding here before the Commission?
Mr. Moore: That is correct. (Rogers Commission 1986, section 1899)

Thomas was asked what would have happened if the Thiokol concerns had been made known to him. He replied: "I can assure you that if we had that information, we wouldn't have launched if it hadn't been 53 degrees." (Rogers Commission 1986, Section 1933)

Nearly seventeen years later (February 1, 2003), the Space Shuttle Columbia disintegrated while returning from space, killing all seven astronauts on board. In this accident too, the investigation committee discovered that the technical cause of the accident was well known *before* senior managers approved the landing. Once again, the engineers did not effectively share critical information with the senior managers responsible for the landing decision (Columbia Accident Investigation Board 2003, 191).

The 9/11 Terror Attacks (2001)

The Central Intelligence Agency (CIA) had been tracking Mohamed Atta, the ringleader of the nineteen 9/11 terrorists, since 2000. During that very same period, almost a dozen U.S. federal and state databases held nonclassified information about Atta's activities inside and outside the United States. For example, the Federal Bureau of Investigation (FBI) and Florida Department of Highway Safety and Motor Vehicles held information about four incidents in which Atta's vehicle was stopped in Florida. The Immigration and Naturalization Service (INS) (today the U.S. Citizenship and Immigration Services [USCIS]) database held five reports on Atta's travel from and to the United States, and three about his domestic travels. The Federal Aviation Administration (FAA)'s Airman Registration and Aircraft Registry databases contained fourteen entries about Atta's efforts to acquire a commercial pilot license and to train in a large jet flight simulator in six different airfields in three states. Private sector databases also held records on Atta's apartment leases, cell phone purchases, aviation fuel acquisitions, new bank accounts, and transfers into these accounts (Bright et al. 2001; FBI 2007; National Commission on Terrorist Attacks upon the United States 2004; U.S. Department of Justice—Office of the Inspector General 2002).

All these pieces of data were useless from the perspective of the agencies owning them. Hence, for even the smallest incentive these agencies would have been happy to provide the information to the CIA. The National Commission on Terrorist Attacks upon the United States (henceforth "The 9/11 Commission") acknowledged this idea, writing: "Information procedures should provide incentives for sharing, to restore a better balance between security and shared knowledge" (The 9/11 Commission 2004, 417).

Alas such an exchange system based on incentives did not exist prior to September 11, 2001. The individual data elements that could have helped the CIA track and stop Mohamed Atta and the other terrorists remained obscure, buried inside silo databases, and inaccessible to outsiders. This sad reality explains why the USCIS granted student visas for two deceased hijackers to attend flight school—six months *after* 9/11 (Chin 2004).

The following congressional statement of Lee H. Hamilton, the former vice chair of the 9/11 Commission remains the most powerful official statement about the cost of agencies' failure to exchange information:

Poor information sharing was the single greatest failure of our government in the lead-up to the 9/11 attacks. The failure to share information adequately, within and across federal agencies, and from federal agencies to state and local authorities, was a significant contributing factor to our government's missteps in understanding and responding to the growing threat of al Qaeda in the years before the 9/11 attacks. There were several missed opportunities to disrupt the 9/11 plot. Most of them involved the failure to share information.

The 9/11 Commission found that the biggest impediment to all-source analysis—to a greater likelihood of connecting the dots—is the human or systemic resistance to sharing information. Hamilton emphasized that the "need-to-share" principle must be accorded much greater weight in the balance with the longstanding "need-to-know" principle of information protection" (Hamilton 2005).

Hurricane Katrina (2005)

On August 29, 2005, Hurricane Katrina struck southeast Louisiana. Levees collapsed and a territory roughly the size of Great Britain including the city of New Orleans succumbed to seawater. 1,800 people died, making Katrina the deadliest U.S. hurricane since 1928. Tens of thousands were left homeless without access to basic supplies; seawater spread lethal pollution everywhere. The total property damage was estimated to be $81 billion, the costliest natural disaster in American history (Spence, Lachlan, and Griffin 2007, 539).

Rescuers had to cope with incomprehensible challenges including the destruction of 90 percent of all essential utility networks (emergency 911 services, energy, communications, water and sewage) (Miller 2006; Spence, Lachlan, and Griffin 2007, 550). At the Superdome where 20,000 evacuees found refuge, police officers had to use bull horns and legwork to communicate with people because nothing else worked (Garnett and Kouzmin 2007, 174). New Orleans and its surroundings descended into chaos. One observer wrote: "Government at all levels was in effect deaf, dumb, and blind blundering about and trying to make sense of an endlessly confusing and rapidly changing situation. This rapidly led to chaos" (Miller 2006, 196–197). Rescuers including police officers became victims. There was no unified command center (Moynihan 2009).

Still, Katrina struck four years after 9/11 and three years after the subsequent creation of the Department of Homeland Security (DHS). Emergency preparedness was a topic high on the agenda of Americans and their government organizations. Years before Katrina, the U.S. Federal Emergency

Management Agency (FEMA) highlighted the threat of the collapse of the man-made levees meant to protect New Orleans that was built below sea level as one of the most dangerous potential disasters the United States faced (Moynihan 2009, 1–2).

After Katrina struck, almost five hundred organizations immediately came to the rescue. Several organizations invested unprecedented resources to help the local population. FEMA sent 11,000 trucks of water, ice, and meals, about three times as many truckloads as used to help with *all* the hurricanes of 2004. The U.S. Department of Defense (DOD) unleashed the largest domestic military deployment operation since the end of the American Civil War 140 years earlier. The National Guard deployment of 50,000 troops was the largest in U.S. history. The Red Cross led a $2 billion 220,000-person operation, twenty times larger than any previous Red Cross mission and providing aid to 3.7 million survivors. The neighboring states of Florida and Texas, the Walmart retail corporation, and even Operation Brother's Keeper (encompassing several hundred churches), all experienced with deadly hurricanes, also helped with the largest-ever evacuation of a U.S. city in such a short time frame (Moynihan 2009).

Yet the various rescue organizations deeply mistrusted each other and therefore refused to share life-saving information. Michael Chertoff, head of DHS, was preoccupied with antiterrorism goals rather than natural disasters. He also had strained relationships before, during, and after the disaster with Michael Brown, the FEMA director. So, the two men in charge of the two most important emergency aid government organizations, DHS and FEMA, isolated themselves, their staff, and organizations from each other during the crisis (Garnett and Kouzmin 2007, 173).

Likewise, Louisiana Governor Kathleen Babineaux Blanco mistrusted federal agencies because she believed that the feds were trying to take over. Blanco rejected the U.S. Army Corps of Engineers' offer to help deal with the flooding levees. She also refused to sign an agreement with the White House to jointly control the National Guard forces (Kapucu and Van Wart 2008, 733). For their part, FEMA officials considered local emergency managers unsophisticated and often treated them with disdain. The U.S. Coast Guard acted heroically but likewise shared no information with other agencies (Garnett and Kouzmin 2007, 181). Municipalities were left to manage on their own. The media stepped in to provide information to citizens. In a defining media moment a frustrated Ted Koppel, the host of the TV news program *Nightline,* asked Brown, the FEMA director: "Do you guys not watch television?" (Garnett and Kouzmin 2007, 184).

Failure to share information resulted in bad decisions. FEMA, relying only on its internal information resources, did not comprehend fast enough the gravity of the situation. FEMA therefore left its high-tech mobile communications truck "Red October" parked idle in Baton Rouge for days after Katrina struck Louisiana. This mobile unit was critical to help reestablish the communication loop around New Orleans. The DHS Homeland Security Operations Center (HSOC), isolated from FEMA's information, decided that the situation on the ground was not serious enough to mobilize the "CEO COM Link," a high-tech system for connecting top government officials with the chief executive officers (CEOs) of Fortune 100 corporations (Garnett and Kouzmin 2007, 179).

On the ground, things were worse. FEMA, Louisiana officials, the DOD, and the U.S. Department of Health and Human Services (HHS) argued over who was responsible for collecting dead bodies floating in the floodwater. Louisiana finally signed a contract with a private company to get the job done, until DOD took over. The Red Cross prepared housing and shelters but did not receive information from FEMA about the number and timing of evacuees arriving; therefore, sometimes large numbers of evacuees reached unprepared locations and, at other times, no evacuees were sent to fully prepared locations (Moynihan 2009).

Frustrated and disgusted by information sharing failures and its cost in human lives, members of the federal Select Bipartisan Committee to Investigate the Preparation for and Response to Hurricane Katrina emphasized the following words in the Executive Summary of its final report: "Better information would have been an optimal weapon against Katrina. Information sent to the right people at the right place at the right time. Information moved within agencies, across departments, and between jurisdictions of government as well. Seamlessly. Securely. Efficiently. . . . One would think we could share information by now. But Katrina again proved we cannot" (Select Bipartisan Committee to Investigate the Preparation for and Response to Hurricane Katrina 2006, 1).

Haiti Earthquake (2010)

On January 12, 2010, a powerful earthquake struck Haiti. More than 230,000 citizens died. International organizations and countries sent people and resources to help the poorest Caribbean and Central American nations. Volunteers even mobilized OD resources to help map and identify emerging needs (Berners-Lee 2010; Noveck 2012).

Poor information sharing hindered the rescue missions. In several hospitals, scraps of papers were taped to each patient indicating name and injury. The more advanced hospitals created their own unique patient information systems. None of the hospitals knew what surgical services other hospitals offered, where to find medical supplies, or even how to transport patients to other hospitals. Failure to share information resulted in over- or under-utilization of scarce medical resources. For example, a dialysis center treating victims with crash injuries operated at 20 percent of its 200-patient capacity because other medical facilities did not know of its existence (De Ville de Goyet, Sarmiento, and Grünewald 2011, 70).

The Pan American Health Organization Haiti report concluded that "Information management, including in the health sector, appears to be one of the weakest points of response in past disasters" (De Ville de Goyet, Sarmiento, and Grünewald 2011, 111). Another international aid organization explained: "However innovative they are, Information and Communication Technologies (ICTs) that operate as islands and silos impede relief efforts and cost lives . . . each system was an island of information, leading to unnecessary duplication, fragmentation, and significant frustration" (Hattotuwa and Stauffacher 2010).

Even after Google established a common standards–based repository to help organizations share information, the international, media, and United Nation (UN) agencies involved refused to share information via this repository or use it (Caribbean Information Society Portal 2010). The most basic questions remained unanswered: Where are field hospitals located? Are they operational and what are their capabilities? What is the water availability and quality in the various field hospitals and rescue camps? What donations have been received and are available? What key supplies are needed?

Influenced by poor information sharing during the Haiti crisis, the Gates Foundation announced a new Grand Challenge competition titled "Increasing Interoperability of Social Good Data," inviting entrepreneurs worldwide to link and connect the different "data islands" of donors and international aid organizations. This grant application call declared: "Interoperability is the key to making the whole greater than the sum of its parts" (Gates Foundation 2013). However, as this book will explain, effective information sharing demands much more than technical interoperability; it requires first and foremost incentivized human agents who are willing to negotiate, agree, and then share their information resources.

The Fukushima Nuclear Power Plant Accident (2011)

On March 11, 2011, following the strong Tōhoku earthquake, a tsunami hit the Japanese Fukushima Daiichi nuclear plant. The 12.1-meter- (40-foot-) high tsunami that struck the plant was twice as tall as the highest wave predicted by officials. Power supply to the plant's cooling systems failed. The ensuing equipment failures, nuclear meltdowns, and release of radioactive materials caused the second largest nuclear disaster since the 1986 Chernobyl disaster. No one died in this accident; its impact on future cancer rates is unknown (World Nuclear Association 2011).

Japanese, American, and international agencies mistrusted each other and refused to share or ignored information. For example, the Japanese Nuclear Safety Division of the Ministry of Education, Culture, Sports, Science and Technology streams data from a national network of detectors called the System for Prediction of Environment Emergency Dose Information (SPEEDI). The Nuclear and Industrial Safety Agency (NISA), Japan's nuclear regulatory and oversight organization, sent SPEEDI data for five critical days (March 12–16) to local Fukushima officials but the emails containing the critical data remained unread and deleted afterward. Likewise, between March 17 and 19, the U.S. military, on behalf of the U.S. Department of Energy (DOE), measured radiation levels within a 45-kilometer radius of the reactors. The information was shared with two Japanese ministries but these ministries did not share the data with the Prime Minister's Office or the Nuclear Safety Commission (Akiyama et al. 2012, 98; Onishi and Fackler 2011).

Information sharing failures led to poor decision making. Prime Minister Naoto Kan delayed the cooling of the reactors by questioning the use of seawater instead of fresh water. Japanese ministries were slow to request help from international organizations. Local officials were incapable of making decisions to mediate the radiation and the situation worsened in the weeks following the disaster (Onishi and Fackler 2011).

By far the worst decision due to insufficient information was the decision to evacuate residents directly into the radioactive plume. The nonshared SPEEDI data included atmospheric radiation dispersion forecasts that clearly demonstrated that a substantial portion of the radioactive material released from the plant went northwest and fell on the ground. Uninformed local officials instructed residents to evacuate north, from lightly to more heavily contaminated areas. In another case, the International Atomic Energy Agency (IAEA) recommended that the population of a village north of Fukushima evacuate south; the Japanese government refused to heed the advice, stating that it needed to investigate the IAEA recommendation (Akiyama et al. 2012, 23–24).

Experts offered reasons for the catastrophic consequences of the nuclear crisis including: (1) an erroneous decision to locate the plant too close to the ocean; (2) a cascading nuclear disaster beyond the coping capacity of any nation; (3) rigid bureaucratic structure in government and in the Tokyo Electric Power Company (TEPCO—the operator of the plant)'s hierarchical management culture; (4) a reluctance to send bad news upward and a need to save face; (5) a politically fragile government; and (6) the need to preserve the public's acceptance of nuclear power (Lovins 2011). These reasons may well be true. However, the more fundamental and immediate reason remains the failure of Japanese local and national agencies to exchange life-saving information during the crisis. As a result, this natural disaster turned into a man-made disaster. This conclusion appears in every report of thirteen different international, national, and independent Fukushima investigation commissions. On July 22, 2013, almost two years after the Fukushima disaster, the media disclosed that, again, TEPCO failed to report information about leaking radioactive water into the Pacific Ocean (Yahoo 2013).

The Information-centric Public Sector

These shocking information sharing disasters are especially troubling due to the new and central role that information plays in redefining the character and function of the public sector. Every generation redefines the concept "public sector" in its image. Woodrow Wilson, in 1887, sought to protect the public sector from corrupt politicians and therefore defined public administration as lying outside the proper sphere of politics (Wilson 1887). The post–World War I, Great Depression generation defined public administration as the sector in charge of eliminating waste and conserving material (White 1926). In 1947, Herbert Simon, still under the spell of

World War II, redefined the public sector as the realm of decision making (Simon 1997).

In 1968, a group of thirty-four young American scholars convened at the Minnowbrook Conference Center of Syracuse University to debate passionately the essence of public administration, and develop a vision that closely reflected the values of the 1960s (Frederickson 1971). This vision emphasized values such as political activism, making the world a better place, participatory democracy, equality among people of different gender, races, and ethnic origins, client service, and smaller and less hierarchical organizations. This vision remained influential well into the 1980s (Stillman 1985). More recent definitions of the public sector have been influenced by globalization and theories of social capital (Bozeman 1987; Pierre 1995).

This book defines the public sector as the collection of institutions whose administrative staff maintains a monopoly over the legitimate process of producing, updating, and disseminating the most extensive and authoritative information in the state. Given the aforementioned defining and redefining of the essence of the public sector, why highlight information ownership as the public sector's defining feature? Three facts point to the centrality of information to the modern public sector. First, the public sector's data elements are ubiquitous. They range from the everyday (e.g., a driver's license number) to the obscure (e.g., Kentucky's Bonus Wildlife Management Area Quota Hunt Deer Permit ID). New missions compel the public sector to collect, store, and disseminate an ever-increasing stockpile of information. So, the public sector becomes a mammoth information storage site that must be maintained to support the daily routines of the modern state.

Second, agencies gain resources when they become the owners of a new data element. For example, in 2000, the U.S. Department of Agriculture (USDA) won new resources to develop standards for organically produced food products. Agency ownership of a particular data element is so important that it is assigned or revoked by law. In a recent case, a U.S. congressional act assigned ownership of Energy Guide labels to the DOE and removed this responsibility from state-level administrations.

Finally, an information food chain, founded on the public sector's data elements, governs our modern economy. Agencies collect information as a side product of executing their legislative missions and programs. Over the years, agencies have accumulated important datasets on which other organizations and individuals increasingly depend. Public, private, and not-for-profit organizations would struggle to operate without access to the most basic data elements that agencies collect and create such as Social Security identification, drivers' license numbers, the registry numbers of land parcels, school records, military identification numbers, and passport information. Every life event is captured in a data element owned by an agency, and by law citizens must provide timely information to update these data elements.

E-government has become increasingly significant to the workings of government agencies. The GAO defines e-government as the government's use of technology, particularly web-based applications, to enhance access to and delivery of government information and services to citizens, business partners, employees, other agencies, and government entities (Kim and Kim 2003). Consequently, in our Big Data age, agencies have become the owners of the biggest and most valuable datasets owned by any organization including private sector organizations such as Google.

Big Data Agencies

Big Data Defined

The business definition of "Big Data" highlights that agencies and corporations collect, store, and analyze large quantities of data and then extract new revenue from data insights (Gantz and Reinsel 2011). The plummeting cost of storage, computing, and network bandwidth and the conversion of everything to digital data facilitate the efforts to collect and analyze Big Data.

The most significant raw source of Big Data is "the digital exhaust." Organizations often collect data about people's digital traces including registering streams of computer mouse clicks, logs reporting where we drive or walk, and our financial transactions. Once aggregated, this digital exhaust reveals previously unseen patterns about people and their actions. This type of thinking emphasizes that people are the sum of their quantifiable social relationships, online interactions, and connections with various types of digital content (Mayer-Schonberger and Cukier 2013).

Scholars define Big Data as a well-designed campaign to collect all data about a given domain (rather than just sample data). Practitioners can then focus less on hypotheses and statistical challenges such as random sampling and more on interesting correlations. Big Data is about the "big picture" or the ability to detect important future trends even before we can explain them. Corporations and individuals endowed with a Big Data mindset often "let the data speak for itself" (Mayer-Schonberger and Cukier 2013, 14).

Big Data involves collecting and drawing insights from "messy" data. For example, Google developed powerful commercial spell-checking and voice recognition software by learning from incorrect data about the common mistakes that people make when they type or speak. With Big Data, practitioners can easily discover nonlinear patterns that statistical methods do not reveal. Big Data enables practitioners to investigate outlier cases that traditional statistics omit. It also allows managers to rely less on their intuition and more on mathematical and correlational data-analysis techniques (Mayer-Schonberger and Cukier 2013, 32–48, 50–72, 192).

Big Data is a buzzword that generates excitement. Practitioners suggest that the possibilities inherent in Big Data are endless (Manovich 2011, 13). Politicians such as President Obama employ Big Data analysts to understand better what voters want (Barton 2012). Readers are taught new words to describe the size of Big Data including petabyte (1,000 terabytes), exabyte (1,000 petabytes), zettabyte (1,000 exabytes), and quintillion (10^{18}) (Gantz and Reinsel 2010). Other scholars remain on guard against some of the less desirable attributes of Big Data. Scholars are alarmed at how Big Data projects are invading privacy and are concerned about Big Data proponents' excessive confidence in the knowledge gained from linking large datasets (Boyd and Crawford 2012). Chapter 7 addresses these concerns.

The Competitive Advantage of Big Data Owners

Scholars and practitioners emphasize that Big Data is an ideal "raw material" because corporations can collect, store, and analyze it effortlessly and cheaply (e.g., recording our mouse clicks when we browse a corporate website). Digital data is never consumed or worn out like other physical materials, can be put to work in parallel to support multiple purposes, and is always available for reuse. The value of data is often dormant and increases over time as businesses use it effectively, often to support secondary uses unanticipated at the time when the data was first collected. Data can also be recombined with other data to generate additional value (Mayer-Schonberger and Cukier 2013, 98–122). Two scholars proposed that we reflect on our Big Data age as the moment when the information society is finally fulfilling the promise implied by its name. They wrote: "The data takes center stage. All those digital bits that we have gathered can now be harnessed in novel ways to serve new purposes and unlock new forms of value" (Mayer-Schonberger and Cukier 2013, 190).

Today, corporate analysts mine Big Data to discover what clients want. In this way, Big Data becomes the competitive advantage of corporations such as Amazon; these corporations appear at times to know ahead of us what we will want to buy next (Mayer-Schonberger and Cukier 2013, 111–115). If data is the new "coin of the realm" then Big Data is the foundation of this new data-centered economy (Economist 2010a, 7). Experts estimate that, since 2005, corporations have increased their investment in the digital universe by 50 percent, to $4 trillion (Gantz and Reinsel 2011, 1). An overwhelming number of corporations (73 percent) reportedly leverage Big Data to increase revenue (Avanade 2012). Big Data analysis also saves lives, including by identifying epidemics more quickly and helping find terrorists (as in the case of helping to find the Boston Marathon bombers in April 2013) (Harris 2013).

Throughout history, people have regarded a certain object or raw material as the most valuable thing to control and exploit in a given period. The Bronze Age and the Iron Age are ancient examples. More recently, examples include Holland's fixation on tulips in the early seventeenth century, and Americans' hunt for gold at the end of the nineteenth century, and, globally, the importance of oil and information assets in the twentieth century. Over time, these objects or raw materials decline in value and corporations born around them lose some or all of their value.

However, virtual Big Data is unique and different from these historical physical objects or raw materials. Big Data can therefore provide a sustainable competitive advantage to those who own it and to those who invest in infrastructure to capture it. It is difficult to quantify this competitive advantage in monetary terms because the value of Big Data is derived from its unknown future secondary uses (Mayer-Schonberger and Cukier 2013, 118, 120, 146–147, 192). Nonetheless, stock markets register well the value of large owners of digital data; in 2013, Apple and Google were the two top corporations in a worldwide assessment of the most valuable brand names (Interbrand 2014). However, Apple and Google are very far from being the biggest Big Data owners, as shown in the next section.

Agencies as the Owners of the Biggest Data

The digital universe expands rapidly. From 2005 to 2020, this universe will grow by a factor of 300, from 130 exabytes to 40,000 exabytes, or 40 trillion gigabytes (more than 5,200 gigabytes for every man, woman, and child in 2020). Experts estimate that by 2015, world digital data will be 7.9 zetta-bytes. This number is the equivalent of 18 million times the digital assets stored by the U.S. Library of Congress (LOC) at the end of 2011 (Ammirati 2011). From now until 2020, the digital universe will double in size every two years (Gantz and Reinsel 2012, 1). Several data-intensive private corpo-rations are growing at an even faster rate:

• In 2007, Walmart's digital data warehouse was almost thirty times bigger than all printed text held by the LOC with its 530 miles of bookshelves and 130 million items (Economist 2010a).

• In 2007, Yahoo's *daily* data intake was about 60 percent of the digital size of all printed items acquired by the LOC since 1815 (Economist 2010a).

• A single international company, Acxiom Corporation, owns the world's largest commercial database on consumers. Acxiom operates more than 23,000 computer servers that process more than 50 trillion data transac-tions a year. Acxiom's database contains information about 500 million active consumers worldwide including the majority of U.S. adults, with about 1,500 data elements per person (Singer 2012).

Yet, worldwide, the public sector's digital data troves are even bigger and growing at a faster rate than those in the private sector. Government agen-cies are often entitled to compel people to provide them with information, without recompense. As a consequence, agencies amass the largest troves of data in the modern state (Mayer-Schonberger and Cukier 2013, 116).

Several U.S. government agencies each own databases that tower over those of the most data-hungry private sector corporations. In 2007, Google's database was about two hundred times larger than that of the LOC, while NASA's database was three hundred times bigger than that of the LOC. In turn, NASA's mammoth data storage pales in comparison to that held by several national security agencies. Consider, for example, the following three facts about the U.S. National Security Agency (NSA) respon-sible for capturing, storing, and analyzing most of the world's electronic communications:

• The NSA has recorded and stored about 2 trillion domestic and international phone calls during the two years following the terrorist attacks of September 11, 2001 (Ayers 2007).

• William Binney, a former NSA official, estimates that the agency has compiled 20 trillion transactions about U.S. citizens and others—who calls whom, emails whom, wires money to whom, and more (Mayer-Schonberger and Cukier 2013, 156). In 2010, the NSA intercepted and stored about 1.7 billion electronic communications daily (Economist 2010a).

• At the end of 2011, the NSA admitted that every six hours it gathers as much data as is stored in the complete printed materials collection of the LOC, including every book or journal that LOC has been storing since its foundation in 1800 (Nosowitz 2011).

The gap between the public and private sectors in terms of how much data agencies and corporations can process in a given year (without storing all of it) is even wider.

Figure 1.1 illustrates the LOC's total volume of digital contents as the length of a bacterium (whose size is 1.8 microns—equivalent in this example to 432 terabytes of data). At the end of 2007, Google's volume of processed data was 20,000 times larger than this bacterium—depicted as the length of a European hornet (also about 20,000 times larger than a bacterium). By 2011, Google's estimated processed data, depicted as the length of a lovebird, was four times larger than that of 2007. Today in 2013, Google's estimated processed data is metaphorically the length of a merlin bird, two times larger than the lovebird. If Google's data processing power continues to double every two years as estimated by the authors of the Digital Universe series, few if any private sector corporations will be able to compete with Google in the data processing domain (Gantz and Reinsel 2012).

But consider the volume of data owned by NASA. In September 2014, NASA will begin operating its latest radio-telescope to map deep space. The area of this project's antennas is one square kilometer. This *single* project of a *single* U.S. agency will process in its first year of operations 25 percent more digital data than Google processed in 2013. Accordingly this NASA project is depicted as a young cat that is 25 percent longer than Google's merlin bird. Readers should note that NASA is but one of America's 200 federal departments and agencies.

Library of Congress (2013)	Google annually processed data (2007)	Google annually processed data (2011 projected)	Google annually processed data (2013 projected)	NASA Telescope Project	NSA Utah center (data storage capacity)	
Bacteria (1.8 microns)	 European hornet (3.6 centimeters)	 Lovebird (14.4 centimeters)	 Merlin (bird) (29 centimeters)	 Young cat (36 centimeters)		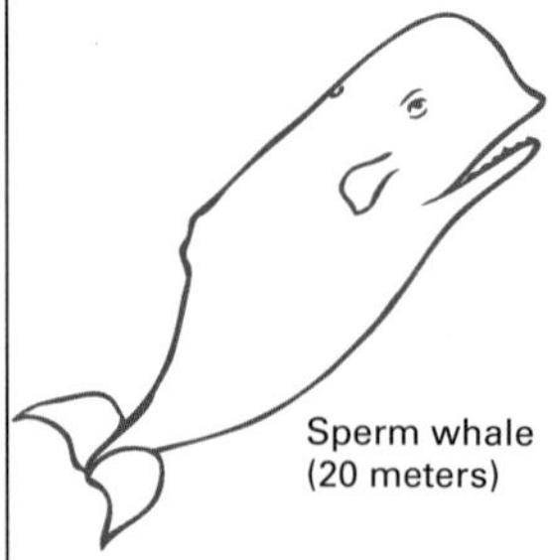 Sperm whale (20 meters)
432 Terabytes	8.4 Exabytes	33.6 Exabytes	67.2 Exabytes	84 Exabytes	5 Zettabytes	

Terabyte = 1,000 gigabytes
Petabyte = 1,000 terabytes
Exabyte = 1,000 petabytes
Zettabyte = 1,000 exabytes

Figure 1.1
The U.S. Library of Congress (LOC), Google, and partial NASA data accumulation compared to the data storage capacity of a single NSA data facility.
Sources: Berkes 2013; Dean and Ghemawat 2008; Harris 2012; Library of Congress 2013; Taylor 2007; Wikipedia 2013.

NASA is not even close to being the most data-rich U.S. agency. In 2013, NSA began operating its latest data center in Utah. This gargantuan $1.2 billion complex features 1.5 million square feet of space. High-performance NSA computers will occupy 100,000 square feet and require 65 megawatts of power (enough for 65,000 homes) and 1.5 million gallons of cooling water a day to keep the machines running. This new NSA data center will have the storage capacity of 5 zettabytes of data, enough to process a century's worth of worldwide communications, phone calls, and emails and have ample storage room to spare. So, a *single* NSA facility can process sixty-nine times more data than the sum total of the data that Google processed in 2013. This is the same as comparing the length of a sperm whale (a single NSA data facility) to that of a merlin bird (all of Google) shown in figure 1.1.

The scope of governmental data collection is unprecedented and increasing in terms of pace and magnitude. No aspect of modern life evades data collection efforts. Already in 2000, the DOD Specimen Repository for Remain Identification was the largest DNA bank in the world with 176.5 million cases, 282 million specimens, and an accrual rate of 20 million new cases every year. This rate grew significantly after 9/11 (Anderlik and Rothstein 2001). Agencies do not know in advance which citizens they will want to scrutinize. So, agencies collect and store information as a preemptive measure, to allow immediate access to data about people who fall under suspicion (Mayer-Schonberger and Cukier 2013, 157).

Public sector electronic records are important because they cover a longer time period and are more reliable and sustainable, and are held by a more neutral guardian than similar private records. These records capture the most important moments in our lives: as babies and as elderly people, as drivers and as pedestrians, as home owners and as homeless people, as business people and as wage earners, as producers and as consumers, as workers and as vacationers, as patients, as children and as parents, as jurors and as criminals, as teachers and as students, and as political contributors (Raul 2002). Over time, governments have become the owners of the largest and most valuable electronic information assets (Solove 2004).

Private sector corporations rely on the completeness, freshness, and availability of public electronic records. For example, the SSA Death Master File (DMF) maintains information about Americans who have passed away. In the United States you may be buried six feet under but, if you are not in this file, private sector organizations will continue to invite you to open retirement accounts, demand that you pay your bills promptly, and inquire why you have not renewed your insurance on time. The smallest change in the procedures of registering people in the DMF immediately impacts tens of thousands of public, private, and nonprofit organizations (Danko 2011).

Governments therefore invest heavily in IT. The U.S. government is the largest producer, collector, consumer, and disseminator of information in the United States (Gelman 2004; Holden and Fletcher 2005; Office of Management and Budget (OMB) 2000). In April 2013, the White House announced that it was budgeting $82 billion for federal IT in fiscal 2014 (Biddick and Kash 2013).

The DOD alone commands the biggest IT budget of any world organization, estimated to be $38.4 billion in fiscal 2012. The DOD's 170,000 IT workers supervise 7 million computing devices, 15,000 computer networks, 10,000 different software systems, and 67,000 computer servers in 772 data centers (Foley 2011; GAO 2012e). Another U.S. government agency, the Internal Revenue Service (IRS), is the largest information processing organization in the world. The IRS collects more than $2.3 trillion in revenues and processes more than 236 million tax returns annually (Holden and Fletcher 2005; IRS 2009). As citizens demand that the government address complex new problems such as biomonitoring (biomonitoring measures the exposure of the human body to toxic chemical compounds, and these measurements are often done in blood and urine), global terror, and green energy, the public sector first responds by intensifying its data collection efforts.

Weber prophesized that modern bureaucracy will "dominate through knowledge" (Weber 1978, 225). Weber himself could not have foreseen the magnitude of the fulfillment of his prophecy. A new type of government has emerged to replace the traditional bureaucratic welfare state: the information state. The information state specializes in the use of information power; its agencies employ information power to redefine control of old domains and to carve out new areas of autonomous influence (Braman 2006). This power depends on how well agencies share information with each other. U.S. agencies such as the FBI, CIA, NSA, and IRS have immense and autonomous power to withhold some data due to national security or privacy considerations. The datasets of many other U.S. agencies are not affected by such privacy and national security considerations; however they lack incentives to share valuable datasets with other agencies, as demonstrated in the next section.

Information Sharing Failures in the Public and Private Sectors

Sometimes, private sector corporations fail to share information. Employees refuse to share in order to secure their jobs. Managers resist sharing information for fear of losing control and power. Companies do not adequately train employees to share information. Corporations purposely erect barriers across departments that curtail information flows to prevent industrial espionage or avert interdepartmental role and authority conflicts (Li and Lin 2006).

However, the private sector also demonstrates information sharing successes such as in the field of "big science" projects (Hara et al. 2003). In the

fiercely competitive semiconductor industry, employees in various firms
have developed private channels to share knowledge (Appleyard 1996).
Knowledge sharing across institutional and company lines explains the
success of Silicon Valley and the relative stagnation of Boston's Route 128,
a similar technological hub, bounded by a tradition of secrecy (Saxenian
1996). There are also some impressive case studies of successful, life-saving
public-private information sharing projects. For example, the FAA successfully integrates aviation safety data including data from the Aviation Safety
Information Analysis and Sharing (ASIAS) system, which connects forty-six
safety databases across the industry and has forty-five participating airlines.
This data-integration effort empowers the FAA to extract life-saving information about accidents and incidents from both public and private sources
(GAO 2012g).

However, regrettably, most public sector agencies function as "islands of
automation," each endowed with its own standalone computer system (Bellamy and Taylor 1996, 55). The advent of e-government increased the pressure on agencies to integrate their separate databases. Citizens demanded
to interact with federal, state, and local government via a single portal
interface such as those used by private sector organizations. Legislatures
in countries such as the United States, Mexico, and China as well as the
EU have approved special budgets to integrate data and build such portals
(Accenture 2004; Pardo and Tayi 2007). Local governments, particularly at
the city level, adopted e-government web portals early on and have made
continuous, incremental progress in this domain (Norris and Moon 2005).
Recently, several local governments in the United States have increased
data sharing to improve their online services. Residents today use local
government portals to pay parking tickets, register for state Department of
Motor Vehicles (DMV) appointments, and pay local taxes. New smartphone
applications empower residents to monitor city council meetings in real
time, confirm bus routes, and contribute to political campaigns. Yet, by and
large federal and national agencies have been less successful than the private sector in integrating data to improve their interactions with the public.

Four differences between the public and private sectors explain why
federal and national agencies fail to integrate data more frequently than
private corporations. First, formal annual budgeting processes command
the daily routines of agencies while private corporations invest flexibly in
innovative technologies to increase their competitive advantage. Private

sector corporations are not required to be representative, and their authority does not flow from elected public officials. Bozeman and Bretschneider, the scholars who pioneered the research domain of public management information systems (PMIS), explained twenty-seven years ago: "There is no private sector counterpart to political control of public organizations" (1986, 479). Public sector agencies are concerned about legislators' response to citizens' reactionary responses to new technologies; in contrast, corporations may lose revenue if they do not adopt new technologies. So, agencies tend to be more hesitant than private corporations to adopt new information sharing technologies (Kamal 2006). Occasionally, this pays off as agencies can learn from the mistakes of private corporations (Rocheleau and Wu 2002). However, at other times, agencies miss opportunities to adopt new technology early on as a means to break down interorganizational information barriers (Mahler and Regan 2003).

Second, by law, agencies are required to uphold higher standards of transparency, accountability, representation, equal access, and privacy protection in matters regarding data integration than those maintained by private corporations. Agencies also cannot treat their information sharing systems as proprietary solutions. They must service the public at large rather than a specific group of clients. Therefore, "blitzkrieg-style" information sharing projects to build information bridges between specific departments and organizations are more likely to occur in the private sector than in the public sector. Public agencies simply are not prepared, by law and practice, to pursue and execute information sharing projects requiring such quick implementation (Kamal 2006).

Third, agencies lack a strong CEO-type leadership. A strong CEO of a private corporation has full discretion to fire or reassign employees and to reward successful employees. Therefore, a charismatic CEO in the private sector can use incentives and penalties to push important information sharing projects to successful completion. Scholars who researched companies such as Microsoft and Hewlett-Packard concluded that information sharing (like knowledge management, business process re-engineering, decentralization, and establishing trust and transparency) in these corporations is directly dependent on the CEO's support and commitment (Akhavan, Jafari, and Fathian 2006). Senior government officers have more limited discretion in such matters. Finally, agencies emphasize soft power measured in terms of reputation, influence, and autonomy. In contrast, the threat of disappointing shareholders drives private corporations to terminate, trim, or redirect floundering information sharing projects much faster than in the public sector.

The Exorbitant Cost of Public Information Sharing Failure

The harshest depictions of information sharing failures appear in legislative minutes, scholarly articles, investigative reports, and practitioner accounts about the public sector. Over the past two decades, the GAO has documented numerous aborted or unsuccessful, large and expensive U.S. information sharing project failures in the DOD, the IRS, the FAA, the CMS, the U.S. National Weather System (NWS), the U.S. Securities and Exchange Commission (SEC), the FBI, as well as the Departments of Agriculture, Housing, Interior, State, Transportation, Veterans Affairs (VA), and Treasury. The GAO lists information sharing failures as a high-risk domain (GAO 2005b, 2007c). Governments worldwide suffer from similar data integration failures (Pardo and Tayi 2007). By some accounts, 80–90 percent of all IT investments in information integration fail for nontechnical reasons (Fawcett et al. 2009; Kamal 2006).

The infamous information sharing failures that opened this chapter are shocking and horrifying. These failures often occur when agency collaboration is crucial to address "wicked problems"—the pressing and complex policy problems that traverse traditional agency boundaries and defy simple single agency-centric solutions. In recent years, such problems have proliferated. They include climate change, environmental disaster and crisis preparedness and response, terrorism, and an aging U.S. population. However, the daily, ubiquitous, and less dramatic information sharing failures of agencies in domains such as homelessness and crime reduction are also enormously costly (Fountain 2013, 13). We analyze this cost in five categories: lives lost, waste and duplication, fraud, data quality, and ineffective government.

Lives Lost

Lives are lost when agencies fail to share data. In Australia, an investigation committee attributed the death of several Northern Territory (NT) infants from malnutrition to agencies' reluctance to share information with each other. In Canada, Paul Bernardo raped or sexually assaulted at least eighteen women and killed three women between 1987 and 1992. Bernardo operated freely because local and provincial law enforcement and forensic agencies failed to share information. A Canadian investigation committee defined this "astounding and dangerous lack of co-operation between police forces" as a "systemic failure" (Campbell 1995, 1, 191). In Israel, the State Comptroller berated emergency and police agencies for failing to share information during a large open forest fire in 2010; 44 prison service officer cadets, policemen, and firemen burned to death due to this failure. In the United States too, the GAO accused the U.S. Department of Interior (DOI) and the U.S. Forest Service for failing to develop and share information to fight forest fires more effectively (GAO 2013e).

Sometimes, information sharing failures thwart the prevention of heinous crimes (The Health Committee 2003; Ritchie 1994). In 2001, a British man who had been investigated in one police district in relation to allegations of eight separate sexual offenses was vetted by another police district and hired as a school janitor. Shortly thereafter, he murdered two ten-year-old school girls in his house. An inquiry committee attributed these murders to systemic information sharing failures within the British police and between the police and social services (The Bichard Inquiry 2004). In 2008 a British mother and her partner starved a seven-year old girl to death, and in 2009, a British mother burned herself and her disabled daughter to death after being abused by a street gang for almost a decade. Investigators of both incidents accused agencies of failing to share information that could have saved the victims (Radford 2010; The Telegraph 2009). In May 2008, the Israeli public was outraged by the murder of four-year-old Rose Pizem whose body was found stuffed in a suitcase in the Yarkon River four months after she disappeared. Her grandfather was convicted of the murder and her mother of soliciting the murder. The Israeli State Comptroller found failures in the way information was shared among the police, educational and health authorities, and welfare services, about women, children, and the elderly at risk (Weiler-Polak 2011).

The lives of all citizens are endangered when agencies fail to share information. The Pipeline and Hazardous Materials Safety Administration (PHMSA) of the U.S. Department of Transportation (DOT) fails to share data with state agencies regarding the safety of more than 200,000 miles of onshore gathering pipelines that frequently transport hazardous liquid and natural gas. Pipeline accidents cost lives and millions of dollars every year (GAO 2012d). The U.S. Customs and Border Protection (CBP), the U.S. Food and Drug Administration (FDA), and the USDA fail to share information about potentially unsafe imported food (GAO 2011g). Within the FDA, twenty-one noncommunicative databases contain different information types that are yet to be integrated to guard the food Americans consume (GAO 2012h). The DOD and the VA have failed for almost two decades now to share electronic data about wounded soldiers transferred from the DOD medical system to the VA's system (GAO 2013a). The House Armed Services Subcommittee on Military Personnel held back all but 10 percent of the funds allocated to build a new DOD-VA Electronic Health Record (EHR) system, until the two agencies could produce concrete plans to merge DOD and VA data in the new system (Federal Computer Week 2011).

Waste and Duplication

The monetary cost of colossal information integration failures is difficult to comprehend. In 1998, Arthur Gross, the former IRS commissioner, terminated an eight-year, $8 billion computer-modernization and data-integration project (Ewusi-Mensah 2003; Committee on Continued Review of the Tax Systems Modernization of the Internal Revenue Service, Commission on Physical Sciences Mathematics and Applications, and National Research Council 1996). In a congressional hearing, Mr. Gross said, "the IRS has created a computer system that does not work in the real world" (Stengel 1997). In 1994, the FAA terminated a twenty-two-year, $25 billion project to connect the agency's standalone computer systems (GAO 1998, 3). Two journalists who documented this failure defined it as "the greatest failure in the history of organized work" (Carr and Cone 2002). Likewise, British taxpayers paid $15.748 billion for a National Health Service (NHS) failed computer integration project (2003–2011) (BBC News 2013).

The investigation committee of the Deepwater Horizon Oil Drill disaster in the Gulf of Mexico (April–August 2010), the worst environmental disaster in U.S. history, stated that information sharing might have resulted in a faster resolution to a disaster that cost billions of dollars (National Commission on the BP Deepwater Horizon Oil Spill 2010). The committee discovered that seven agencies failed to share spill-control data, skills, and expertise in the two decades preceding the disaster (GAO 2011i).[1] In the taxation domain, the IRS, the SEC, and the U.S. Commodity Futures Trading Commission (CFTC) do not share information on corporate derivatives trades whose total notational amount outstanding grew from $32.7 trillion in 1999 to $231.2 trillion in 2010 (GAO 2011d). In the disaster recovery domain, FEMA spent seven years and $40 million on a failing computer project to unify flood insurance policy and claims data; the agency currently has no way to centrally analyze and compare its insurance premium payments and claims data (GAO 2011g). In the energy domain, in 2012, the DOD spent $372 million on 600 renewable energy projects, but the DOD's separate departments responsible for these projects do not share best-practices information with each other (GAO 2012m).

U.S. Representative Darrell Issa (R-California), who has been serving as the chairman of the U.S. House Oversight and Government Reform Committee since January 2011, claims that information sharing failures result in even greater financial loss than reported. The U.S. federal government spends $81 billion every year on technology. Members of Congress who supervise this investment estimate that between $20–21 billion are wasted on unsuccessful computer integration projects. However, according to Congressman Issa, the real waste lies in the untapped alternative uses for these funds that could significantly impact the annual $17 trillion U.S. economy (Issa 2012).

Fraud

In 2010, the GAO tested U.S. welfare agencies resilience to fraud. The GAO filed for childcare support using false or deceased individuals' names and false employment details. The claims were awarded. The claims succeeded because U.S. welfare agencies do not share data on people seeking such support (GAO 2010g).

In other cases, con artists extract millions in benefits from the U.S. federal government by pretending to be disabled veterans who own small businesses. The DOD, the U.S. General Services Administration (GSA), the U.S. Small Business Administration (SBA), and the VA fail to share information about these alleged veterans, and so the fraudulent claims are processed and paid as legitimate (GAO 2012t).

Fraudulent welfare claims also affect the housing domain: the U.S. Federal Housing Administration (FHA) provides billions of dollars in mortgage insurance payments to people who have failed to pay their taxes and who are not eligible to receive these funds. FHA officials argue that the IRS does not share information with them due to confidentiality concerns. However, the FHA did not ask the IRS to share the relevant information; Congress approved such sharing in similar circumstances (GAO 2012q).

Data Quality

When information is not shared, fewer people have the opportunity to view it and to correct problems, and data deteriorates. For example, the U.S. federal government manages about 650 million acres, or 29 percent, of land in the United States. Four agencies—the U.S. Bureau of Land Management (BLM), the U.S. Fish and Wildlife Service (USFWS), the U.S. National Park Service (USNPS) in the DOI, and the U.S. Forest Service—manage about 95 percent of these acres. The U.S. Bureau of Reclamation (USBR) manages another 1 percent. The five agencies collect data to help manage land under their jurisdiction and store this information on agency computer systems without sharing it. As a result the data quality of U.S. land records is compromised (GAO 2012a).

Ineffective Governance

Good programs accomplish little due to information sharing failures. The Child Care and Development Fund (CCDF) of the HHS received $7 billion in 2009 including $2 billion from the American Recovery and Reinvestment Act of 2009. Congress instructed CCDF to use the funds to subsidize childcare for children under age thirteen from low-income families, whose parents work or attend educational or job training programs. HHS estimated that information sharing failures resulted in payments to ineligible recipients, duplicate payments, and payments for services not received collectively totaling $833 million (11.9 percent of the funds appropriated to this program) (GAO 2010g).

In 2011, four agencies—the U.S. Department of Commerce (DOC), U.S. Department of Housing and Urban Development (HUD), the USDA, and the SBA—ran eighty programs to award economic aid to underserved communities, worth a total of $2.9 billion. These organizations did not share data with each other: every single one of the eighty programs overlapped with at least one other program. Fewer deserving communities received the help they needed due to this duplication (GAO 2012o). In 2013, the GAO accused agencies of failing to share information that resulted in failure to actualize President Obama's orders to make America more economically competitive (GAO 2013b).

In summary, citizens and residents suffer from public sector information-sharing failures that lead to disappointing results and sometimes tragic consequences in terms of human lives and billions of dollars lost. Improved information sharing is needed to support the day-to-day, back office tasks of agencies in an age when these agencies are required to tackle complex, interdisciplinary challenges. How do scholars account for such information sharing failures? How have practitioners attempted to improve information sharing over the past two decades? Answering this question is the objective of the next chapter.

2 Coerce, Consent, and Coax: Existing Information Sharing Approaches

The chapter defines the key concepts of "data," "information," and "knowledge." It suggests that we must enable agencies to discover and acquire access to data that other agencies possess before we can discuss the acquisition of knowledge. Next, the chapter proposes that legislatures employ three approaches to encourage agencies to improve information sharing: "coerce," "consent," and "coax." Theoretical arguments and case study analysis demonstrate that these three approaches are unsuccessful. Finally, the chapter introduces the book's novel approach to information sharing that emphasizes incentives and exchange.

Defining Data, Information, and Knowledge

Data is a set of discrete objective facts that form a record. Individual data elements contain a partial record of events and therefore lack meaning and purpose (Davenport and Prusak 1998, 2–3; Newcomer and Sharon 1991). Data is more lightweight, replicable, and faster to transmit than any other physical raw material in history (Carr 2003). This has led to rapidly increasing digitization. All organizations depend on digital data and manage and track it as records inside information systems. Vibrant information economies are born and digital dossiers increasingly shape our lives. Data elements are the raw material for the creation of information (Shulman, Thrane, and Shelley 2005; Solove 2004).

Information is "data endowed with relevance and purpose" (Drucker 2006, 129). People contextualize and categorize data in order to convert it into information. Information is a message created by senders for receivers. The information sender aims to impact the receiver's perception and behavior (Davenport and Prusak 1998, 3–4). Organizational information is more than the sum total of the individual data elements used to create it. A government official in the U.S. Centers for Disease Control and Prevention (CDC) may analyze and merge numerous data elements while writing a report about seasonal flu. However, when this CDC report is published, it acquires a new meaning: it now represents the CDC's official position on seasonal flu, and may prompt external entities (organizations and individuals) to act based on the report.

Knowledge is deeply embedded in individuals. It is framed experience, values, contextual information, and insights. Knowledge assets originate and are applied in the knowers. The human members of an organization transform information into knowledge by comparing information, connecting it, and discussing its implications for decisions and actions. Frequently, knowledge is deeply rooted in action, experience, and specific context and cannot be easily extracted from its human carrier (Alavi and Leidner 2001; Argote and Ingram 2000; Iverson and McPhee 2002; McLure Wasko and Faraj 2000). Organizations strive to embed knowledge in organizational practices and norms of behavior (Davenport and Prusak 1998, 5–6).

While using the common terms "information" and "information sharing," this book primarily focuses on government agency exchange of *data and datasets*. In our Big Data age, organizations that own raw data, the royal merchandise of our time, possess a distinct advantage over other organizations. Even latent data, whose value is not obvious to the organization, constitutes a valuable raw material in the information state due to its potential secondary uses (Mayer-Schonberger and Cukier 2013, 134). Most government organizations are aware of the latent value of their datasets and guard them tightly, as demonstrated in chapter 3. However, in order for data to have "secondary uses" there must be "secondary users." Agencies today cannot easily explore other agencies' datasets, and therefore cannot mesh these datasets with their own in the process of converting data to information and information to knowledge. This book's primary goal is to develop new theoretical foundations to empower incentivized agencies to share data more effectively.

The Coerce, Consent, and Coax Information Sharing Approaches

Scholars emphasize that information sharing is context-specific; it is not always positive. In some circumstances sharing information may even cause harm, while in others, not doing so may have harmful effects. Whether or not to share information must be considered in context and on a case-by-case basis (Thomas and Walport 2008). Still, scholars and laypeople alike are dismayed to discover information sharing failures in domains where information sharing is strongly merited (as exemplified in chapter 1). Until the late 1990s, the information sharing topic elicited little research interest. Since then, the number of scholarly papers on information sharing has grown (Wilson 2010).

Three main approaches dominate the information sharing literature: coerce, consent, and coax. The coerce approach mistrusts agencies and seeks to impose information sharing. In contrast, the consent approach argues that agencies can and do consent to share information to promote a greater common good. The coax approach is located in the middle of a theoretical continuum, between coerce and consent. It nudges agencies to improve information sharing by establishing mechanisms to support sharing.

The Coerce Approach

The coerce approach views government officials as selfish agency-centric actors who use computers as tools to increase their agency's reputation and autonomy (Kling 1980; Kling and Iacono 1984; Kraemer and King 1986; Ardichvill, Page, and Wentling 2003; Constant, Kiesler, and Sproull 1994; Jarvenpaa and Staples 2001; Jian and Jeffres 2006; Kolekofski and Heminger 2003; Marks et al. 2008; Yang and Maxwell 2011; Zhang, Dawes, and Sarkis 2005; Lazer and Maria 2004). Agencies mobilize new technologies to improve their standing in a political power game (Maor 2010; Maor and Sulitzeanu-Kenan 2013). They use information assets to promote their power, reputation, and autonomy in power struggles with other agencies. Concerns about narrow agency gains and mistrust drive agencies to hide information from each other. Agency-centric actors invest in data integration only if it furthers their own agency's interests (Fountain 2007; Hilgartner 2000; Krause and Douglas 2005; Moffitt 2010; Rourke and Edward 1961; Schneider and Ingram 1990; Stone 2002).

The coerce approach argues that agencies refuse to share information because the exposed information might reveal organizational weaknesses such as poor data quality. The agency might lose its discretion to publish only positive news or to "cook" the data to promote specific goals. Outsiders could use the information to discount the organization's reputation.

The exposed information might reveal overlaps among agencies. The legislature could then abolish programs and slash budgets. This argument explains the information-hiding behavior of public, private, not-for-profit, and even academic organizations (Accenture 2004; Akbulut 2003; Dawes 1996; Fountain 2007; Landsbergen and Wolken 1998; Pardo and Tayi 2007; Rocheleau 2003; Vangen and Huxham 2003).

In the United States, agencies must be coerced to share information because, at a systemic level, American government structures work against cross-agency information sharing. The U.S. system of governance was designed with the explicit intention of fragmenting authority and coordination across government. Every institutional feature of the American federal government including statutes, regulations, procedures, processes, and culture drives agencies toward differentiation and away from integration (Roberts 2006b, 314–315). Only Congress is authorized to appropriate funds for agency programs; congressional subcommittees are concerned with appropriating funds to support their narrow missions. Large agencies, such as the Environmental Protection Agency (EPA) and DHS, report to over seventy committees and subcommittees often with differing priorities (Fountain 2013). Congressional committees frequently promote single-issue legislation and even promote legislation to discourage agencies from sharing data. The U.S. law requires agencies to secure permission from Congress to develop shared interagency budgets for joint projects or operations. Even newer cross-agency legislative efforts such as the 2010 Government Performance and Results Act Modernization Act (GPRAMA) are layered on top of old legislative acts, institutions, and program charters that interfere with information sharing; these old acts are never removed from the law books and remain in effect (Fountain 2013).

U.S. federal IT vendors must be coerced because they are primarily concerned with maintaining current publicly funded projects rather than investing in new types of information sharing projects that Congress may cease to fund. For their part, senior public officials do not wish to defend (in public hearings and to the media) spending taxpayer funds on failing computer integration projects, so they further reduce the scope of IT projects including the elimination of interfaces between these projects and other existing IT systems. Fountain summarized the situation: "In a profound sense, the institutional underpinnings of U.S. federal government design—primarily the authorizations and appropriations processes and the practices that flow from them—strongly work against cross-agency collaboration" (2013, 46–47).

Over time, the proliferation of standalone agency systems complicates the job of integrating governmental data. Agencies view this integration work as a public good that must be paid for with nonagency resources to ensure that agency developers are not distracted from higher-priority tasks. This myopic and selfish behavior propels agencies to use but not contribute to new interagency information-sharing solutions until these solutions become so dated and poor in content that no one wants to use them (Flanagin, Monge, and Fulk 2001; Fountain 2007; Fulk et al. 2004; Krause and Douglas 2005; Premkumar 2003).

The coerce approach is pessimistic. It suggests that only politically powerful champions in positions of influence can coerce agencies to share (Srivastava, Bartol, and Locke 2006). However, such champions are rare, require political support, and drain efficiencies from other projects (Beath 1991; Kamal 2006; Kamal and Themistocleous 2006). Each administration differently defines the avenues for such champions to emerge. During the Clinton administration, leaderless and self-managing cross-agency working groups were formed with mixed results. During the Bush administration, "lead programs" with goal leaders located within the lead agency were used to more clearly define authority. During the Obama administration, cross-agency appointees are drawn from the Executive Office of the President (EOP) rather than from agencies (Fountain 2013, 59).

Yet the American president and his staff cannot champion every cross-agency information-sharing project without becoming stretched beyond their capacity across numerous projects. In a recent example, continuous Presidential efforts to increase information sharing among agencies to increase the volume of American exports have resulted in mixed results because the information barriers are simply too numerous for the small Presidential team to overcome (Fountain 2013; GAO 2013b).

The coerce argument is also tautological—successful information sharing projects become "evidence" that strong champions have overcome selfish interests; unsuccessful information sharing projects become "evidence" that champions have yet to emerge; one cannot refute this argument with empirical data. Most important, the coerce approach fails to address the fundamental challenge of overcoming agencies' disincentives to share information willingly. One unsuccessful DHS project illustrates this argument.

Failing to Coerce Agencies to Share: The Homeland Security Information System (HSIN) Case Study   The HSIN project's history exemplifies why information sharing cannot be commandeered by a single agency even in the most critical domain—combating terrorism. Prior to the creation of HSIN, local security officials complained that counterterrorism information received from federal agencies was not timely, accurate, or relevant (GAO 2003b). In 2003, DHS began designing HSIN as a nationwide collaboration for sharing Sensitive But Unclassified (SBU) data with partners who were engaged in preventing security threats. The system was designed to address the needs of thirty-five communities of interest (such as emergency management) operating within eighteen critical infrastructure sectors (such as commercial nuclear reactors). In 2007, DHS spent $70 million to build HSIN (GAO 2007a, 2007b, 2008d).

However, state and local agencies did not cooperate with the HSIN initiative. Local security officials resented the fact that DHS perceived the fight against terrorism as an exclusive federal responsibility. They wanted concrete benefits in exchange for providing data to DHS (GAO 2003b, 2006a, 2007a). Agencies chose to upgrade their own information sharing networks rather than join HSIN (GAO 2006a). Security managers questioned why DHS built HSIN from scratch instead of adopting an existing network such as one operated by the Department of Justice (DOJ), or the successful nationwide Regional Information Sharing System (RISS), operational since 1974 (GAO 2004b, 2007a, 2007b). In September 2007, DHS decided to terminate HSIN and then immediately launched a follow-up project called "HSIN Next Gen." DHS continued to employ a coerce approach while designing and building HSIN Next Gen.

In October 2010, DHS terminated the HSIN Next Gen project. This termination reduced DHS IT costs by nearly $129 million. DHS cited, among other things, continuing cost, schedule, and performance shortfalls and the lack of key IT management controls and capabilities that are essential to mitigating such shortfalls and ensuring successful system delivery (GAO 2013c). But in fact, the HSIN project failed twice because DHS did not treat other agencies as information sharing peers. DHS wanted other agencies to provide data and to let DHS alone "connect the dots" to prevent

terrorist attacks (GAO 2003b, 13). Given this approach, DHS did not create new information sharing partnerships, and did nothing to leverage
information sharing mechanisms in the private sector. HSIN's sad history
is not an outlier; selfish bureaucratic interests often confound coerce-type
information-sharing projects (GAO 2003d, 2008b, 2008c; White House
2010). In most cases, agencies have the means and the arguments to resist
sharing when it is imposed.

The Consent Approach

The consent approach emphasizes that government officers have a moral
obligation to serve the public. Agencies should use this moral obligation to
promote a culture of serving the greater common good. Moral interest and
community interest can then grow to become the dominant motivations
for sharing information (Ardichvill, Page, and Wentling 2003; Constant,
Kiesler, and Sproull 1994; Jian and Jeffres 2006; McLure Wasko and Faraj
2000). Scholars who subscribe to this approach contend that continuous
information sharing failures merely suggest that we have yet to find the
correct path to convince agencies to improve sharing for the greater common good.

Consent scholars correctly emphasize that, almost always, agencies do
not know what useful datasets other agencies own. Therefore, agencies'
consent to share information willingly with other agencies is imperative
(Kelman 2009; Noveck 2009). The key question is how to nudge officials
across agencies to communicate so that agencies can discover useful information for exchange (Robbins 2006). Consent scholars emphasize that
effective inter-organizational information exchange must be voluntary and
in service of common goals (Akbulut 2003; Hara et al. 2003; Dawes and
Prefontaine 2003; Jian and Jeffres 2006; Kolekofski and Heminger 2003;
Mayer-Schönberger and Lazer 2007b).

Agencies often prefer cooperative methods to the enforcement of legislation to coerce information sharing. The OMB has a statutory obligation to
enforce laws and rules. However, senior agency officials prefer to resolve
interagency challenges in collaborative ways. In a 2013 study published by
the Administrative Conference of the United States, government officials
testified that such collaboration is the best course of action and preferred to
focus OMB statutory powers only on impasses that resist solution (Fountain
2013, 38).

Similarly, EPA officials have argued that information sharing is context-specific and is not best pursued via means of legal coercion (GAO 2009d). In 2012, the EPA rejected a GAO recommendation to build a nationwide centralized database in which all state and local New Source Review (NSR) permits issued to fossil fuel electricity generating units would be deposited. As in other cases, the GAO had identified a complex information sharing flow that appeared to be broken. Information about NSR permits did not appear to flow from state agencies to EPA regional offices and then to the EPA itself. The GAO attempted to apply a template coercion solution to this problem: build a central database, compel all stakeholders to channel data into the database, and, then, analyze the data (in this case to understand who is polluting the air that Americans breathe). However, the EPA rejected the GAO recommendation, explaining that each NSR permit requires a case-specific analysis that is dependent on the particular state or local emissions requirements. Therefore, the analysis of NSRs is better performed by the ten EPA regional offices that maintain more intimate and consensual working relationships with state and local agencies that issue NSR permits (GAO 2012f).

Still, the consent approach is overly optimistic. It does not pay sufficient attention to the fine details of information sharing failures. It also ignores selfish and calculative aspects of human behavior. The consent approach disregards the dual nature of legislative power that can facilitate or impede information sharing. Sometimes legislation encourages information sharing, as occurred after the 2008 global financial meltdown, when The Dodd—Frank Wall Street Reform and Consumer Protection Act (2010) created the Office of Financial Research (OFR) as a mechanism to improve financial information sharing among U.S. regulators. However, more often than not, the U.S. Congress has enacted laws that have created information sharing barriers. In 2006, Congress barred by law the use of the creative budget-sharing mechanism of grants.gov, a joint federal grants online application program created by twenty-five agencies. Congress was concerned that such a bottom-up budgeting information sharing solution would limit congressional discretionary programming power over the executive branch; so representatives in the House passed a bill to stop this information sharing solution (Dawes 1996; Fountain 2007; Gil-Garcia, Chengalur-Smith, and Duchessi 2007; Gil-Garcia and Pardo 2005; Zhang and Dawes 2006).

Even agencies sometimes use legal means to resist consensual sharing. The DOE, the DOT, and the EPA refuse to share information about diesel emission reduction programs. The three agencies each separately run several programs (for a total of fourteen programs) to reduce mobile source diesel emissions that expend a total cost of $1.4 billion over five years (2007–2011). The GAO reported this refusal, admonished the agencies, and demanded that they begin coordinating their efforts to share information in this domain. Rather than follow this recommendation, the agencies mobilized the law to defend their right not to share information. One DOE official declared that diesel emission reduction is not even a "secondary responsibility" of his department according to the laws and regulations that govern DOE's functions. Likewise, a DOT official explained that diesel emissions reduction is an "out of scope" goal for DOT according to the legal mandates provided to his department; therefore, the official added, it is not "appropriate" for DOT to establish or share existing quantifiable diesel emissions measures (GAO 2012j, 49–51).

Consent scholars also emphasize technology as a silver bullet that can overcome narrow-minded organizational politics. But information systems, even the best of them, are merely tools. They cannot create goodwill and trust in places where these do not exist. Most important, the consent approach does not explain why agencies would agree to "free" precious information willingly. Today, useful data has a currency value—it is not free. The Obama administration's open data program, discussed in chapter 3, illustrates well the reasons why the consent approach often fails.

The Coax Approach
The circumstances surrounding the adoption of the coax approach are always the same. An urgent interdisciplinary problem captures the media attention. The public pressures politicians to "do something." Powerful agencies resist sharing. Legislatures decree the creation of a new information sharing mechanism. These mechanisms come in three varieties: coax via office, coax with standards, and coax through system-of-systems.

Coax via Office Legislatures create a new information sharing office because it is the easiest, fastest, and cheapest way to "do something." At first, everybody celebrates how the new office has advanced the intangible goal of creating a new information sharing culture. Several years later, the legislatures, the media, auditors, and the public discover that the office in fact had limited or no impact on actual information sharing.

Failure to Coax via Office: The PM-ISE Case Study After the 9/11 information sharing fiasco (see chapter 1), U.S. politicians demanded that the American intelligence community adopt a "need-to-share" attitude (Hamilton 2005). Following section 1016 of the Intelligence Reform and Terrorism Prevention Act of 2004, President George W. Bush ordered the creation of the office of the Program Manager of the Information Sharing Environment (PM-ISE) in the homeland security domain (http://www.ise.gov/background-and-authorities). The PM-ISE office was not created as a traditional program and therefore possessed limited means to promote information sharing (Program Manager Information Sharing Environment 2011). Its official goal was to: "Provide the means for sharing terrorism information in a manner that—to the greatest extent practicable—ensures a decentralized, distributed, and coordinated environment that builds upon existing systems and leverages ongoing efforts" (GAO 2011h, 6).

More specifically, the PM-ISE was tasked to (1) create a culture of sharing; (2) reduce barriers to sharing; (3) improve information sharing practices with federal, state, local, tribal, and foreign partners; and (4) institutionalize sharing (GAO 2011h, 11). The PM-ISE office coaxed sixteen powerful agencies including the CIA, the DOD, the DHS, and the FBI to cooperate. In July 2009, a Presidential committee was established to further oversee and guide the PM-ISE office.

In 2011, the GAO blamed the PM-ISE office for creating incomplete technology guidance documents, failing to engage key homeland security stakeholders, and not estimating the cost of its work. GAO staffers wrote: "More than 6 years after the enactment of the Intelligence Reform Act and initial efforts to create the ISE, there is not a clear definition of what the ISE is intended to achieve and include" (GAO 2011h, 14). Yet GAO staffers never asked the key question: was it reasonable to expect that a handful of officials and consultants in the PM-ISE office would successfully coax the intelligence community of about two thousand organizations and close to one million employees to improve information sharing (Washington Post 2010)?

Coax with Standards Legislatures also try to improve interagency information sharing by funding programs to develop interoperability standards.

"Interoperability" is defined as the ability of two or more systems to exchange information and to use the information that has been exchanged. At its highest level, interoperability empowers one agency to receive electronic and computable data from another agency and process the received data automatically. At lower levels of interoperability, agencies use computers to exchange data that is viewable but not computable (GAO 2009c, 4–5).

Failure to Coax with Standards: The VA-DOD Case Study   Over the past fifteen years, the U.S. Congress has generously funded the efforts of the VA and the DOD to create information sharing standards in the domain of electronic medical records. Jointly, the two departments operate one of the largest health care organizations in the world, providing care to sixteen million beneficiaries for an annual cost of $102 billion (estimate of 2013). However, the two departments had initially maintained separate health care organizations and incompatible IT systems (GAO 2012r).

The VA and DOD's first effort to build a joint Government Computer-based Patient Record (GCPR) system failed (1998–2002). By 2005, the two departments served the medical needs of fifteen thousand American servicemen and servicewomen wounded during the wars in Iraq and Afghanistan. The American public was outraged by reports on the VA-DOD failure to electronically exchange patients' medical records. Scholars, auditors, and media commentators demanded to know why American soldiers could not receive seamless medical service while being transferred between DOD and VA hospitals and clinics. Politicians responded quickly. In 2003, a Presidential taskforce demanded a "seamless transition from military service to veteran status" in health care, especially in the domain of sharing accurate and current medical information (GAO 2006d, 9). A Presidential Executive Order in April 2004 mandated a "widespread adoption of interoperable electronic health records" (GAO 2009a, 7). Twelve congressional hearings and twenty-three GAO reports between 2001 and 2011 addressed this topic (Panangala and Jansen 2013, 15–25).

The VA and DOD reacted slowly and partially. They established some standards to share limited information. For example, one system supported unidirectional transfer of information from DOD to VA about members who left active duty. Three other systems shared laboratory, clinical, pharmacy, and drug allergy data. The two departments referred to these systems as the "short term" solution. The GAO continuously reprimanded DOD and VA for failing to establish the desired long-term solution of adopting fully interoperable standards to exchange all medical data about all beneficiaries (GAO 2006d, 9–11).

Congress then passed the 2008 National Defense Authorization Act (Section 1635) requiring that the two departments build a "fully interoperable electronic personal health information" system and create a new interagency program office to advance this goal (GAO 2008f, 1). In response, at the beginning of December 2010, DOD and VA began designing the integrated Electronic Health Record (iEHR) and promised to complete it by 2017. However, in February 2012 DOD and VA abandoned the iEHR project after investing $1 billion in it. Officials from both departments concluded that iEHR would cost $12 billion as opposed to the original estimated cost of $4 billion. VA then decided to modernize its own electronic health records system relying on its existing open source (OS) software solution. DOD decided to search for a commercial solution to unify its different electronic health records systems (some of them are still paper-based) (Johnson 2013; Panangala and Jansen 2013).

This painfully slow information sharing progress is partially due to the immense size of the medical operations of the two departments and the need to protect patients' privacy (e.g., as stipulated by the Health Insurance Portability and Accountability Act of 1996). A deeper reason for this slow pace is that the VA and the DOD lack incentives to act faster and more vigorously. American taxpayers have already paid billions of dollars to address this problem. Was there no other way to spend the money more wisely to incentivize the two departments to act more effectively?

Coax with System-of-Systems The strongest coaxing mechanism is a system-of-systems. This concept highlights interoperability among different systems as the single most important feature of system design. Therefore, interoperability is built in parallel to the construction of individual systems. This change in thinking represents an improvement over the traditional and costly approach of developing individual systems first and then attempting to integrate them later on (GAO 2003c, 2). However, system-of-systems projects are difficult to execute. Their builders chase moving targets because whenever the underlying individual systems change, the overarching networking system must also change. Unless project requirements are defined well and in advance, these projects quickly become complex, extremely expensive, and prone to fail.

Failure to Coax with System-of-Systems: The FCS Case Study   The U.S. Army's Future Combat Systems (FCS) project (2003–2009) exemplifies the promise and pitfalls of these projects. With FCS, the U.S. Army wanted to create new brigades equipped with new manned and unmanned vehicles linked by an unprecedented fast and flexible battlefield network. This project involved creating fourteen completely new weapon systems all connected by a powerful wireless network. FCS remains the greatest technology integration challenge that the DOD and the U.S. Army have ever faced (Klein 2007; GAO 2008e).

The FCS project schedule was overly ambitious as the U.S. Army planned to build and deploy fourteen different combat vehicles and fifty different critical technologies in twelve years (the Army, in its entire history, has not deployed a single new tank that involves five critical technologies in less than five years). Demonstrations of the new technologies were small and inefficient. Requirements came in late and were incomplete. Three years into this project, the Army added three new combat systems and pushed the project deadline by four years. These changes increased the number of lines of software code to support the overarching networking system from 61.4 million to 95.1 million, three times more than the most complex software projects in DOD's history including the Joint Strike Fighter (22.9 million lines of code) and the Multi-Mission Maritime Aircraft (24.5 million lines of code). Correspondingly, the program cost increased from the original estimate of $92 billion in 2003 to $162 billion in 2008, making FCS the second-costliest weapon project in history after the $256 billion Joint Strike Fighter program (Capaccio 2006). GAO officials described the abysmal status of the program: "Almost 5 years into the program, the Army and LSI have not yet fully defined how the FCS network is expected to function, how they plan to build it, and how they plan to demonstrate it" (GAO 2008e, 2). In April–May 2009, the FCS program was terminated. Other failing and expensive system-of-systems American federal projects include the FAA project (1980–2000, estimated waste: $35 billion) and the IRS project (1994–1998, estimated waste: $8 billion) (Carr and Cone 2002; Stengel 1997).

Comparing the Coerce, Consent, and Coax Approaches

The coerce, consent, and coax approaches contradict one another in their explanation of information sharing failures. The coax approach emphasizes the dense nature of federal computer systems that defies all attempts at modernization (hence, the need to coax sharing among electronic mountains), while the coerce approach claims that agencies can reengineer such systems if ordered to do so. In explaining the cause of information sharing failures, the coerce approach highlights selfish human motives while the coax approach emphasizes complex man-machine relationships.

In explaining the driving force of information-sharing projects, consent scholars highlight altruism while coerce scholars emphasize obedience and discipline. In measuring the success of information-sharing projects, consent scholars emphasize soft human factors such as enthusiasm and willingness to use new social media technologies to promote the greater common good, while coax scholars stress more tangible factors such as changing legislation and centralizing information sharing flows.

The consent approach predicts that successful information-sharing projects can change the nature of modern government while coerce and coax approaches consider failure to be the standard output of such projects. Overall, information sharing scholars oscillate between doomsday information-sharing failure accounts (the coerce approach) and naïve expectations that technology or legislation can overcome these failures (the consent and coax approaches).

Legislatures sometimes oscillate in choosing which approach to use. For example, in 2003, the European Union (EU) decided to employ the consent approach to encourage European agencies to release datasets voluntarily. In 2013, EU legislatures changed direction and adopted the coerce approach, ordering agencies to release their datasets (European Commission 2013). Such changes accomplish little concrete information sharing results. Agencies' datasets remain duplicated, fragmented, or inaccessible to outsiders. Agencies also remain concerned about how they will be able to control their vital information resources and how to receive fair compensation for granting access to their datasets.

Above all else, the coerce, consent, and coax approaches fail because they do not address the root cause of the public sector's information sharing failure—how to change the behavior of the officials in command of public sector informational resources. It is not easy to change this behavior. Public sector culture is risk averse and highlights accountability over and above entrepreneurship (Janssen, Charalabidis, and Zuiderwijk 2012, 12). However, with some small, carefully designed incentives it might be possible to nudge officials to begin engaging each other in a serious discussion about improving information sharing as explained in the next section.

Introducing the Incentives-Driven Information Sharing Approach

The previous section raised the key information sharing questions: how can we entice senior public officials in command of agencies that know little about each other to *want* to share information? How can we change these officials' basic predisposition from being overly information protective to becoming information-sharing oriented?

Mancur Olson proposed one answer to these questions. Olson argued that members of a large organization would not act in the group's common interest unless motivated by selective incentives. He defined a selective incentive as one that applies to the individual members of the organization depending on whether they do or do not contribute to the provision of the collective good. He distinguished between membership in large and small groups. Small groups are able to motivate members with a shared objective. In contrast, large groups must provide selective incentives in order to motivate their members to contribute to the common good (Olson 1971, 1982).

Researchers have documented how Olson's selective incentives have successfully promoted information sharing. One such study demonstrated how a performance-based reward system significantly affected the willingness of staffers in Korean organizations to share knowledge (Kim and Lee 2006). The information revolution provided additional evidence in support of Olson's ideas. For example, eBay (where sellers are eager to maintain their high buyer approval ratings) and Travelocity (where frequent flyer miles are used to encourage travelers to remain loyal to the same airline) illustrate how small, selective incentives can nudge people to change their economic behavior. The media has also taken notice of the power of incentives to nudge agencies to share data (Economist 2010a, 11). Simply put, in a capitalist society where our self-worth and social position are often economically based, the provision of small but concrete financial rewards for those who contribute to an institution's information sharing mechanism is the most effective way to influence the behavior of the entire workforce.

Olson's theory emphasized individuals rather than organizations. Subsequent scholars expanded his theory and described how selective incentives could be used to entice organizations to reduce costs and improve efficiency and performance (Rainey, Backoff, and Levine 1976). Scholars also noted how selective incentives can improve inter-organizational knowledge sharing (Dawes 1996; Akbulut 2003; Vann 2005; Kim and Lee 2006; Clarkson, Jacobsen, and Batcheller 2007; Willem and Buelens 2007). One study explained how organizations nurture their reputation as honest traders to support future trades with other organizations (Barzelay and Kaboolian 1990; Tomz 2001). Another study explained how the provision of organizational incentives helps build a critical mass of participants in a new information system (Monge et al. 1998). Organizational selective incentives, unlike coercion and penalties, also appear to be effective in enticing smaller organizations to share information with larger ones (Hart and Saunders 1997; Iacovou, Benbasat, and Dexter 1995). This book emphasizes *organizational* selective incentives because information sharing is a big job that requires agencies to collectively demonstrate willingness to share information. In contrast, *personal* selective incentives might lead to information sharing improvements that are myopic and nonsustainable. For example, government officers who receive information sharing bonus points in performance reviews may increase sharing to win such points irrespective of the quality or importance of the shared data. Certainly, there is an important place for awarding personal selective incentives in large and hierarchical organizations; however, the improvement of information sharing among numerous agencies requires more than awarding selective incentives to individuals.

The incentives-driven approach seeks to nudge agencies as *institutions* to interact with other agencies via frequent information sharing exchanges. Such interactions are expected to generate deeper trust among agencies that, in turn, will generate increased exchange. Organizational trust refers to the commonly held belief in one agency that, in the future and in an uncertain environment, another agency will behave in a predictable, reciprocal, and fair manner. Trust enables an agency to take risks and accept vulnerabilities in a relationship with another agency irrespective of the trustor's ability to monitor the trustee (Dirks and Ferrin 2001; Dyer and Chu 2003; Hart and Saunders 1997; Mayer, Davis, and Schoorman 1995; Vangen and Huxham 2003; Zaheer and McEvily 1998). Scholars, in fields as diverse as management and education, depict a virtuous cycle in which trust and information sharing are an antecedent and an outcome of each other (Piderit, Flowerday, and Von Solms 2011; Tschannen-Moran 2001).

Opposition to the idea of using selective incentives to improve information sharing remains strong. Several scholars argue that exchange rationale would not help to advance information sharing (Culnan and Armstrong 1999; Jarvenpaa and Staples 2001; Kim and Mauborgne 1998). Jacobs emphasized the "guardian syndrome" of agencies whose role is to act as guardians who embody the ethos and virtues of the traditional Roman Praetorian Guard including obedience, hierarchy, honor, the shunning of trade, and the dispensing of largesse. She warned that agencies that adopt exchange logic would grow to become "monstrous moral hybrids" whose guardian ethos is corrupted by greed. She claimed that a public agency must not run like a business and should not try and copycat the business practices of private sector corporations (Jacobs 1992). Other scholars have suggested that government officers are endowed with sufficient intrinsic moral obligation to improve information sharing; extrinsic incentives would cause this moral obligation to degenerate into selfish acts (McLure Wasko and Faraj 2000; Osterloh and Frey 2000). One scholar argued that incentives would further empower data-producing agencies to exploit weaker data-consuming agencies. He asserted that agencies should charge other agencies only the cost of reproducing and disseminating data (Prins 2004). An EU directive (2003) adopted this approach.

This book advances the practical approach of using organizational selective incentives to improve interagency information sharing rather than relying on the naïve expectation that agencies will behave altruistically and agree to share information. It proposes to provide selective incentives to entice self-interested agencies to develop information assets and sell access to these assets to buyer-agencies. Like Bliss who displayed goodwill and offered small concrete incentives to develop a new science of biblical archeology, the book claims that such incentives can prompt agency officials to engage each other in new information sharing conversations and, later on, improve actual interagency information sharing. Before developing this idea, the next chapter empirically examines the consent approach that currently enjoys media attention and public support in more than forty countries worldwide.

3 Why Open Data Finds Agencies' Doors Closed

The chapter defines the open data (OD) concept and narrates the historical evolution and vision of OD programs. It explains why critics predicted that agencies would not cooperate with these programs. Next, the chapter discusses why agencies' OD compliance was poorly measured, then describes the first empirical, rigorous study of the pioneering U.S. federal OD program (2010–2012). The study reveals that while agencies claimed to comply with OD, they did very little to justify this claim. Studies of non-U.S. OD programs reinforce this conclusion. The chapter concludes with a discussion of agencies' resistance to fully cooperating with OD programs. This discussion reinforces two lessons revealed in the discussion of Bliss's archeological work practices in the preface: (1) the need to carefully observe the information policies of previous generations that are inscribed into legacy systems and accept the limitations these policies impose on information sharing efforts; and (2) the requirement to adopt an incentives schema to nudge government officials to share information resources.

Defining Open Data

OD is non-privacy-restricted and nonconfidential data that is produced with public funds and is made available without any restrictions on its distribution (Janssen, Charalabidis, and Zuiderwijk 2012, 2). OD programs attempt to satisfy the requirement that governments release high quality, complete, and timely data in a downloadable and license-free format that computers can automatically discover and exchange (Harper 2011, 1). The key idea behind the OD initiative is to create an environment where agencies release valuable data free of charge and the public builds applications to analyze the data. The hope is that this combination of liberated data and open source applications will increase transparency, participation, and collaboration (Lakhani, Austin, and Yi 2010).

Normative OD scholars emphasize that excessive bureaucratic secrecy is corrosive because it exacerbates mistrust, promotes corruption, and is undemocratic in nature. They claim that citizens have a right to be informed about what the government is doing (Moynihan 1999; Stiglitz 2003). Recent developments in digitization, the Internet, and social media provide new opportunities to release such governmental information to the public (Berners-Lee 2010; Noveck 2012). Instrumental scholars claim that OD is an effective error-correction system and that it also diminishes corruption (Florini 2004, 21). Normative and instrumental scholars rely on three assumptions: (1) politicians will agree to cede control over some information; (2) agencies will release data willingly; and (3) citizens will use the published data. Critics argue that empirical evidence does not support these assumptions (Janssen, Charalabidis, and Zuiderwijk 2012, 3).

Proponents also intend that OD programs will advance economic prosperity and the Open Government vision. This vision includes citizens harnessing social media tools to participate actively in governmental workflows. Open Government, in turn, is expected to contribute to transparency. Transparency is openness to public scrutiny as defined by the rights and abilities of organizations and individuals to access government information and information about government (Bannister and Connolly 2011, 5).

President Obama's OD Blitzkrieg Campaign

While campaigning, Obama promised to reverse the post 9/11 "retreat from openness" (Roberts 2006a, 19). During the seventy-seven days between Election Day and Inauguration Day, the Obama-Biden transition crew commissioned a team to prepare the Open Government initiative. This team identified organizations that were willing to support a transparency agenda. President Obama aimed to establish an "unprecedented level of openness in government" (Millar 2011).

American Open Government architects then launched a blitzkrieg-style campaign to enforce openness on agencies. On his first full day in office (January 21, 2009), at the height of the worst economic crisis America had experienced since the Great Depression, President Obama signed three memorandums and two executive orders. Four of these five documents promoted Open Government and one of them was the official Open Government Memorandum (White House 2009). In March 2009, Vivek Kundra was appointed as the first-ever federal chief information officer (CIO). In early 2009, rank and file government officials were invited to provide the administration with direct input (instead of commenting via their agencies). In March 2009, U.S. Attorney General Eric Holder reversed the Ashcroft memorandum of October 2001, which advised agencies to employ caution in cooperating with the Freedom of Information Act (FOIA). Holder declared: "in the face of doubt, openness prevails" (Holder 2009). A barrage of Open Government initiatives surfaced including eRulemaking, IT Dashboard, Recovery.gov, and USAspending.gov. The administration showcased Open Government stories and ensured that senior appointees adhered to Open Government principles (Millar 2011).

On May 21, 2009, the 120-day anniversary of the President's Open Government Memorandum, a team headed by the CIOs of the DOI and the EPA launched www.data.gov (OMB 2009). The architects of data.gov were determined to make it the premier web publishing location for important federal datasets. Then, on December 8, 2009, the OMB published the Open Government Directive (OGD). The OGD ordered agencies to make as much information as possible available online (Economist 2010a). At the outset, agencies were instructed to publish *at least* three high-value datasets on the web. High-value datasets were defined as containing: "information that can be used to increase agency accountability and responsiveness; improve public knowledge of the agency and its operations; further the core mission of the agency; create economic opportunity; or respond to need and demand as identified through public consultation" (OMB 2009).

These datasets were required to have never before been made available or published in a downloadable and open format (OMB 2009). These first three datasets were considered a down payment, or a minimum; agencies were expected to continually make new datasets available to the public (McDermott 2010). The OGD specifically demanded that agencies "identify additional high value information not yet available and establish a reasonable timeline for publication online in open formats with specific target dates" (OMB 2009, 7).

Through these executive acts, senior level appointments and positive government rhetoric, OD grew from an idea to a doctrine. New OD supporters joined the government including Beth Simone Noveck, a law professor and social networking entrepreneur, who was appointed deputy chief technology officer (CTO) of the White House Office of Science and Technology Policy. She argued that common people's expertise combined with the limitless potential of social networking would create a new federal knowledge ecosystem (Noveck 2009).

OD architects created a public relations (PR) buzz that continues to characterize the program to date (Lakhani, Austin, and Yi 2010). OD architects continue to claim that OD mobilized the expertise of the masses, harnessed the hidden desire of agencies to share data, and gave birth to a community of innovators. In the OD jargon, individuals are "called to arms" to support the OD program, everything associated with "the government of the past" is brushed away, and the spirit of openness and innovation is contagious (Noveck 2011). The Obama administration and the media highlighted how OD helped the economy and lowered the cost of governmental operations (White House 2010). Police crime maps and school performance tables attracted millions of visits. Stories appeared about organizations that used OD to build life-saving applications such as one that helps people make informed decisions about heart surgeries (http://www.scts.org).

President Obama's OD blitzkrieg campaign also inspired politicians and governments worldwide to adopt OD principles. British Prime Minister Brown launched his "Making Public Data Public" campaign in March 2010, two months after the United Kingdom (UK) OD site became operational (http://data.gov.uk). The European Commission (EC) launched an OD portal at the end of December 2012 (http://open-data.europa.eu/en). At the end of 2013, the U.S. OD portal displayed the flags of forty-three countries, four institutions, and thirty-nine U.S. states that operate OD portals (http://www.data.gov/opendatasites). On the third anniversary of the American OD portal (May 21, 2012), the U.S. General Services Administration (GSA) in partnership with India's National Informatics Centre produced an open source product called Open Government Platform (OGPL) so that other countries could copycat the American example. The OD program promotes a world in which agencies and laypeople share data and applications altruistically.

Early Predictions of Agencies' Willingness to Support OD

U.S. OD architects quickly announced that all agencies succeeded in releasing high-value datasets by the designated deadline (Data.Gov 2010). Proponents explained that agencies understood that they are the mere custodians of the information they collect and that society will be more innovative once this information is released. Supporters predicted that agencies would continue to embrace the OD vision (Mayer-Schonberger and Cukier 2013, 116–117).

In contrast, other scholars hypothesized that senior agency officials would resist cooperation with OD programs due to three reasons: (1) the OD program's unrealistic goals; (2) lack of funding to support OD; and (3) a contradiction between the OD vision and agencies' own views of their data-managing function. First, scholars claimed that OD proponents promoted an unrealistic goal of maximizing transparency that did not take bureaucratic culture into account. Agency officers are rewarded for secrecy not openness; they are not accustomed to live in glass houses. So, critics hypothesized that OD might alarm agency officers who are wary of absolute transparency (Bannister and Connolly 2011, 16; Coglianese 2009; Huijboom and Van den Broek 2011, 7). In addition, the OD concept and goals were not clearly defined. To some people, OD meant the release of downloadable data. Others interpreted OD to imply the release of data to boost the economy. Still others considered OD to be a program designed to release data about the government. Critics predicted that agencies would find it difficult to cooperate with ill-defined OD goals (Yu and Robinson 2012).

Second, critics proposed that proponents ignored the nonfunded cost of OD programs. To cooperate with OD, agencies would need to hire additional staff, adjust data to different formats, and improve metadata. These activities are costly and were not funded (Bannister and Connolly 2011, 10). OD architects pressured agencies to adopt a corporate attitude. Noveck advised agencies to study how Facebook governs "900 million inhabitants" with only 3,000 employees (2012). But as discussed earlier there are good reasons why agencies do not function like corporations. U.S. federal web designers comply with numerous regulatory regimes (Robinson et al. 2009, 162), and agencies rely on legacy systems that were not designed to support the continuous provision of data. Therefore, OD critics suggested, agencies would have to pay programmers to manually construct "datasets" from legacy databases.

Finally, OD critics hypothesized that the OD vision might clash with how agencies see their role as data managers. These scholars argued that agencies might not wish to be associated with a program that increases information overload, and could tarnish their reputation as collectors and users of data. Evans and Campos described citizens' task of sorting out the relevance and reliability of released OD datasets as a confusing, "herculean task" (2013, 172). In May 2010, the UK Treasury published the Combined Online Information System (COINS) data. This data was so voluminous and poorly documented that the British Broadcasting Commission (BBC) and the *Guardian* newspaper had to hire software developers to decipher it (McClean 2011, 8–9). Agency officials also noted that, in practice, only 1 percent of all www.data.gov visitors have downloaded a dataset (White House 2013, 17). Other scholars even hypothesized that agencies might promote OD as a means to deflect attention from their unwillingness to support other transparency channels such as the freedom of information (FOI) program (Horner 2012; Rosenberg 2013).

In conclusion, critics proposed that OD programs would not overcome agencies' resistance to releasing data. These critics used early empirical observations to support claims that some agencies refused to publish data about their internal operations; others refused to share their data release plans; and still others did not live up to the goals that they themselves created. Critics used anecdotal data to propose that agencies repackaged data previously published elsewhere and that the data lacked descriptions and, sometimes, could not be downloaded. Agencies released datasets about their regulated domains and not about their own operations. Data was duplicated on several web portals. Scholars hypothesized that this dense and incomprehensible cloud of datasets of little value was a smokescreen to promote the perception of transparency (Bass et al. 2010; Coglianese 2009; Evans and Campos 2013, 174; Harper 2010, 1, 2012, 2; Hendler 2009, 2010; Janssen 2012, 8; Shkabatur 2012, 65).

Measuring U.S. Federal Agencies' OD Compliance

The first studies of OD empirical performance mostly used anecdotal data to suggest that agencies were not fully cooperating with OD dictates. An early consortium of volunteers conducted its own evaluation of the first OD datasets released and discovered that initial datasets were a "mixed bag," meaning that they contained both high-value and non-high-value datasets (Harper 2010; McDermott 2010, 402). Harper argued that agencies did not release basic data including the U.S. government's organization chart (2011, 2). The Congressional Research Service (CRS) conceded that there was no enforcement mechanism in Open Government to ensure agency compliance (Ginsberg 2011).

U.S. Open Government architects introduced an evaluation of the Open Government project (the "Open Government Dashboard") based on a self-assessment questionnaire completed by the agencies. Not surprisingly, agencies awarded themselves high marks despite significant discrepancies in degrees of compliance with the assessment criteria. A comparison of the self-assessments of two agencies illustrates this inconsistency. The GSA and the VA awarded themselves high marks on the questionnaire for meeting expectations. However, to meet project expectations the GSA created a website with hundreds of new web pages available via the site, while the VA indexed three documents and two links to older information that existed on the VA's website prior to the launch of the OD program. None of the agencies awarded themselves the red "Fails to Meet Expectations" marks.

To date, agencies' OD compliance is a relatively new research field in which little systematic research has been performed (Zuiderwijk et al. 2012, 169). OD research reports mainly include conceptual arguments, anecdotes, and technological discussions (Janssen, Charalabidis, and Zuiderwijk 2012, 3). OD supporters continue to argue that "bottom-up demands for OD are mounting everywhere" (Fioretti 2012, 2). Critics respond that neoliberal politicians have manipulated OD to mobilize public pressure to expand governmental services outsourcing (Bates 2012, 7; Longo 2011, 44–46). Yet, proponents and critics alike use little systemic quantitative analysis to substantiate their arguments.

Developing an independent method to empirically measure the impact of OD was challenging. Data.gov did not respond to inquiries requesting that the site release data about itself (surprising as data about open data should perhaps be the most open data); however, it was possible to measure how agencies truly responded to the program by downloading performance data that data.gov published. Anticipating that this performance data may one day be removed, the research team downloaded it weekly and during one full year (May 16, 2010–May 8, 2011). The analysis that follows is the first systematic empirical study of U.S. federal agencies' *actual* OD compliance.

U.S. Agencies' Passive-Aggressive OD Attitude

An initial empirical examination supports OD's assumptions. The OD program successfully recruited agencies to index data via data.gov (during the surveyed fifty-two weeks the number of participating agencies grew from 105 to 169). Over the same period, participating agencies more than doubled the number of datasets that they indexed (3,252 datasets in May 2011 as compared to only 1,283 datasets in May 2010). The public registered over one million downloads of datasets. Logarithmic panel regression analysis provides further support for OD's assumption: an increase by 1 percent in the number of indexed datasets is correlated with an increase in the number of downloads.

Yet, a closer examination reveals a different story. Figure 3.1 presents OD's history in pictorial form. It shows that most agencies met the minimal OGD requirements by publishing a small number of datasets (the dotted line: the scale of 0–2,000 measures the aggregated number of high-value datasets agencies indexed on the OD website) and did virtually nothing thereafter. The public consequently discovered that data.gov is of little value and the number of downloads from data.gov did not significantly increase (the solid line: the scale of 0–60,000 measures the weekly number of downloads of all datasets. Note that, without direct access to the raw OD weblogs, it is impossible to determine whether these downloads were carried out by government employees or private individuals. Another early empirical OD study similarly concluded that the public did not "participate meaningfully" in the program (Lukensmeyer, Goldman, and Stern 2011).

A further examination of the September 2010 spike in the number of high-value datasets supports the argument that most agencies provided minimal data to data.gov. The spike is principally accounted for by an increase in mid-September 2010 in the number of EPA high-value datasets from 330 to 1729. These datasets (and their corresponding downloads) comprised numerous Toxics Release Inventory (TRI) reports, each reporting data for a single state and a single year (from 1986 to 2010), which the EPA had been publishing on its own website since 1998. Furthermore, the EPA's

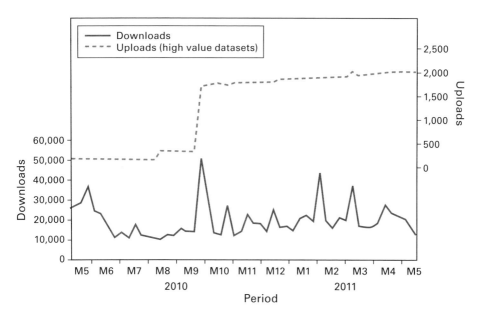

Figure 3.1
Growth of indexed high-value datasets and downloads to and from the U.S. open data portal (www.data.gov).
Source: Peled 2011, 2087.

CIO was one of the two founding CIOs of data.gov, providing further motivation for the EPA to support the project.

Since its inception, data.gov has grown to become the playground of a tiny group of agencies. Kundra emphasizes that, during its first two years, data.gov has grown from 47 to 389,681 datasets and applications (Kundra 2011). However, in May 2011, only 5 out of 169 participating agencies accounted for 99.37 percent of all datasets and applications (378,488 of 380,879 datasets as measured on May 8, 2011) as shown in figure 3.2.

Almost all uploads were geographical datasets and applications (98.90 percent or 376,678 of 380,879 datasets); these artifacts consisted of data maps that existed, in one form or another, on the U.S. Census Bureau (Census) website, the U.S. Geological Survey (USGS) website, and the U.S. National Oceanic and Atmospheric Administration (NOAA) website, before data.gov was launched. The Census and the USGS remain the *only* two agencies displaying a "negative ratio" on indexed datasets and applications, to number of downloads. The Census has indexed almost fourteen times more

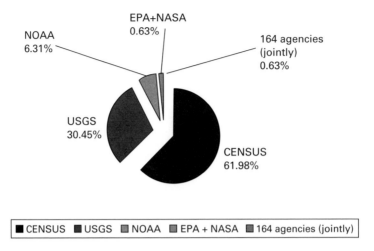

Figure 3.2
Uploads (data and applications) by agency to the U.S. open data portal (www
.data.gov).
Source: Peled 2011, 2088.

data artifacts than the number of downloads received via data.gov. This is
likely due to the fact that the public can find similar data for free elsewhere
(via Google Maps, for example) or can directly access the data on the websites of the Census, USGS, and NOAA. A CRS report noted that USGS and
NOAA accounted for the "vast majority" of all datasets published on data.
gov. The author of this report added: "many agencies provided three or
fewer datasets to the site" (Ginsberg 2011, 15).

Even excluding these geographical postings, data.gov remains the
domain of a small number of agencies. Five agencies jointly command
58 percent of all indexed nongeographical datasets (with the EPA alone
owning more than 47 percent of all nongeographical indexed datasets).
Likewise, four agencies jointly possess 58 percent of all nongeographical
applications indexed on data.gov. The same is true for high-value datasets:
the EPA alone commands almost 70 percent of these datasets. Four agencies
own over 56 percent of all high-value applications. The small club of active
data.gov players includes the EPA, Census, USGS, NOAA and to a lesser
extent NASA and DOD.

Almost all agencies were equally unlikely to update previously uploaded
datasets or to upload new ones. Figure 3.3 measures the median number

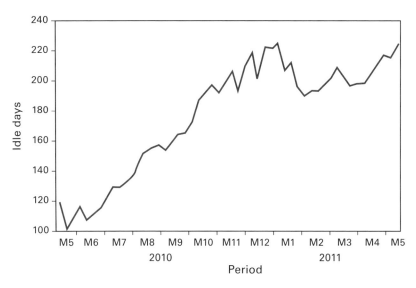

Figure 3.3
Median number of idle days since last update/upload to the U.S. open data portal (www.data.gov).
Source: Peled 2011, 2089.

of idle days since an agency last updated an existing dataset or uploaded a new one. The Y-axis measures the number of days since an agency last updated or uploaded new datasets. The linear growth displayed in figure 3.3 shows that agencies increasingly declined to update or upload datasets. As of May 2011, the average participating agency had not returned to data. gov for 222 days since its last data.gov transaction. Almost 30 percent of all agencies (50 out of 169) have remained idle in data.gov for one full year or more. Moreover, one organization (Nextgov.com) reported that on January 26, 2010, many of the datasets that agencies claim to have posted on the website on January 22, 2010, were not available on data.gov on January 25, 2010 (Ginsberg 2011).

Figures 3.1, 3.2, and 3.3 suggest that only a handful of agencies remained active in data.gov as of mid-2011. The average agency did the minimum required in order to qualify as a "participating agency" and, shortly afterward, stopped cooperating with the program.

These trends intensified in the years after the OD site launch as evidenced by the fact that in the beginning of 2011, OD architects lowered the "participating agency" requirements. On average, the forty-two agencies that joined data.gov between May and December 2010 published seven times more datasets on their first appearance in data.gov than the twenty-two participating agencies that joined data.gov between January and May 2011. Most important, about 80 percent of all agencies (no matter when they joined data.gov) did not publish high-value datasets on their first appearance on data.gov.

For its part, the public noted the meager and stale content available on data.gov and did not increase the number of downloads from the site. In May 2011, 75 percent of all participating agencies and subagencies experienced fewer than 100 downloads each week. Over a period of one full year, 54 percent of all agencies experienced fewer than 1,000 downloads of their datasets and applications. The same tiny club of agencies that indexed most of the datasets and applications received the lion's share of all downloads. The EPA alone commanded 27.51 percent of the aggregated downloads. The trends described earlier are the same for both independent and nonindependent agencies (a nonindependent agency is subordinate to the White House or one of the cabinet departments such as DOJ or DHS).

Recently, the CRS, the *Economist* magazine and several scholars published new empirical evidence demonstrating that most agencies shared little and non-meaningful data via OD portals. For example, agencies released datasets concerning entities that they regulate but did not release data regarding their own internal operations (Bingham and Foxworthy 2012; Economist 2012, 35; Ginsberg 2011; Lukensmeyer, Goldman, and Stern 2011). These studies support Wonderlich's claim that OD architects created "wiggle room" that enabled agencies to evade the White House's best OD intentions (Wonderlich 2011, 2).

Non-U.S. Agencies' OD Resistance

Non-U.S. agencies also reluctantly cooperated with initial OD programs. Janssen, Charalabidis, and Zuiderwijk described the first European OD datasets: "The adage 'garbage in, garbage out' certainly holds true for open data" (2012, 16). One government officer explained the OD strategy of many European agencies: "Only data that is relatively safe is publicized and dropped in the larger pile . . . some of them even hope that the data will not be discovered in this pile . . . there are no mechanisms for gaining any feedback about its use" (12).

Likewise, a British audit report revealed that the evolution of the UK OD program was similar to that of its earlier American sister program. British politicians pressured government officers to adopt the OD program. However, British agencies were well aware of their data's value. Several agencies regularly trade information assets with other agencies. Therefore agencies uploaded datasets of uneven quality to the UK OD website. They did nothing thereafter to track the cost and benefits of uploading the datasets. Most of the uploaded data was already available in a more useful format on these agencies' websites. Agencies reported that they were "in compliance" with the instruction to "free data." The PR image of the UK OD program remains stronger than the program's results (UK Comptroller and Auditor General 2012).

Citizens in these countries discovered the low value of the uploaded data and opted not to download it. Initially, software developers enthusiastically developed applications for newly released data. However, these early applications were plucking the low-hanging fruit, which was quickly depleted, after which developers lost interest in the harder task of sifting through freed valueless data. In New Zealand, an OD project died prematurely after developers discovered that facts were dumped into cyberspace without purpose, and refrained from developing applications for them (Economist 2010b).

Andrew Scott, a former governing Director of Transparency and Digital Engagement, and a member of the British Transparency Board, named the reluctance of British agencies to release information "data hugging." He explained that one reason why agencies "hugged" their data so closely, refusing to release it, was the issue of data ownership. Like their American counterparts, British agencies believe that they have ownership over data and are therefore reluctant to release it for free (Halonen 2012). Similarly, in several European countries, agencies that trade data are reluctant to free it (Van Den Broek et al. 2011).

In the developing world, OD programs are still new. Initial evidence suggests that here too there is a significant gap between OD rhetoric and actual performance. For example, in November 2012, after two years of planning, Tim Berners-Lee proudly announced the birth of Ghana's OD portal (http://data.gov.gh), but one year later Ghana features the same 122 raw datasets, one application, no high-value datasets, and no participating agencies on its U.S.-style OD site (Berners-Lee 2012).

Two important caveats apply to these findings. First, we must remember that an agency's seemingly valueless OD dataset may contain hidden value due to unanticipated "secondary uses" (Mayer-Schonberger and Cukier 2013, 104–105). Second, OD is an emerging transparency program. It takes a long time for such a program to mature. For example, ninety countries have passed right to information (RTI) legislation since the birth of the RTI movement in Sweden nearly 250 years ago (1766). So, we must grant the OD program more time to grow. Still, for the information sharing purposes of this book, it is important to explore why agencies resisted cooperation with the first OD programs.

Why Agencies Resist OD

The prerogative to decide how, when, and why to disseminate data has always been the source of bureaucratic power. OD architects failed to consider that datasets are valuable assets that agencies work hard to create and expect to be compensated for releasing. OD architects disdainfully call this argument "the nasty, brutish, and short worldview of government" (Noveck 2009, 190). However, government officers understood that, in the name of transparency, OD architects were demanding agencies to give up possession of that which defines their status and identity in the new information era— electronic data. Disinclined to openly confront the popular OD program, agencies adopted a passive-aggressive stance.

Scholars noted that certain agencies were reluctant to free datasets because they derived income from selling these datasets (Huijboom and Van den Broek 2011, 9; Van Den Broek et al. 2011, 2). In Britain, the Met Office, Ordinance Survey, Land Registry, and Companies House operate as trading funds: they partially depend on data sales. A Public Accounts Committee member explained that the trading funds would have lost "millions and millions of pounds" had they cooperated fully with the UK OD program (Public Accounts Committee 2012, EV-6). The UK government had to purchase data from its own trading funds in order to release it to the public. Cole described a case in which a U.S. state legislature opposed releasing a dataset because the state was selling copies of it for $90,000 per sale (2012,

2). At no time did politicians bar interagency data-trading practices or the selling of valuable datasets to the public; hence, agencies remained first and foremost motivated to protect tradable information assets from the requirement to release them free of charge.

Agencies are not the only actors seeking to benefit from their investment in enriching information assets. The web culture itself has evolved from its infant "everything-for-free" phase to its current for-profit condition. Companies such as Apple, Amazon, and eBay developed exchanges where digital products are cheap but not free of charge. These companies reap significant gain because even a cheap product yields profits when multiplied by billions of split-second transactions executed in a digital exchange arena. Agencies, too, employ "cheap but not free" courses of action. Beginning in April 2012, the state of Georgia lowered the cost of records obtained by the public from 25 cents to 10 cents a page and began requiring agencies to alert requesters if records will cost more than $25 to provide (Economist 2012, 36).

It is unfair and unfeasible to demand agencies to free valuable information assets without compensation. It is also not wise to do so. Agencies labor hard to create and improve these assets. If agencies are forced to free information assets without compensation, they will lose motivation to invest resources in extracting insights and additional value from their raw and unprocessed data.

So why didn't agencies inundate OD web portals with countless datasets that they cannot trade with other agencies or sell to the public? After all, in the age of social networking it is easy and cheap to generate valueless data. Only a small number of agencies took advantage of this fact. The GSA posted on data.gov a searchable version of its 1,700-page semiannual regulatory agenda, including the administration's proposal to set standards for a "retirement home for chimpanzees used in federal research" (Noveck 2009, 125); similarly, the EPA, the Federal Communications Commission (FCC), and the U.S. Forest Service published datasets containing millions of nonsearchable public comments. However, these are the exceptions. So why does the data analysis suggest that agencies did not upload massive amounts of valueless datasets?

The answer is that agencies understood that the uploading of *any* dataset had the potential to exacerbate three data integration problems related to releasing datasets. First, the *problem of inclusion* concerns what data is included or excluded from the dataset. Misleading data could be intentionally released in order to damage or promote the cause of certain groups. For example, the U.S. Centers for Medicare & Medicaid Service (CMS) might choose to release positive datasets about surgeons without indicating which ones were involved in malpractice court cases. Second, the *problem of confusion* refers to the fact that it is impossible to rectify confusing or bad data once it is released because it trickles *downstream* to numerous databases that are not controlled by a single entity. The OMB is exacerbating the confusion problem because it lets agencies decide what to publish on federal OD portals. In cases where program areas overlap, the data is reported and defined inconsistently (Fountain 2013, 58). Over time these numerous data definition inconsistencies trickle down and feed thousands of databases in the public, private, and not-for-profit sectors.

Finally, the *problem of diffusion* is created by the fact that OD did not offer a mechanism to retain historical versions of the same dataset, to create historical integration points among datasets, or to allow data to expire. Knowing how different data elements regarding a specific citizen appeared to officials at a given point in time is critical to understanding key information such as why citizens were arrested or deemed qualified to receive particular benefits. Without mechanisms that allow citizens to integrate datasets at different historical points in time, an OD portal is a useless index where one cannot connect datasets in a meaningful way.

Even the most recent and progressive U.S. federal legislation fails to address the time-version challenge. The GPRAMA has defined and promoted the important concept of Cross-Agency Priority (CAP) goals. Currently, only the most recent quarterly progress report for each CAP goal is available on the Performance.gov website. This renders the task of tracking progress toward achieving a CAP goal impossible. It also means that every time a CAP goal changes (as is the case when the U.S. federal government approves a new budget with new CAP goals), information about old CAP goals will disappear from Performance.gov (Fountain 2013, 34–35).

Agency officials understand well the time-versioning challenge. They know that data wrapped in context and traceable to its sources is a record. Records are the blood cells of governmental work. Agency officials were concerned that OD would separate datasets from their source records thus eliminating the ability to link datasets while creating a long-term maintenance nightmare (Bass et al. 2010, 1; Evans and Campos 2013,

175; Thurston 2012, 3; Zuiderwijk et al. 2012, 157). The GAO and the U.S. National Archives and Records Administration (NARA) admitted that the flood of unsorted information into public databases creates uncertainty and degrades the quality of these databases (GAO 2010b; NARA 2006).

Over many years, agencies have fine-tuned routines to tackle the problems of inclusion, confusion, and diffusion. The OD program threatened to nullify these routines. Instead, it offered agencies a bad trade: OD receives recognition for freeing data, and at the same time robs agencies of their ability to trade data and passes on to them the tedious work of resolving data quality problems that the OD program itself exacerbates. Agencies' technical managers understood the true cost of supporting OD and therefore reduced their involvement with the program to a minimum.

So agencies opted to appear as if they were complying with OD programs while, in effect, not supporting them. This is not the first time that agency officials have countered unwelcome instructions by appearing to be in compliance with a given order while in fact not complying. Recently, the OMB sought to consolidate federal data centers that grew from 432 in 1998 to 2,094 in July 2010 by closing down 650 centers by 2015. Agencies were not eager to comply for fear of losing control over resources. So, agencies submitted apparently comprehensive inventory reports that lacked critical data (GAO 2011a). As with OD compliance reports, agencies appeared to comply while, in effect, not cooperating.

In mid-2011, Kundra resigned in protest at the harsh cuts in the federal OD program budget (Wadhwa 2011). However, this program encountered problems long before its budget was slashed. Two important lessons emerge from the early OD experiments. First, like Bliss in his excavation of the pottery of ancient civilizations, OD programs encountered historical limitations inscribed into legacy databases. These limitations teach us the importance of adopting the humble attitude that Bliss displayed toward the archeological mountain. With sufficient humility and appreciation of these limitations, we can design better information sharing programs. Second, early OD programs teach us that vision, excitement, and goodwill are not enough to support a long-term information sharing solution. Some incentives are necessary to prompt human actors to engage each other in developing such a solution. Chapter 4 will reveal that agencies have already discovered the value of such incentives.

4 How Data Trade Opens Agencies' Closed Doors

Keenly aware of the value of their data, American agencies were trading data with each other before the onset of the Internet age (GAO 1991). However, agencies have an ambivalent attitude toward their datasets. On the one hand, they are aware of the economic value of their data and know how to increase this value by mining data with BI tools and linking it to external datasets. On the other hand, agencies have no incentives to utilize their datasets beyond supporting their chartered missions. Current U.S. interagency data exchange practices reflect this debilitating lack of efficacy: the practices are innovative and mutually beneficial for buyers and sellers, but also encourage data monopolies and waste. This status quo can change. This chapter highlights the little-known history of one creative, incentives-driven information-sharing solution in the Australian public sector. This case study underscores the argument that minor monetary incentives are an effective means to unleash a new information sharing ecosystem inside government.

How Agencies Develop Information Assets

Agencies understand that data is the wellspring of their autonomy and power. The UK government estimates that public sector data contributes 16 billion pounds annually to the UK economy (UK Comptroller and Auditor General 2012). U.S. officials sometimes refer to public data as the currency of their agencies. One official said: "in this business, you are as good as your data is" (Flanagin, Monge, and Fulk 2001, 78). Private-sector exchanges worth billions of dollars depend on harvesting information from public sector databases. In the genetics data domain, U.S. companies such as First Genetics, Trust Inc., The Gene Trust, and Genomics Collaboration

Inc. are heavily dependent on government data (Anderlik and Rothstein 2001). Sometimes, Congress even intervenes to curb agencies' desire to sell data to the private sector. In 1994, Congress passed the Driver Privacy Protection Act to curb the practice of state agencies selling personal information such as drivers' license numbers to outsiders (Grupe 1995; Roberts 2006a). Information powerhouses from the public and private sectors often strike data access deals. In 2005, Google signed an agreement with NASA to access NASA's data (Sternstein 2005). European agencies also understand the economic value of their data; they grant free access only to old, non-downloadable or nonprintable data, and direct clients to public-private partnerships where clients can purchase more useful information at market prices (Burkert 2004).

Agencies know how to extract value from their existing data by meshing it with data purchased from other sources. At times, these "other sources" can be highly profitable but morally questionable. In 2008, German tax authorities purchased a disk from Heinrich Kieber, a forty-two-year-old former bank employee. Mr. Kieber stole confidential information on customers of a Liechtenstein bank. The disk contained foreign banking data about 1,400 wealthy individuals. The German tax authorities meshed the purchased data with German tax data to identify citizens who apparently failed to report their true income to the German government. The German authorities paid four million euros for the disk and recovered about 180 million euros in tax payments (much of it from wealthy individuals who turned themselves in) (Landler 2008). Such ethically questionable transactions can backfire. A similar story in 2010 led to a breakdown in the diplomatic relationship between Germany and Switzerland (Jolly 2010).

Public organizations also extract value from their data by meshing it with data acquired legally and freely on the web or from the private sector. Consider the following two examples:

• *Central Banks and Google Analytics Data:* Central banks in the United States, Israel, Chile, the United Kingdom, and Spain mesh their data with Google Analytics data that aggregates hundreds of billions of web searches by keywords. Traditionally, these central banks relied on economic indicators to determine important decisions such as setting the national interest rate; however, economic indicators are not always current for the time these decisions are made. So, in recent years, central banks have developed their own indices based on Google data to forecast future consumer behavior.

These indices, alongside more traditional aggregated numbers, are presented to central bank governors before they set the benchmark interest rate for their countries. Using the Google Analytics data, the Chilean and UK central banks also predict the number of job seekers and employees concerned about losing their jobs (based on Google search words related to unemployment benefits); the Spanish Central Bank forecasts how many British tourists will visit Spain in the next month; and the twelve branches of the U.S. Federal Reserve Bank forecast auto, home, and retail sales. These central banks even use Google search data to run "sentiment analysis" to assess if the public is more or less optimistic about the future of the national economy (Ito and Odenheimer 2012).

• *FEMA, Waffle House, and Disaster Relief:* FEMA applies the same data integration and BI techniques in the disaster relief domain. When a disaster strikes in the United States, FEMA officials must swiftly assess and rank the disaster's severity and scope. Thousands of lives and billions of dollars depend on the accuracy and timeliness of these decisions. To improve its decision-making capability, FEMA acquires data from the Waffle House Corporation. Waffle House is a large American food chain open 24 hours a day 365 days a year, and known for remaining open as long as reasonably possibly during disasters or crisis events. After a disaster strikes, Waffle House must decide whether to keep its stores in the disaster area open—which managers strive to do unless there is present danger to employees' and customers' lives—and determine how to stock stores in that area. To aid in these decisions the Waffle House Corporation built a "Waffle House Index" that collects and processes real-time information on the scope and intensity for each disaster affecting its stores' operations. FEMA officials now mesh their own collected data for disasters with the Waffle House Index to make better decisions (Bauerlein 2011).

These examples illustrate how agencies expand the economic value of their datasets by meshing them with nontraditional data. Agencies also invest in various data mining technologies to extract more value from their existing data. Data mining enables corporations and agencies to analyze massive volumes of data quickly and relatively inexpensively. Already in 2004, half of all U.S. agencies were using or planning to use such techniques and this trend is intensifying (GAO 2004a). The examples that follow illustrate some of the insights U.S. agencies derive from mining their data:

• The USDA mines hundreds of terabytes of raw satellite image data to estimate the overall food supplies of the United States (Anderson 2008). The
USDA also used BI tools to uncover fraudulent crop-loss claims (White 2007).

• The U.S. Centers for Medicare & Medicaid Services (CMS) recently
launched an Office of Information Products and Data Analytics. This office
will oversee CMS's comprehensive information portfolio (Biddick and Kash
2013, 12). The Department of Health and Human Servicer (HHS) also built
an enterprise data warehouse to monitor potential national blood supply
shortages (White 2007).

• The U.S. Department of State (DOS) uses data mining to detect employees' fraudulent use of government credit cards (White 2007).

• The U.S. Department of Education (ED) uses data mining to identify
fraudulent Pell Grant payments (White 2007).

• The IRS uses data mining to distinguish between tax evaders and those
who make genuine errors on their tax returns (White 2007).

• The U.S. Navy and the Marine Corps use BI tools to assess how many
training personnel they need, what the failure rates of all parts on deployed
ships are expected to be, and what the uniformed personnel turnover might
be (White 2007).

• The U.S. Treasury uses artificial intelligence to detect suspected financial
crimes in data that the Treasury began accumulating following the Bank
Secrecy Act of 1970 (White 2007).

Agencies even use BI tools to predict how citizens will behave. They
model complex political, economic, and social realities so that they can
respond to changing conditions faster and more efficiently (Ayers 2007).
Recently, the investment arms of the CIA and Google created a joint company to examine in real time Internet chatter and links among millions
of web pages in order to predict events and relate these events to specific
individuals, locations, and times. The CIA and Google chose an apt name
for their joint venture—"Recorded Future" (Shachtman 2010).

Why and How Agencies Fight over Data Ownership

Agencies that win data ownership in a new domain acquire new revenue
sources. In 2005, the OMB designated the Office of Personnel Management
(OPM) as the agency responsible for security clearance investigations of

new federal employees. The DOD then transferred this function to the OPM. The OPM acquired 1,800 new investigative job positions and received a onetime fund transfer of $49.4 million from the DOD. The DOD and the OPM also signed a contract specifying their mutual obligations in this domain (GAO 2012p). This DOD-OPM deal was part of an overall effort to reorganize the chartered responsibilities of the two agencies including capital assets, contractual responsibilities, employees, and information sharing responsibilities.

Agencies compete with each other to acquire ownership over new information assets. The DOC and the DHS are battling each other over the ownership of a new online ID. The winner will receive funding to issue an online national ID to every U.S. citizen or U.S. resident that requests one, a new data element that might become as important as the Social Security Number (SSN) is today (June 2011). Similarly, the EPA and the DOE have been battling for years, far from the public eye, over ownership of new data elements that define green standards for energy consumption (Olsen 2007; Thormeyer 2006). Ownership of a single data element such as an SSN or a driver's license ID means long-lasting influence for a federal or state agency.

Agencies also compete for ownership of new information sharing standards. Such ownership empowers one agency to enforce data standards on other agencies; these agencies, in turn, pay a substantial monetary price for having to comply with the new standards. In 2007, an internal DOD report urged the department's senior echelon to become engaged in the effort to set new biometrics information sharing standards. The author explained: "Reportedly, the Program Manager [of the Information Sharing Environment (ISE) office] is actively seeking candidate projects to demonstrate and advance cross-organizational architecture and data sharing, and this is an opportunity the Department should not miss" (Office of the Under Secretary of Defense for Acquisition Technology and Logistics 2007, 66).

Timing is a critical factor in data ownership battles. The EPA created the first set of data standards for the physical safety of facilities that treat drinking water, wastewater, and storm water. In 2002, the EPA hired consultants to develop the standards, risk-assessment methodologies, and guidance documents. The EPA also developed risk-assessment software tools, installed software in water-purification facilities, and trained employees. The EPA even reorganized itself internally to improve the handling of water safety issues; the agency nurtured close working relationships with organizations such as the National Association of Clean Water Agencies (NACWA) and the National Drinking Water Advisory Council (NDWAC). The DHS, born in early 2003, began a battle for ownership of the data standards too late. Empowered by Congress, the DHS began investing in the development of water safety data standards in 2005. Yet, by 2006, the EPA had already decisively won this battle. The EPA even issued its own report highlighting the agency's legal authority and its data ownership in the water safety domain. Shortly afterward, the DHS adopted the EPA standards (GAO 2006c, 2011b).

Data Trade in the American Public Sector

Tradable Types of Information Products

U.S. agencies exchange three types of information products. First, they trade in primary data that are observable facts such as a person's age. Some observable facts are generated (such as passport numbers), others are received from citizens (such as place of residence), and still others are hybrid pieces of data (such as Social Security benefits). Next, agencies trade in secondary information products that grant insights into the relationships among primary data elements. For example, the GSA sells BI reports to the DHS. The DHS employs these reports to lower the cost of contracting with external vendors (GSA 2006).

Finally, agencies sell information services to other agencies. An information service is a data product combined with contractual delivery of data updates. For example, according to the Social Security Act, the Social Security Administration (SSA) must provide six benefits-providing agencies with access to the *full* version of the Death Mater File (DMF) database containing information about 98 million deaths of people with SSNs. The law grants free access to the DMF data to one agency (VA). Another agency (OPM) gets access to DMF data based on a data-for-data exchange agreement with the SSA. The other four agencies pay the SSA for monthly DMF updates, including the Defense Manpower Data Center, which pays the SSA over $40,000 annually for the updates, and the CMS, which pays $10,000 annually for updates (GAO 2013d).

The SSA also sells an information service based on a *limited* version of the DMF database—a database containing 87 million deaths of people with SSNs. For the period between October 1, 2012 and September 30, 2013 the SSA sold to the National Technical Information Service (NTIS) the limited

DMF database as well as weekly, monthly, and quarterly updates for an annual fee of $210,200. SSA officials inserted a clause into the agreement with the NTIS that allows SSA to monitor who accesses the DMF data. This clause declares: "upon request by SSA, NTIS will provide an analysis of the DMF customer base in an appropriate format agreed upon by the parties" (NTIS and SSA 2013). For its part, the NTIS developed a thriving business of selling differential, on-demand, subscription, or batch based access to DMF data to organizations and individuals (GAO 2013d; NTIS 2014).

Payment Mechanisms in the Data Exchange Arena

Agencies adopt explicit exchange language while selling information products to other agencies. The GSA advertises its schedules containing information on how to contract with vendors on a web page titled "For Federal Agency Customers—Ordering Form" (U.S. General Services Administration 2013). Likewise, on a web page designed for agencies, the SSA declares: "SSA will look at the return on investment for any information exchange" (SSA 2012).

Agencies sign contracts that define the terms of selling information to and buying information from each other and punish agencies that violate these terms. In 2007, the DOD stopped using the DOI's GovWork assisted acquisition information service for all orders worth more than $100 thousand and demanded that GovWork return all funds worth more than $100 thousand that were not already under contract. The DOD's Inspector General claimed that GovWork agents did not uphold their contractual obligation to the DOD (Miller 2007).

Four payment mechanisms exist within this internal data exchange: pay with dollars, pay with data, pay with additional budget, and pay with functions and human resources. First, agencies pay for data with dollars. In 2008, the SSA received reimbursements from 32 federal and 251 state data exchanges for data it provides to support non-SSA programs (GAO 2008a). Similarly, the HHS, the managing partner of grants.gov (a joint federal grants online application program) requested to restructure the program on a fee-for-service payment model by which each of the twenty-five participating agencies would pay its share based on the volume of online data transactions it receives from grants.gov (GAO 2011f). The DHS paid the SSA $14 million to isolate E-Verify (an Internet employment verification system)'s data transactions from other SSA workloads in order to speed up the execution of transactions. This payment was in addition to payments that the SSA received from the DHS for the data itself ($3.5 million in 2007 and $7.6 million for more data in 2009) (GAO 2010c).

Frequently an agency prices data sold to another agency based on the full-time equivalent (FTE) salaries of those who prepared the data. For example, the USGS priced a report sold to the USFWS based on the number of FTEs that USGS claimed to invest to develop the report (USGS and USFWS 1990). This practice is common because it transfers the capital cost associated with the development of the report from the agency that prepares the report to the agency that purchases it. This practice is supported by U.S. tax laws and the manner in which research and development (R&D) investments are depreciated for tax purposes over time.

In tough budgetary times, agencies are eager to be paid in dollars for information. A retired CMS official explained that such payment arrangements are internally known as "charge-back fees." He described a project in which the DOJ paid the CMS charge-back fees for CMS reports that enabled the DOJ to identify physicians suspected of submitting fraudulent claims to the government. CMS officials disliked the idea of someone using their data in pursuit of physicians. They consented to share the data only after the DOJ agreed to pay charge-back fees (Moscoe 2011). Charge-back fees constitute a small portion of the receiving agency's overall budget; however, these fees are a source of discretionary income (unlike larger congressional funds which are tied to specific programs). Moreover, the client agency periodically returns to the seller agency to purchase data updates.

Second, agencies pay for data with their own data. For example, the FBI, the DHS, and the DOS maintain separate biometrics databases. The three agencies signed a Memorandum of Understanding (MoU) empowering each other to access the biometrics data records of the other agencies (GAO 2008b). The SSA also exchanges data for data with the social services agencies and motor vehicle departments of various states (GAO 2009g).

Third, an agency may receive special funding for providing data to another agency. The SSA received additional budgetary funding for providing data to support CMS's Medicare Part C and Part D (GAO 2008a, 2011a, 2012). During the 1990s, Congress collectively awarded the states $2.3 billion to build a new Statewide Automated Child Welfare Information Systems (SACWIS) to integrate data about children living in foster homes and children at risk. The states signed agreements to share SACWIS data with the federal Temporary Assistance for Needy Families (TANF) system.

However, special funding arrangements sometimes turn into entitlements. Today, the states still receive SACWIS payments but they do not comply with the TANF information sharing agreement that they signed more than a decade ago (GAO 2011j).

Congress sometimes conditions program funding on the free release of data to other agencies. The DHS's E-Verify program grew slowly from 1986 and then more quickly after September 11, 2001. This program directly addresses two key public concerns: national security (i.e., not hiring terrorists) and illegal immigration (i.e., not losing American jobs). Even at the height of the 2008 economic crisis, Congress generously funded this program. In return, Congress instructed the DHS to exempt state employment agencies from paying program subscription fees (GAO 2010c). Interesting to note, a similar Australian program has adopted a data-for-dollars model (see chapter 6).

Finally, Congress sometimes compensates an agency for data integration services provided to other agencies by transferring budgetary and personnel resources from the receiving agencies to the providing agency. For example, Congress authorized the new Terrorist Screening Center (TSC) to establish its Terrorist Threat Integration Center (TTIC) Identities Database partially by taking over data, functions, and personnel from the DOS's older TIPOFF counterterrorist program, the FBI Watchlist Unit, and the Transportation Security Agency's No-Fly and Selectee List program (Secretary of State et al. 2011).

Conditions for Awarding Free Data Access

Agencies award other agencies free access to valuable information if at least one of three conditions exists. First, sometimes, agencies sign generic information sharing agreements. These agreements use vague language and include clauses that protect the signing agencies' information ownership rights. These agreements also include clauses stating that specific information sharing acts require signing an additional information sharing agreement. Recently, federal and state agencies signed such an agreement to share information to protect Arkansas forests (Arkansas Forestry Commission (AFC) et al. 2011).

Second, an agency sometimes agrees to grant another agency free access to its information if it furthers a specific agency interest. The U.S. Forest Service is concerned that the State of Alaska is overdeveloping its rich forest and coastal resources and might cause irreversible damage to habitat life. To assess such damage, the U.S. Forest Service agreed to grant Alaska access to its data. The agreement signed between the U.S. Forest Service and the State of Alaska lists the rich data menu that the former vows to provide to the latter. The agreement even specifies penalties for not providing data access (State of Alaska and USDA Forest Service Alaska Region 2000).

Finally, sometimes agencies adopt an information branding strategy based on the free distribution of data, to secure continuous congressional funding. Most agencies are the exclusive data owners within a certain domain. Sometimes, technological changes empower private corporations to challenge the data monopoly of an agency. For example, the USGS and the NOAA face competition from Google Earth, as they are no longer the only organizations that can map America's lands, seas, and skies. USGS and NOAA's challenge is to convince Congress to continue awarding them billions of funding dollars to develop the same datasets that are published free of charge on the web. Under such (rare) circumstances, agencies freely publish their best datasets and distribute them aggressively through many channels. The hope is that private corporations will lose their motivation to develop competing datasets, and that Congress will continue funding the agencies' programs because, now, more organizations are dependent on the agencies' data. In 1995, the NOAA developed its Science-on-Sphere (SOS) 3D display program that museums use to display NOAA datasets. Since then, the NOAA has provided all the data updates to support SOS displays free of charge. The SOS program manager claimed that NOAA only provides free *data* to museums. However, the director of education in a low-budget museum reported that NOAA had provided his museum with grants to fund SOS hardware purchases, receive technical support, and extend the existing SOS display (Shanahan 2012; Russell 2012).

Public Sector Data Trade Outside the United States

European agencies also trade data with each other and rely on privacy exemption rules to do so. These rules are similar to the U.S. "routine use" exemption stated in the American Privacy Act of 1974, which allows agencies to disclose personal information to other agencies if the information is for "a routine use" (Prins 2004). Each European country has developed a unique identifier for every resident, and shares this identifier across its government (Otjacques, Hitzelberger, and Feltz 2007b). This identifier is a necessary data element to support interagency data trade. In several

European countries and in Canada, agencies are legally defined as the owners of the data elements they collect, create, or update. The EU created a broker agency to establish best practices for interagency data exchanges.

Successful Implementation of Incentives-Driven Information Sharing

Several countries demonstrate the potential of implementing incentives-driven information sharing arrangements. In Brazil, a web-based system called Bacenjud provides the Brazilian Central Bank with incentives to share information with the courts. The Bacenjud system empowers judges in thirty different courts to request that the Central Bank freeze or liberate the bank accounts of individuals and companies, or declare an entity as bankrupt. A Bacenjud request costs the Brazilian Central Bank less than 80 cents to process as opposed to the $10 cost of a request before Bacenjud was introduced. Every Bacenjud request can be addressed in less than twenty-four hours as compared to five to twenty days previous to Bacenjud (Joia 2004; Machado 2007). In Finland (and to a lesser extent also in Sweden and Denmark), the Population Register Centre has been selling census data to other state and municipal agencies as well as to private-sector corporations and individuals for more than two decades. The Finnish Population Register Centre covers about 70 percent of its budgetary expenses through revenues derived from such data sales. Other Finnish agencies also sell and buy data from each other. Despite minor complaints regarding this data trade practice (e.g., these complaints are discussed in chapter 7), the Finnish interagency data trade framework is considered successful in terms of improving interagency information sharing and also in terms of contributing to market-oriented reforms in the public sector as well as to budget transparency and performance management (Erkkila 2012, 129–171).

The little-known history of the Australian Public Sector Mapping Agencies (PSMA) provides another interesting, innovative, incentives-driven information sharing solution. This case study also reveals important insights on how such solutions emerge.

The Australian PSMA Incentives-Driven Information Sharing Case Study

The Birth of PSMA   During the early 1980s governments worldwide converted their maps into digital format. In the late 1980s, the Australian

Bureau of Statistics (ABS) searched for a digital mapping solution to facilitate the Census of Population and Housing (Australian Census) that the ABS carries out every five years in a thinly populated country that is slightly larger than the United States (excluding Alaska). Geospatial data was available via ten national mapping cadastral agencies (NMCAs): one for each of Australia's six states and two territories and two for the Commonwealth. Tensions existed among the agencies. The two Commonwealth agencies, the Australian Land Information Group (AUSLIG) and the Royal Australian Survey Corps (RA Svy), competed with each other. RA Svy maintained a good working relationship with the state and territory mapping agencies. These agencies generally mistrusted AUSLIG.

Organizations (the ABS included) would have had to negotiate data access and pricing separately with each agency. Each agency maintained data in a different format that was generally incompatible with those of other agencies. Their datasets used contrasting technologies and different data models. They used different coordinate systems and their data differed in quality and accuracy. The ten mapping agencies were concerned about ownership rights to data that they had captured at great cost over many years. The agencies were also nervous about the prospect of another agency "fiddling" with their data (Mobbs 2012c). Prior to 1992, no organization managed to negotiate ongoing access to the datasets of the ten mapping agencies or to construct a high-quality map of Australia (Holmes 2009).

The ABS's willingness to pay for such a map triggered the interest of the surveyors-general in charge of the Commonwealth and state agencies. The ABS planned to use a national digital base map for the planning and conduct of the Australian Census, and to distribute its "CDATA96" CD software product to the Australian public free of charge with digital mapping data embedded in it. Digital mapping data represented the "crown jewels" of mapping agencies back then. So, the surveyors-general wanted to ensure in advance that they would be able to maintain ownership rights and possible revenues from any arrangement with the ABS. On January 31, 1992, they met to discuss the creation of a national dataset that would include Digital Cadastral Data Base (DCDB) data and selected topographic data. Mutual acrimony and mistrust among the mapping agencies was high. Some believed that supplying data for the national dataset would be a distraction. Others were concerned that their datasets would be degraded by incorporating them into a unified national dataset. All feared that they might lose Intellectual Property (IP) rights over their data.

Complicating matters further, AUSLIG insisted that the ABS digital mapping solution be based on its own digital product called GEODATA, suited for small- to medium-scale geographic information system (GIS) applications. AUSLIG proposed that all mapping agencies pour their data into GEODATA to make a national digital map for the ABS. However, the other mapping organizations rejected this suggestion because they were determined to protect their sovereign rights as owners of their own mapping datasets (Waters 2006b). Determined to become the supreme mapping organization in Australia, AUSLIG decided to create a separate, commercially oriented bid for the ABS project in partnership with a well-known commercial publisher of Australian street directories.

This created an impossible situation for the ABS—AUSLIG was a key member of PSMA and yet it planned to compete with the PSMA bid (Mobbs 2012c). So, in response to the "Expression of Interest" document that PSMA submitted to the ABS on May 1, 1992, the ABS decided to publish a public tender inviting other vendors to submit bids for the provision of mapping support. The Australian Parliament released the ABS from a standing legal obligation to use exclusively black-and-white paper AUSLIG maps, freeing the ABS to publish the public tender for a digital mapping solution. In July 1992, the ABS informed PSMA that the agencies' proposed solution would not address all ABS requirements and therefore PSMA would not be invited to the tender despite ABS's preference for PSMA data. The acrimonious relationships within the PSMA played a key role in the ABS decision to reject the PSMA bid (Holmes 2009).

The surveyors-general did not want to lose the ABS contract. They understood that the Australian Census mapping project offered them a once in a lifetime opportunity to unify their data into a single Australian digital mapping and cadastral database at little or no cost. They also knew that other nonpublic sector organizations would be willing to pay to access this database in the future. Early on, a value-added reseller (VAR) called Peripheral Systems (later to become MapInfo Australia) made it known that it found the task of negotiating licensing arrangements to obtain data from the ten separate mapping agencies laborious and unnecessary (a VAR sells national datasets with value added components such as a digital national map of Australia that empowers end users to superimpose data or graphics). Peripheral Systems expressed willingness to pay for a well-integrated digital map of the whole of Australia. The surveyors-general were eager to develop potential new revenue streams for their agencies because they were increasingly subject to cost-recovery budgetary frameworks that compelled them to generate revenues from maps and digital map data sales.

The surveyors-general worked jointly to convince the ABS to give PSMA another chance to bid. They mobilized the Land Ministers of their various governments. They designated as their leader Don Grant, the New South Wales (NSW) surveyor-general. Grant, himself a former military surveyor, was a skilled negotiator and an astute political operator. He recruited the support of his own NSW government and the cooperation of the surveyor-general of Victoria. Yet, the other agencies remained suspicious when Grant raised the idea of creating a national mapping dataset using the ABS contract as a launch pad for a new public institution. Grant testified that, initially, he only had a "dream and a concept" to offer to the other agencies (Grant 2012b).

Grant was bold when needed: several times he embarrassed AUSLIG at meetings for their noncollegial behavior toward PSMA in pursuit of AUS-LIG's commercial interest. The meetings were frequently heated. Grant kept all participants focused on the goal—creating Australia's first digital map. He testified that building PSMA was an act of "perseverance and coopera-tion" (Grant 2012b). He was convinced that "without some fierce inter-play we would have lost the opportunity" (Grant 2012a). Grant's leadership style was defined as "brinkmanship" (Mobbs 2012c). Persistence paid off. All agencies, including AUSLIG joined PSMA on day one and remain mem-bers to date.

Grant also commanded the Land Information Centre (LIC), the NSW mapping agency that had the sophisticated personnel and digital equip-ment to bind together the mapping agencies' data. He employed these resources to recruit reluctant agencies. Early on, Queensland and West-ern Australia admitted that they were yet to bring their datasets up to the required standard. Grant used funds available to him to assist these agen-cies so they too could participate in the ABS contract bid. At the time, Grant had no guarantee that PSMA would win the ABS contract (the funds were paid back to NSW after the contract was won).

Grant played an instrumental role in hiring effective staff members for PSMA aided by Des Mooney, his general manager at the LIC who facili-tated the engagement of John Mobbs as project manager for the ABS project (later on, Mobbs became PSMA's first CEO). Mobbs was a twenty-five-year veteran as a topographic surveyor with RA Svy. He used his expertise and good working relationships with the mapping agencies to resolve the difficult technical issue of unifying the data. Mobbs described Grant's leadership: "The creation of the PSMA bid would not have happened without [Grant's] intervention, initiative and encouragement with the other jurisdictions, his disciplining influence on AUSLIG, and his commitment of a significant part of his technical workforce at Bathurst over a period of some 3 years" (Mobbs 2012c).

The members of the new PSMA organization frenetically prepared proof of concept, data validation, hardcopy output examples, and cost and specification documents. Just before Christmas 1992, the ABS confirmed that PSMA had been chosen to supply base map data. In June 1993, the ABS and PSMA signed a commercial agreement. The ABS agreed to pay A\$3.4 million Australian dollars to license the data from PSMA (paid in installments between July 1993 and July 1996). The agreement also provided a small royalty return to PSMA from the retail sale of products, and an annual data maintenance fee of 100,000 Australian dollars. PSMA now had the seed money to build the first whole-of-Australia digital map (Holmes 2009; Mobbs 1998).

PSMA's Unique Incentives-driven Information Sharing Solution   The ABS contract marked the beginning of the hard work to create the first whole-of-Australia digital map. Mobbs's first order of business was to convince the "die hard cartographers" in the different agencies that it was neither "heresy" nor "pollution" to mix their data with the data of other agencies (Mobbs 2012b). Mobbs administered the ABS seed money and NSW's sophisticated mapping capabilities, to manage the data integration work on schedule and on budget (Mobbs 1998). The agencies received their first selective incentives from PSMA (i.e., a share of the ABS contract funds) if they actively worked with Mobbs and his team to integrate their data.

Data resolution was the first problem to overcome. Mobbs reduced CDATA96, the first whole-of-Australia digital map, to one-seventeenth of its original size to make it fit on a disk. The Reduced Output Spatial Dataset (ROSD) was then born as the foundation for all PSMA products to come. Mobbs toiled to convince cartographers that the differences between thinly and thickly populated areas mandated the creation of a nontraditional map, more accurate where accuracy was needed and, potentially, less accurate in other areas. Cartographers cooperated with Mobbs partially because they received monetary incentives that helped them pay for upgrading the quality of their data.

PSMA successfully delivered the first digital whole-of-Australia map to the ABS. By 1996, the ABS grant was depleted. The prospect of acquiring VAR revenues was tempting. However, a Queensland official warned that PSMA should not exploit such revenues without a transparent business plan. So PSMA launched an independent review that led to the creation of PSMA Australia Limited. The surveyors-general hired a legal counsel to develop the legislation to support their incentives-driven framework. The new entity embedded selective incentives (i.e., royalties and dividends) in the PSMA Australia Limited constitution. These incentives are small in comparison to the public sector budgets of the mapping agencies. Therefore, the agencies view their foremost obligation to develop the best digital data, each for its own jurisdiction. PSMA Australia Limited remains a "serendipitous by-product" which provides just enough incidental revenues to keep agencies focused on PSMA's success (Mobbs 2012b).

Since 2000, the new PSMA Australia Limited has acted as a wholesaler to clients but with responsibility for facilitating the assembly and maintenance of the national mapping datasets, which are outsourced through competitive tendering. PSMA Australia Limited seeks to avoid competing with its member agencies by focusing on *national* applications for its data assets. Recently, PSMA Australia Limited facilitated the rollout of the fiber and infrastructure for the National Broadband Network that is designed to connect every Australian home, school, and workplace to high-speed Internet services. Figure 4.1 below visualizes the PSMA vision.

PSMA Australia Limited has adopted a unique business model to motivate stakeholders to share data. The state, territory, and Commonwealth mapping agencies are shareholders and data suppliers. These relationships are legally distinct and dealt with separately. Australian legislation defines the nature of the shareholder relationship; PSMA Australia Limited's structure is the same as that of listed companies on the Australian Stock Exchange although PSMA Australia Limited remains an unlisted public company. Each of the nine agencies holds a single share in PSMA Australia Limited. The latter has a board of ten directors—one from each state or territory government plus an independent chair—with a CEO, a chief operating officer, and a small team of employees.[1] At the direction of

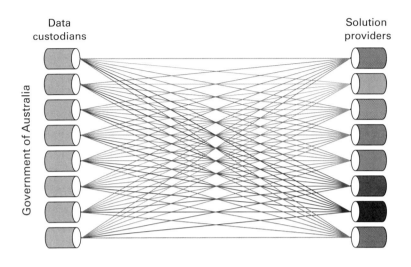

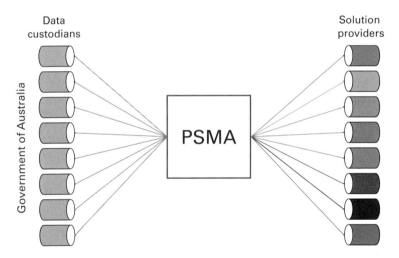

Figure 4.1
How PSMA Australia adds value.
Source: Paull and Lovell 2010, 4.

the board, PSMA Australia Limited can return dividends to shareholders, when a surplus exists at the end of the year. As data suppliers, the agencies always receive a license fee from PSMA Australia Limited for the use of their datasets (Paull and Lovell 2012).

PSMA Australia Limited generates revenues by signing license agreements with VARs. VARs pay PSMA Australia Limited an annual access fee and royalties based on sales of the VAR product. The latter then uses the revenues to create new national datasets and to improve existing ones. PSMA Australia Limited's data products are distinct from those created by the agencies; often PSMA Australia Limited licenses its datasets back to the agencies so that the latter can take advantage of the national consistency and improved data quality. Such licensing may occur directly between PSMA Australia Limited and the agencies but more commonly it will occur through an intermediary VAR where there is additional value desired by a particular agency. PSMA Australia Limited has remained lean, focused, and not dependent on government funding (Littlewood, MacDonald, and Stanley 2010; Paull and Lovell 2012).

Most important, the founders built PSMA (and subsequently PSMA Australia Limited) to be an institution that does not compete with the business lines of its shareholding agencies. PSMA Australia Limited focuses on developing national datasets that otherwise would not be available. It refers clients who seek high-resolution maps to the shareholding agencies. Those who seek whole-of-Australia mapping products can purchase these from PSMA Australia Limited.

This sophisticated incentives-driven framework increased cooperation and information sharing among the agencies. After the birth of PSMA, officials from the different NMCAs began meeting each other more frequently. They engaged with each other to create new geospatial products (see http://www.psma.com.au/list-products). By working closely together, the Australian NMCAs were able to remove duplicate products and save money. They also developed an entirely new data network connecting the providers and users of spatial information (Littlewood, MacDonald, and Stanley 2010).

Over time, the Australian NMCAs began delegating increased electoral and financial powers to PSMA Australia Limited. The 2001 constitution contained no special voting privileges for NSW or Victoria (the states with the largest populations). Since then, the agencies have voted several times to further ease PSMA Australia Limited's internal voting mechanisms. On

July 4, 2001, the constitution was changed to declare that any two directors and the secretary could sign, draw, endorse, or execute a negotiable
instrument (Paull and Lovell 2010). A simple majority is needed for most
board of directors' decisions. A special majority (75 percent) is required for
rare special resolutions. A unanimous vote is required only to approve the
annual program and constitutional changes (PSMA 2008).

Shareholding agencies became increasingly willing to nominate independent, professional directors to the PSMA Australia Limited board. Each
agency nominates one director to the board for a total of nine directors.
There is an option to elect an additional three independent directors contributing economic, accounting, marketing, pricing, and licensing expertise, who also ensure that board meetings do not deteriorate into a political
stalemate. The first independent director was elected in 2001 (with skills in
marketing and licensing), another in 2003, a third in 2007, and one in 2011
to replace a retiring independent director. So, since 2007, the PSMA Australia Limited board included the maximum allowed number of independent
directors. In addition, the chairperson has always been an independent
director. In 2001, after Grant declined an offer to become the first PSMA
Australia Limited chairperson, the board elected an independent director
who served as chairperson until 2012 when he was replaced by another
independent director.

Over the years, the agencies have continuously expanded the scope of
issues that PSMA Australia Limited is authorized to deal with. They empowered PSMA Australia Limited to build the LYNX system to manage all data-
contribution and data-access transactions. LYNX is a spatial data warehouse
that serves as the infrastructure for all network activities. Data providers
can upload their data directly into LYNX, and VARs receive data products and updates directly from LYNX. LYNX (called PSMA Systems today)
grew and has automated all the transactions between PSMA Australia Limited and its shareholding agencies. Beginning in 2008, the agencies decided
to cease paying themselves discretionary royalties and, instead, to use the
funds to develop the second LYNX generation. Recently, the agencies began
decommissioning their own address verification services in favor of PSMA
Australia Limited's national service (Paull 2012).

The PSMA (and subsequently PSMA Australia Limited) business model
has been successful commercially. In 1997, PSMA Australia Limited signed
its first contract with a VAR. Today PSMA Australia Limited licenses its

products to more than thirty VARs. Over the years, PSMA Australia Limited has increased the number of new products and the intensity of releasing updates for existing products, has improved the quality of datasets, increased the number of data release formats, and expanded its relationships with mapping agencies worldwide. PSMA Australia Limited motivated Australian mapping agencies to improve the quality of their datasets. The agency won national and international prizes for its innovative products. LYNX has also won several prizes (Dixon 2010; Holmes 2009; Paull 2011).

Withstanding Crisis with Incentives   Before the 2008 economic meltdown, PSMA Australia Limited shareholders paid themselves 20 percent mandatory and an additional 20 percent discretionary royalties based on annual revenues. They voted to stop discretionary royalty payments after the crisis erupted and continue to refrain from doing so to date. Commenting on this crisis, the current PSMA Australia Limited general director wrote that the PSMA business model created a "pragmatic and agile philosophy that has enabled success." He emphasized the members' willingness to consider any alternative "to overcome roadblocks" (Paull 2012). This approach helped PSMA Australia Limited sail successfully through the 2008 crisis.

Two years later, the global OD movement introduced another challenge to PSMA. In 2010, Australian Secretary Drew Clarke of the Department of Resources, Energy and Tourism consulted Vanessa Lawrence, head of the British NMCA, about improving Australia's spatial infrastructure. Lawrence recommended to "license at zero price" some of the PSMA Australia Limited outputs to the public sector (Lawrence 2011, 53, 60). PSMA Australia Limited and its shareholding agencies resisted this proposal. Eventually, Clarke understood that if PSMA Australia Limited provided data at no cost (especially to the biggest prospective client—the public sector) its business model would disintegrate. The government rejected the recommendation to reform PSMA Australia Limited arguing that it is a "matter for the PSMA to decide" as legally mandated (Office of Spatial Policy 2012, 12–13, 19–20). The agencies then decided to invest new negotiation powers in PSMA Australia Limited, to negotiate on their behalf a for-profit whole-of-Australia license with the entire public sector.

At the height of the 2008 economic crisis, the agencies decided to expand their unique PSMA information sharing solution by building a new subsidiary organization called PSMA Distribution to take over demand functions including production definition, product life-cycle management, marketing, licensing, pricing, distribution, and sales (Paull 2012). PSMA Australia Limited remains the single shareholder of PSMA Distribution. The latter organization has no assets of its own, acts on the basis of a license from PSMA Australia Limited, returns revenues to the parent organization, and reports annually about its activities as a PSMA group. Yet, PSMA Distribution has its own board of directors, with an even higher proportion (than the PSMA Australia Limited board) of independent directors with marketing skills.

Key PSMA Lessons   The history of PSMA and PSMA Australia Limited provides several powerful lessons that bode well for the incentives-driven model. First, initial discord and acrimony among stakeholder organizations can be overcome. Second, changing existing law is a critical first step to improving public sector information sharing. The ABS needed to be released from the legal obligation to exclusively use AUSLIG maps, before ABS could publish a public tender for a digital mapping solution. Technical and economic breakthroughs such as this occur only where a supportive legal-institutional framework exists. Third, seed money is critical to motivate agencies to set aside long-standing rivalries and engage each other in foundational conversations about improving information sharing. Mobbs describes the initial grant offered by the ABS: "The PSMA dataset simply would not have been created without this financial stimulus, as each agency was operating in fairly austere circumstances. To suggest that each agency should somehow divert some of its operating budget to a national initiative would have been regarded as heresy at that time" (Mobbs 2012c).

Fourth, a skilled negotiator-leader (Grant) and management team (Mobbs and Mooney) can play a critical role in developing trust and convincing all stakeholder organizations to cooperate. Deeper information sharing among the mapping agencies evolved as they began working together to unify their data. Mobbs wrote: "As the joint venture progressed successfully, it was through our regular social interactions around Board meetings that we learned each other's foibles and fears and came to trust each other better" (Mobbs 2012c).

Fifth, a successful incentives-driven information sharing program can create a "snowball effect." In 2000, after completing seven years of service in PSMA (and PSMA Australia Limited), Mobbs was immediately recruited to resolve the lack of information sharing among Australian policing organizations. Mobbs's subsequent successful efforts as the inaugural executive director of CrimTrac, detailed in chapter 6, include the effective use of an incentives-driven information sharing framework. This demonstrates that public sector entrepreneurs who successfully launch an incentives-driven information sharing framework in one domain can replicate their success in other domains.

The PSMA project highlights several additional key features of the incentives-driven information sharing approach. It demonstrates that the proposed approach works well to increase information sharing horizontally and vertically within a large bureaucracy. Grant and Mobbs built a long-term incentives-driven business framework that generated interagency goodwill. Some agencies gain more than others in this exchange game; yet, even agencies that gain less receive enough benefits to remain engaged in the new exchange arena. The PSMA project also demonstrates that multilateral information sharing exchanges are superior to bilateral information sharing agreements. Regrettably, bilateral agreements are the dominant method agencies use to share information, despite the negotiation and implementation challenges, described in the next section.

Monopoly and Waste: The Limits of Bilateral Information Sharing Agreements

Economists may argue that existing bilateral interagency information sharing agreements are sufficient within government. By this line of argument, the maximum action that governments could carry out to improve information sharing would be to create fairer cost-accounting rules to structure reimbursement for sharing data. However, the current bilateral information sharing regime suffers from two problems: (1) it benefits only a handful of data-monopolist agencies; and (2) this regime wastes taxpayer funds and consumes time because each agency must discover what data other agencies own and then spend years negotiating standalone bilateral agreements to share the data. The current bilateral information sharing regime therefore cripples agencies' capability to react effectively and in real time to crises such as Hurricane Katrina and the Deep Horizon oil spill in the Gulf of Mexico.

Data-Monopolist Agencies

Current data-sharing arrangements unevenly benefit agencies that have a monopoly over serving the common needs of other agencies in a given domain. OPM holds a data monopoly in the federal employment domain. Between 2004 and 2011 it supervised USAjobs.com, a web portal that advertises federal job vacancies. In September 2011, OPM terminated the contract of Monster.com, a leading private-sector online job placement vendor, in favor of its own USAJOBS 3.0 software, promising to save taxpayers $5 million over the next ten years. The agency ostensibly terminated the Monster.com contract to ensure that sensitive applicant information would not be "co-mingled in a commercially-operated web site" (Lipowicz 2011a). But USAJOBS 3.0 software was buggy. Vendors argued that OPM violated the Clinger-Cohen Act (1996) by not verifying if better software already exists in the federal sector. In addition, OPM was now engaged in anticompetitive activity because it regulated agencies and also sold them an information service. Shortly after deploying USAJOBS 3.0, OPM hiked the fees for posting job vacancies by 19 percent. Senator Kerry commented: "It seems to me that if it was going to cost less to operate the service, then the fees to agencies should not be going up" (Lipowicz 2011b). But OPM's monopoly in this domain enabled it to do as it pleased.

OPM also holds a data monopoly in the domain of background checks for hired federal employees. In 2011, OPM collected more than $1 billion from agencies to conduct two million background checks. By law, agencies must use OPM checks, so OPM had no incentive to improve efficiency. The agency developed an electronic case-management program to support background checks but continues to convert to paper 98 percent of the electronic data received. OPM justifies this absurd practice with the claim that a small number of customer agencies do not have electronic capabilities. OPM's cost of running background checks increased by 79 percent over six years (from $602 million in 2005 to $1.1 billion in 2011) even though the workload actually decreased from 2008 onward. OPM's IT investments in background checks increased by 682 percent during the same period. Agencies believe that they are overcharged for background checks but can do nothing to challenge OPM's monopoly in this domain (GAO 2012p).

The SSA's Consent Based Social Security Number Verification Service (CBSV) is another example of an agency exploiting a data monopoly. U.S.

federal, state, and local agencies subscribe to use CBSV to verify SSNs. Because only the SSA can provide this service, it imposes harsh contractual terms on subscribing agencies. A new client agency must pay a one-time nonrefundable enrollment fee of $5,000. The SSA collects a $1.05 transaction fee for each SSN verification. Agencies must pay all fees *in advance* at the beginning of each year. The SSA then draws out of the deposited funds as verification services are rendered. Services stop as soon as the funds run out; interest is not accrued on deposits. The SSA has the right to raise fees at will. After sending a fee-hike notice to subscriber agencies the SSA is entitled to withdraw additional funds from subscribers' accounts. Subscriber agencies are charged the full transaction fee if they make an error in submitting a verification request. When the SSA makes similar errors, the agency is exempt from any liability and the subscriber agency must pay—again—for reprocessing the data to remove the SSA error. The SSA can also change at will the method of receiving verification requests or the method of providing results to subscribers. Subscriber agencies are then responsible for all costs related to such changes. The SSA has the right to suspend or cancel any agreement by sending the subscriber agency an email. On signing the CBSV agreement the subscriber agency waives all of its judicial review rights. The SSA is not liable for any damage due to delaying or failing to provide CBSV data. The SSA can impose the draconian CBSV contract on client agencies because these agencies do not have a better option (U.S. Social Security Administration 2009).

Lack of transparency, increased fees, expensive technologies, and cumbersome workflows are symptoms of a bigger problem. When a single agency is the sole provider of information to other agencies, and is protected by law from competition, it loses any incentive to improve workflows, to increase transparency, and to reduce transaction fees. Moreover, agencies such as SSA exploit their information monopoly over critical data elements and impose harsh information sharing terms on other agencies. Chapter 6 will demonstrate how a selective-incentives multilateral information-sharing exchange can overcome this problem.

Wasteful Bilateral Information Sharing Agreements

The current information sharing regime wastes agency time and resources. Agencies sign what are typically bilateral Memorandums of Understanding (MoUs), known as "data use agreements," to share information. MoUs are contracts and other written agreements that describe and prescribe the structures and processes of information flows (Fountain 2013, 48). Two types of information-sharing MoUs exist. A department can sign an agreement with another department to share specific information. For example, if the SEC's Division of Trading and Markets is investigating broker activities associated with the Bank of America (BoA) they will sign an agreement with a Federal Reserve department to share information about the BoA. A different type of data use agreement is signed when agencies share information in a broad domain in which data has not previously been shared. For example, the SEC and the Federal Reserve's governing boards will sign a generic data use agreement to share information in the general domain of over-the-counter (OTC) markets (Jung 2012).

Even the most daring and exciting cross-agency information sharing initiatives must undergo the tedious process of developing bilateral information-sharing MoUs among the collaborating agencies. Agencies signed such bilateral agreements with the GSA before engaging in the Integrated Acquisition System (IAS). Important shared federal websites such as USASpending.gov (operated by GSA) or regulations.gov (operated by the EPA) also require agencies to each sign a bilateral information sharing MoU with the site operator. Agency general counsels must develop, review, and approve each MoU. The volume of interagency agreements keeps growing, burdening agency general counsels and attorneys (Fountain 2013, 99).

Information sharing negotiations are lengthy; it often takes years for agencies to prepare and sign an MoU. The SEC and the Treasury's Financial Crimes Enforcement Network (FCEN) negotiated for years over the sharing of suspicious activity report (SAR) data that tracks money laundering transactions (Jung 2012). Since 1992, HUD and the VA operate a joint program to help homeless veterans find shelter but have yet to sign a data use agreement; many homeless veterans receive excessive or insufficient assistance because this agreement is not signed (GAO 2012s). The Federal Energy Regulatory Commission (FERC) and the Nuclear Regulatory Commission (NRC) negotiated for six years (2003–2009) before signing a data use agreement; the negotiations began in August 2003 when critics attributed an inefficient response to the blackout in the Eastern Interconnection of the U.S. power grid to information sharing failures (Sanders 2009). The DHS and the DOJ labored for seven years (2003–2009) to develop a biometrics data use agreement (GAO 2011e). Each agency sought to protect its biometrics assets and was only willing to share them in the context of a fair data-for-data deal; the protracted negotiations process became a subject of GAO scrutiny (GAO 2011e). The DHS and the DOS spent four years (2008–2011) developing a biometrics data sharing agreement (GAO 2011e).

Even offices within the same agency take years to sign mutual data use agreements. In September 2011 the U.S. Air Force's Office of Special Investigations, the Air Force Contracting unit, and the Air Force General Council for Contractor Responsibilities signed an agreement to share data on fraud and contractor misconduct after a long negotiations period (Weigelt 2011). Sometimes, after years of negotiations, agencies produce a meager "agreement to agree" on how to share information. The GSA and the DOD negotiated for years before agreeing on a common language to be used in future data use agreements (Miller 2007). A retired official commented that protracted data use negotiations indicate that at least one agency feels that it is not getting fair compensation for its data (Moscoe 2011). These time-consuming MoU negotiations waste precious agency resources and yield meager results.

In the current information sharing regime there is a proliferation of bilateral agreements. One amusing incident illustrates how endemic this problem is: The HHS responded to the GAO's complaints about the proliferation of homeland security information sharing networks by arguing that the GAO failed to take notice of six *additional* HHS standalone information sharing applications (GAO 2004b). Today, government officers cannot find answers for simple questions such as "Which agency owns this data?" An SEC official explained that he could only find relevant data in "obvious places" such as the IRS (Jung 2012). Agencies cannot even find information about older data use agreements. Such agreements exist mostly on paper even when the shared data is electronic. The GAO criticized data use agreements as "complex and involving numerous processes" and remains concerned about the length of time it takes to develop such agreements (GAO 2002, 14; GAO 2012b). An official commented on a recent NASA-DHS scientific data sharing agreement, saying: "these agreements rarely produce anything of value" (Dizard 2005).

The current information sharing regime actually discourages agencies from developing mutually beneficial information sharing agreements. Because there is no clear rewards system for producing valuable data, agencies do not exploit information sharing opportunities. Consider, for example, the potential for information sharing cooperation between the U.S. Census Bureau (Census) and the U.S. Postal Service (USPS) in the execution of the constitutionally mandated decennial census. The 2010 census was the most expensive population count in American history; it cost $13 billion, exceeding the cost of the 2000 census by almost $5 billion (in 2010 dollars). A good portion of this increase is attributed to finding the correct addresses of housing units. In 2010, the Census hired 585,000 temporary workers to count 46 million households that did not mail back census forms. At the same time, the USPS was in deepening financial trouble. Total mail volume peaked in 2006 and has been in decline ever since. The cumulative net loss of USPS was almost $23 billion for the five years between 2007 and 2011. In 2011, USPS reached its $15 billion borrowing limit. The USPS subsequently suspended employer contributions to employees' retirement plans and shut down 3700 retail stores. The USPS's financial condition appeared on the GAO's 2011 list of high-risk programs (GAO 2011g, 44–48).

The Census's cost problem opened a business opportunity for the USPS. The two agencies did collaborate on a small scale during the 2010 census. The Census used a new USPS Intelligent Mail Barcode product to track mail packages en route to delivery. This allowed the Census to determine which census forms were being returned by post, remove these from the replacement mailing list, and save on postage costs. In addition, the USPS agreed to destroy, rather than return, undeliverable census mail pieces, which resulted in cost savings for both the Census and the USPS. However, the USPS and the Census share information based on an old 1995 data use agreement that benefits the Census more than the USPS. Following the signing of this agreement, Congress mandated that the USPS deliver its entire address database to the Census biannually and free of charge. So USPS officials are wary to commit to a new, long-term information sharing agreement that may once again force them into an inferior data trading position.

These concerns stop the USPS and the Census from tapping mail carriers' extensive address knowledge (e.g., in 2010, a retired mailman knew which survey addresses to remove or add due to Katrina's devastation). The Census estimates that 53 percent of the nineteen-million nondelivered 2010 census surveys were mailed to vacant housing units. The Census is planning to hire an army of $15-per-hour temporary staffers to deliver the 2020 census forms. The Census calculated that employing mail carriers to do the same job would cost more. However, the Census only needs the mail carriers' intimate address knowledge (not their feet). An opportunity exists for the USPS to develop an "is-anyone-still-living-here?" information service and to sell it to the Census. In fact, about 40,000 state and local agencies maintain address lists for emergency responses and property assessments. With the proper incentives in place, the USPS could purchase some of this data, merge it with its own data, and sell a higher-quality information service product to the Census. This product could save the Census millions of dollars. However, in the current information sharing regime, the USPS has no incentive to develop the product. So, two large and financially strapped agencies remain locked into a rigid and inflexible data use agreement (GAO 2011c).

Finally, the most costly waste lies in agencies' failure to exploit information sources that they own. Between 2000 and 2008 the Administrative Office of the U.S. Courts (AOUSC) paid $156 million over ten years to two companies, WestLaw and LexisNexis, to publish AOUSC records online. WestLaw and LexisNexis digitize, organize, and add search features to these records. During this period, these two corporations have earned an estimated $2 billion annually from selling U.S. court rulings and case reference guides to organizations, including selling these records back to the U.S. federal government for $30 million (Economist 2010a, 11). In our Big Data era when data ownership is so valuable, could not AOUSC, at minimum, have negotiated a better agreement with WestLaw and LexisNexis that exempts U.S. federal agencies from the need to buy these records?

Despite their special position in capturing information and enjoying data mining capabilities, agencies hoard huge quantities of digital data instead of using it to energize the economy (Mayer-Schonberger and Cukier 2013, 116). All too often, agencies hug valuable data closely, unaware of the good causes that the data could serve to support other organizations inside and outside government.

Occasionally, agencies do not want to share information. Agencies then use legal, security, and privacy justifications to avoid sharing. However, more frequently, agencies are willing to share information if compensated. Still, the existing information sharing regime is cumbersome, wasteful, and discourages agencies from proactively seeking new information sources.

Several agencies have already discovered the important relationship between incentives and information sharing. The DHS, the DOJ, and the DOD, as well as the Office of the Director of National Intelligence (ODNI) have made information sharing a factor in their incentives programs by offering employees awards based on their contributions to information sharing and collaboration practices (GAO 2011h, 11). However, these incentives address only individual federal employees and do not support institutional information sharing arrangements such as those introduced by PSMA. Chapter 6 will demonstrate how an incentives-based information sharing program can address the problems identified with current information sharing practices. To do so, the chapter will examine the concept of a "contested commodity exchange."

5 Public Sector Data as a Contested Commodity

This chapter first defines this study's key economic concepts. These definitions highlight the challenge of exchanging a good or service whose insertion into the exchange is ethically contested by the public: a contested commodity. The chapter examines the histories of exchanging thirty ethically contested commodities, to understand which public sector data types are good candidates for incentives-driven exchange. These histories also provide insight into desired conditions to erect an agency data-exchange arena. The gruesome history of commoditizing cadavers for anatomical dissections in Britain at the beginning of the nineteenth century deepens the understanding of the relationships among these conditions. The cadavers case study also underscores the importance of defining a "person" while designing a new contested commodity exchange. In addition, it provides insight into the relationship between supply and demand and the role of law and public opinion in erecting a new contested commodity exchange.

Defining Commodity, Commoditization, Exchange, and Value

The Commoditization of Ordinary Goods and Services

The book proposes to consider governmental data as a valuable commodity that agencies could exchange with each other. Economists define a "commodity" as an object that is produced, exists, and circulates through the economic system as it is being exchanged for another object, usually for money. The value of an object as a commodity becomes known only at the moment of the exchange. Gifts usually beget a chain of counter-gifts and nonmonetary obligations. In contrast, the exchange of commodities is discrete and finite. It is difficult to withdraw commodities from an exchange arena because once formally sold, commoditized objects such as cars and houses possess a resell value and remain potential commodities for another exchange transaction (Kopytoff 1986).

Commoditization is the process whereby an object becomes a commodity. In this process, singular objects are homogenized and sold in bulk. Objects must undergo a process of conversion from their original state to acquire a new status as commodities with an exchange value recognized by the marketplace. Objects are selected, homogenized, and made cognitively similar by placing them within the same for-sale category where they can be sold in bulk. The process of commoditizing objects pervades almost every aspect of our existence (Kopytoff 1986).

Exchange is the hallmark of the commoditization process. The exchange of commodities must be voluntary (the seller is willing to sell and the buyer wants to buy). Exchanges are facilitated by an exchange technology. Money is the most important exchange technology. Humans continue to invent exchange technologies to facilitate the commoditization of new objects. For example, eBay uses online auctioning exchange technology to successfully convert new singular objects into commodities with an exchange value. In a modern society, the value-homogenizing drive of the exchange system and its underlying exchange technologies has an enormous momentum limited only by the capability of the exchange technology (Kopytoff 1986).

Schemes exist to create an exchange arena for private data, and determine a monetary value for this data so that data owners can decide on what terms to sell access to it (Bollier 2010, 24; Laudon 1996). Several exchanges have sprung up to test different strategies to price data. For example, DataMarket (http://datamarket.com), founded in Iceland in 2008, provides access to free datasets from sources such as the UN or the World Bank; this company earns revenue by reselling data from commercial providers like market research firms. Windows Azure Marketplace (http://datamarket.azure.com/) focuses on pricing premium datasets (Mayer-Schönberger and Cukier 2013, 121–122).

The Commoditization of Ethically Contested Goods and Services

Some valuable objects are never commoditized. Anthropologists and political theorists have discovered that multiple different exchange systems coexist within the same society. In tribal societies certain sacred objects never become commodities and other objects are commoditized based on rules of distinct spheres of exchange (Kopytoff 1986, 71). Advanced societies also have not-for-sale objects including public lands, monuments, state art collections, the paraphernalia of political power, royal homes, the insignia of chiefs, and ritual objects. Advanced societies maintain multiple separate exchange systems such as "collectibles exchange systems" that are devoted to the discovery and exchange of ethically sensitive commodities such as currency used in Nazi concentration camps (Appadurai 1986).

An object's value changes as it ages, and according to market circumstances and demand. The "biography of things" concept introduces the idea that objects have biographical possibilities inherent in their current status (Kopytoff 1986, 66). Data elements too have a "biography" that describes their historical evolution and the possibilities of using them to support secondary purposes. Sometimes, *metadata* (information about the data elements themselves) contains such important biographical information.

Empirical studies with the highest theoretical value are those that examine objects that move between the categories of not-for-sale objects and commodities. These cases reveal how to convert objects into commodities. These cases include those where it is difficult to separate a person from an object as in the cases of selling human organs, surrogate motherhood, prostitution, and slavery (Kopytoff 1986). For this book, these cases are important because they teach us ethical lessons that can be applied to the exchange of data about the digital "personhood" of citizens (based on linking numerous data elements in many governmental databases).

It is not easy to specify the *value* of data in terms of a common metric such as money; the same data contains different value and saliency for different stakeholders. As a virtual good, data is not consumed; the same data could be resold numerous times. Data is an "experience good"—a client agency needs access to some of the data in advance in order to assess its usefulness. Even passive spectators contribute to data's monetary value. Individuals browse data and click through. In doing so, they fuel a sophisticated rating industry and increase the value of the browsed data (Fulk et al. 2004; Monge et al. 1998).

Agencies frequently block external access to their most valuable datasets, as described in chapters 3 and 4, thus making it almost impossible to assess their value. Agencies then receive congressional budgets to maintain and develop these datasets. Taxpayers pay billions of dollars annually to support this process. One effective way to discover the value of the most important datasets in the public sector is to erect an internal, electronic data exchange system inside government as described in chapter 6. To do so, we must first explore in depth the process of commoditizing and setting a value for goods and services in a new contested commodity exchange.

Four Lessons from Historical Contested Commodity Exchanges

Public data is a political good. Mill, Marx, Kant, Waltzer, and Radin have argued that every society has nontradable higher goods such as political power and judicial decisions (Radin 1996; Waltzer 1983). Sandel explained: "Putting a price on the good things in life can corrupt them" (Sandel 2012, 5). Conversely, market proponents have argued that trading is built into human nature. Every civilization, they have suggested, has enlarged trading by increasing its outreach across time and space. Mutually beneficial exchange overcomes objections to exchange certain goods. Market proponents argue that it is unfair to decide for others what goods can or cannot be sold. For example, if by selling their labor children can avoid dire poverty and, possibly, starvation, should they be permitted to work (Basu 1999; Basu and Van 1998)? Removing a good from the exchange also limits our ability to learn from market failures (Leebaert 1998). Exchange critics concede that some incentives can be provided for the donation of a contested commodity such as a body organ (Phillips 2011).

Public data is a contested good because its introduction into an exchange arena provokes ethical misgivings. Public data is a contested commodity because agencies hold sensitive information about citizens, which may not be suitable for trade. There are no studies about trading public data as a contested good; however, studies exist about trading other contested commodities. Table 5.1 below provides a brief overview of thirty such goods. At least one scholarly source is cited for each contested good for the benefit of readers who wish to further investigate the ethical debate surrounding it.

The thirty contested goods are divided into four categories. The first includes contested commodities that are parts of the human body. Due to advances in medical technology, the economic value of body parts is unprecedentedly high. Some contested body parts (such as blood) are fully commoditized. Others (such as kidneys) continue to stir ethical debates. The second category deals with consumable materials. It includes well-known commodities such as carbon emissions as well as lesser-known ones such as nitrogen. The third category, "objectifying the self," includes humans who,

Table 5.1
Contested commodities: history and ethical concerns

Category	Name	Ethical concern	Period	Sources
Human body	Hair jewelry	Convert human hair into a market commodity but allow jewelry to transcend market associations	1770–1910	(Sheumaker 2003)
	Blood	Establish blood as a commodity rather than as a charitable contribution	1936–present	(Cooper and Culyer 1968)
	Sperm	Overcome accusations that human insemination is a criminal offense or an act of adultery	1790–1977	(Fader 2014)
	Ova	Misgivings about large cash incentives offered to upper-class females willing to donate their eggs	1978–present	(Blackley 2003)
	Solid organs	Concerns that the rich will purchase the organs of the poor for large sums of money	1972–present	(Becker and Elias 2007; Cohen 1989; Kaserman 2001; Schwindt and Vining 1986)
	Tissues	Fears of an unregulated black market for human tissues	1949–present	(Mahoney 2000)
	Genetic data	Collection of genetic data is crucial for research but can lead to discrimination	1990–present	(Parry 2004)
	Biotech samples	Fear that private companies will collect samples in unethical ways	1993–present	(Andrews and Nelkin 1998)
	Saintly relics	Black marketeering in the relics of saints required for construction of church altars	750–1150	(Geary 1986)
	Medical services	Transforming doctor-patient relationship into merchant-consumer relationship	1910s–1970s	(Tomes 2003)

(continued)

Table 5.1
(*continued*)

Category	Name	Ethical concern	Period	Sources
	Memorial services	Exploiting for profit the emotions of the grieved kin of a deceased person	1910s–1930s	(Tharp 2003)
	Cadavers	Digging out fresh cadavers and selling them to medical schools (Great Britain)	nineteenth century	(Ross and Ross 1979)
	Federal data	Converting federal data into an internally traded commodity within government while overcoming concerns regarding governmental greed, privacy, and Big Brother government	2010–present	(Radin 1996)
Consumption products	Emissions	Treating pollution as a commodity that can be traded on an open marketplace	1967–present	(Ellerman and Joskow 2008)
	Nitrogen	Proposing trade in nitrogen pollution credits to reduce fertilizers' damage to the environment	1971–present	(Hey, Urban, and Kostel 2005)
	Nano-materials	Concerns that the nano-materials humans breathe and digest pose future health risks	1950s–present	(GAO 2010e)
	Fair trade coffee	Demanding to label coffee to raise awareness of the exploitation of poor, small-scale farmers	1989–present	(Rice 2001)
	Blood diamonds	Buying diamonds, mined in an area of conflict, that help finance belligerent war efforts	1990–2000	(Le Billon 2006)
	Animal fur	The killing of animals to make luxury clothing artifacts	1960s–present	(Muth and Jamison 2000)

Objectifying the self	Slavery	Negating the slave's humanity by treating him/her as an object (United States)	1619–1865	(Sowell 1981; Wolff 2002)
	Prostitution	Anger due to the objectification of women's sexuality	1960s—present	(Head 2010)
	Surrogate motherhood	Concerns about the creation of a poor childbearing underclass	1976—present	(Anderson 1993)
	Detailed marriage contracts	Conflicts with a romanticized notion of marriage as an institution of love and trust	1760—present	(Anderson 1993)
	Child labor	Objectifying children as laborers at the expense of the children's education and well-being	1992-present	(Basu and Van 1998; Basu 1999; Basu, Chau, and Grote 2006)
	Military service	The rich exempting themselves from conscription by paying the poor to fight for the homeland	1789—present	(Adams 2005; Sarkesian 1972)
	School vouchers	Sacrificing the ideal of universal education for a for-profit schooling system	1955-present	(Stanley 2004)
Sacra	Death bowls	Creating sacred ritual objects and keeping them away from the marketplace (Solomon Islands)	Current	(Davenport 1986)
	Saintly land	Converting saintly land into a commodity (Mexico)	1775-1810	(Fisher 2003)
	Silk	Emphasizing the superior ethical value of homemade garments over British garments (India)	1905-1947	(Bayly 1986)
	Ghee	Adulteration of ghee stirs ethnic riots between the Hindu and the Marwari communities (India)	1917	(Hardgrove 2003)
	MSG	Trading in MSG as a commodity synonymous with the national movement (China)	1910s-1940s	(Gerth 2003)

in one way or another, are commoditized by other human beings. This category encompasses slavery, prostitution, and surrogate motherhood, as well as lesser-known commodities such as detailed marriage contracts. Finally, the fourth category, "sacra," contains objects that are sacred to certain cultures. Ranging from wooden burial bowls to ghee (the purest form of butter fat used by Hindus in sacred rituals), these objects stir emotions, and even riots if the trader is suspected of meddling with the pure substance during trading.

The arguments for or against treating public data as a tradable good do not depend on whether other contested goods can be commoditized. Nonetheless, metaphors are "tools of the trade" in contested goods scholarship. They are ideas borrowed from one domain that function literally rather than figuratively in another domain. Metaphors also dominate the public IT domain. For example, the IRS suffered from decades of technological fiascos. At the beginning of the 2000s, the IRS adopted the metaphor of "the virtual value chain" in all its IT projects as part of the IRS's efforts to modernize and facilitate citizen services. The adoption of this metaphor proved to be successful. The public and the media noted the positive change in IRS IT initiatives (Holden and Fletcher 2005; Vann 2005; White 2007). Proponents of transplant organ exchange also developed positive metaphors to recruit public support (Crespi 1994). Positive data exchange metaphors include the image of freeing locked public data via eBay-style exchange and the comparison of public databases to the undiscovered goldmines in the mythical Old West—awaiting a crowd of adventurers to tap their potential. This chapter focuses on thirty contested commodities to glean four important lessons to assist the design of PSIE.

The Information-Type Lesson

The histories of the contested commodities illustrate the intersection between a commodity's market value and ethical sensitivity, and reveal the most promising combination for successful contested commodity trade. During research for this book, several hundred sources on the thirty histories of contested commodities were reviewed. Then, they were independently ranked on two scales of 1–10 according to the following criteria: (1) the degree to which the ethical debate surrounding the commoditization of a contested commodity is resolved (10 meaning that the ethical debate is resolved (e.g., blood) and 0 meaning that the ethical debate is entirely

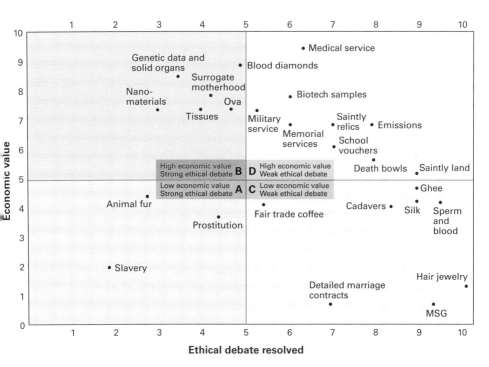

Figure 5.1
Measuring contested commodities for ethical debate and economic value.

unresolved (e.g., slavery)); and (2) the contemporary market value of a given commodity (10 meaning that the commodity ranks highly in terms of market value (e.g., medical services) and 0 meaning that the commodity currently has little market value (e.g., hair jewels)). The independent rankings were averaged to produce figure 5.1. The purpose of this thought experiment was to expand our conceptual thinking about public data as a contested commodity.

The contested commodities in the lower left cell of figure 5.1 (marked with the letter "A") are the ones least likely to be commoditized, as they have a low market value and unresolved ethical debate. Aggregated demographic data falls into this category. Such information can be found free of charge on commercial OD sites. Nonetheless, ethical concerns prohibit agencies from trading in such data. U.S. college boards harvest demographic data about college applicants from Facebook but would not dare ask an agency for the same data (Jaschik 2007). Contested commodities that reside in cell B have a higher market value than those in cell A, however they too present unresolved ethical concerns. National security data belongs in this category; secrecy concerns regarding trade in such data overrides their potential market value. The ethical debates regarding contested commodities in cell C are resolved but the incentive to trade in them is limited due to their low economic value. Geographical data falls into this category. Trade in this data does not raise strong ethical debate; however, today, such data can be found free of charge on the web (e.g., Google Earth). Finally, contested commodities in cell D are the "sweet (trading) spot" for a public data exchange program. These commodities have a high economic value and their trade evokes little ethical debate. Environmental and disaster-relief data conform to this category. The value of data is high; at the same time politicians and the public demand interagency information sharing.

Note that none of the thirty commodities were placed in the right uppermost corner of figure 5.1. Contested commodities are never completely "ethically resolved." Even blood still evokes some ethical misgivings. For example, people believe that it is better to "donate blood" rather than to "sell blood" but almost always give blood in a blood bank. Similarly, the ethical debate over PSIE will never be completely resolved.

The Cresting Moment Lesson

The thirty histories demonstrate that a "cresting moment" usually exists in the life span of a contested commodity, at which point scarcity of a product meets a promising new technology that provides a solution to this scarcity. Jointly, the scarcity and the new technology overcome ethical concerns and assist the emergence of a new contested commodity exchange. For example, before World War I (WWI), commercialized blood donation was believed to be a sacrilegious act. However, WWI demonstrated the lethal consequences of blood shortages, prompting scientists to develop new technology to support the mass storage and transfer of blood. By the time World War II (WWII) broke out, the moral debate over selling blood was nullified by the life-saving benefits of these new techniques on the battlefield. The term "blood bank" was coined in 1937 (Cooper and Culyer 1968).

The histories of commoditizing sperm and ova echo that of commercializing blood. When the artificial insemination procedure was first published in 1954, U.S. courts declared that, regardless of a husband's consent, a married woman's insemination by another person's sperm would be considered an act of adultery, the child born from such insemination would be ille-gitimate, and the husband would possess no rights over the child. As soon as the technology for preserving human sperm by cryogenic methods matured, and the demand for this commodity was clear, the moral debate regarding sperm donation faded away (Fader 2014). Likewise, the develop-ment of in vitro fertilization in the UK (1978) and the first pregnancy using donated ova in Australia (1983) ended the debate regarding the morality of selling ova (Blackley 2003).

A contested commodity exchange is unlikely to emerge if either one of the two conditions (scarcity and new technology) is absent. The debate regarding prostitution still rages today because there is neither a scarcity of prostitutes nor a new technology to meet the need for prostitution in an innovative way. Likewise, the moral debate regarding surrogate moth-erhood is unlikely to disappear as there is neither a scarcity of surrogate mothers nor a new technology to provide an alternative to surrogate moth-erhood (Anderson 1993). A new technology alone is insufficient to over-come moral concerns. Technology exists to collect human cells from the floors of surgery rooms and extract genetic data from them. However, there is no scarcity of a product in this case, and the debate regarding the use of such procedures without the explicit consent of the cells' owners is still raging. Some ethical concerns override the conditions of scarcity and tech-nology. The complete commoditization of one human by another is con-sidered taboo. Slavery and child labor were once "profitable commodities" (Basu and Van 1998; Wolff 2002). Fortunately, ethical and legal support for trading in humans no longer exists.

Public data as a contested commodity has reached its cresting moment. Information sharing failures are expensive and lethal as demonstrated in chapter 1. However, a solution technology has emerged during the past decade: automated electronic information exchanges like those used by eBay, Amazon, and Apple's iTunes. Chapter 6 provides more information about these automated exchanges and how they could be adopted to sup-port a new internal public sector electronic information exchange.

The Restricted Commoditization Lesson

The thirty histories reveal a third lesson: contested commodity exchanges are successful if they are subjected to trade limitations at their inception. Such restricted arrangements ban advertisement, limit the number of potential buyers, decouple demand and supply, mandate nonmonetary payments, or set terms for the future removal of a commodity from the exchange (Agnew 2003; Schwindt and Vining 1986). Restricted commoditization also allows a contested commodity to benefit simultaneously from voluntary exchange and trade. Such arrangements helped blood become the established commodity it is today (Cooper and Culyer 1968). The thirty histories suggest that full commoditization and noncommoditization are but end points in a continuum. The interesting questions are found in between these two extremes: what limits will be set on trading? How effective will these limits be?

Restricted commoditization arrangements exist in every successful contested commodity exchange. The first sperm banks only permitted semen storage to men facing the possibility of sterilization. Later on, these banks began receiving semen donations from the broader population, concurrently applying new restricted commoditization arrangements such as establishing donor anonymity (Fader 2014). Plans to commoditize cadaveric transplant organs detail how funds will be deposited (e.g., paid directly to kin or deposited in the college accounts of the donor's children) (Schwindt and Vining 1986). Contested commodity exchanges often ban advertisement. The early decision of the American Medical Association to curb advertisement for medical services helped to professionalize the medical field. Similarly, the FDA's strong regulatory power is rooted in the American tradition of viewing medical services as a contested commodity (Tomes 2003). At times, the private sector also adopts restricted commoditization. Ever since the Quakers boycotted slave-derived goods in 1827, there is a growing demand to label products that are produced by ethical standards. In 2002, the fair trade coffee movement developed an international certification system designed to ensure that poor growers receive adequate compensation for their labor (Rice 2001).

New contested commodity exchanges evolve only after provisions are made to ensure that less advantaged populations do not suffer due to changing rules of the game. An exchange for luxurious coffins evolved in America during the 1750s, only after free simple coffins were first offered to paupers (Tharp 2003). School voucher systems evolved only after the state installed measurements to ensure that wealthy populations do not use the new system to reject responsibility toward less advantaged children (Stanley 2004). Sometimes, provisions are made in advance for the removal of contested commodities from the exchange. The struggle to ban trading in blood diamonds and animal fur demonstrates such stipulation (Le Billon 2006; Muth and Jamison 2000). Such restrictions are not new. In the Solomon Islands, natives cannot trade hand-painted wooden bowls that were used in a death ritual (Davenport 1986). Similar to the foundations of a good marriage, restrictions on contested commodity trade must be supported by formal rules. Romantic notions regarding how a selfless marriage or a restricted market ought to function must be embedded within official stipulations (Anderson 1993).

The early adoption of restricted commoditization arrangements applies well to the idea of trading public data as a contested commodity. Some data cannot be traded (e.g., predictive genetic data discovered via a routine blood test should not be used in custody fights over children). Like slavery, such sensitive data is a "product" that is barred from the exchange. In the United States, Title II of the Privacy Rule of the Health Insurance Portability and Accountability Act (HIPAA) limits the portability of sensitive medical data. This act requires that all organizations acquire authorization from individuals before releasing personal and medical information about them. In contrast, data such as vehicles' license numbers is tradable. In between these extremes, most public data can be traded as a contested commodity based on restricted commoditization arrangements.

Fraud and Black Markets Lesson

The thirty histories teach that contested commodity exchanges can effectively overcome the challenges of black markets and fraud. "Body snatching" and murderous practices disappeared after the passage of the UK Anatomy Act of 1832 as described in the next section. The black market for saintly relics (necessary for the construction of medieval church altars) vanished after sacred icons became commoditized, and became the preferred source of religious power (Geary 1986). The histories of legalizing exchanges for prostitution, alcohol, smuggled goods, and transplant organs also support this argument.

Fraud is effectively stemmed in new contested commodity exchanges through self-policing, peer outrage, and network communication. The establishment of formal exchanges to trade in ova, human tissues, and fair trade coffee instantaneously reduced fraud by providing buyers and sellers with a rule-driven exchange arena in which they can execute transactions;

self-policing and peer outrage play an important role in reducing unethical behavior in these new exchanges (Mahoney 2000). Utilizing network communication, eye and tissue banks stem fraudulent behavior in the purchase of corneas from coroner offices, ensuring that useable corneas are prioritized for seriously ill individuals (ibid.). The EU's emissions trade system increased trust among member countries, thus removing certain countries' concerns that other countries were "cheating" in their pollution reports (Ellerman and Joskow 2008). The emissions exchange also caused honest information brokers to emerge, which decreased fraud (EU ETS 2010; Premkumar 2003).

A Public Sector Information Exchange (PSIE) can also eliminate fraud and eradicate information black markets. Today, more outsiders execute public sector functions than ever before. Exchange among strangers is characterized by problems regarding the authentication and verification of data quality and property rights, which can result in information fraud. Trading in public data can eradicate fraud and information black markets by providing a legitimate exchange arena where information quality and property rights are verified. It will be cheaper and more convenient for an agency to acquire the data it needs via this exchange than search for it elsewhere.

In addition, information trading agencies reputed for selling inaccurate, misleading, or dated information products will discover that, in the future, fewer agencies will agree to trade with them. This reputation-based mechanism will serve as a powerful deterrent for agencies from purposefully selling poor-quality or dated information products to other agencies. One scholar has already examined how the use of agency reputational mechanisms effectively stems corruption and fraud (Picci 2011). PSIE could be an important addition to such reputation-based governance mechanisms. An efficient information sharing arena will also eliminate citizen fraud such as false claims for social benefits.

Lessons from the Cadavers Exchange System

The case study of the commoditization of cadavers for anatomical dissections in Britain during the eighteenth and ninteenth centuries demonstrates the dependencies among the aforementioned contested commodity exchange lessons. In that era, cadavers were a contested commodity that belonged to cell B in figure 5.1 (e.g., high market value and unresolved ethical dilemma). Medical and anatomical schools suffered from an acute shortage of cadavers for anatomical dissections, but the breakthrough technology to address this shortage (e.g., virtual dissections) would not emerge until almost two hundred years later. Therefore, a horrific black market evolved to provide cadavers to medical schools. Restricted commoditization arrangements were imposed on cadavers exchange. These arrangements helped vanquish the most egregious symptoms of the black market including murder and body snatching. However, other black market syndromes persisted for another 100 years because the cadavers exchange did not experience a cresting moment when an acute supply problem meets a breakthrough technology. The cadavers case study reveals two additional lessons: (1) PSIE will need a good definition of the "virtual person" concept and what it encompasses; and (2) public opinion and the law must change to support a new contested commodity exchange such as PSIE.

From the Birth of the Cadavers Supply Problem to Body Snatching

British medical students began acquiring knowledge of anatomy through clinical dissection in the seventeenth century. Medical schools then needed access to cadavers for training. In 1540 King Henry VIII followed a Scottish precedent and granted an annual right to dissect the bodies of four hanged murderers. In 1752, another royal act empowered the courts to punish murderers with a public dissection immediately following their hanging. The 1752 royal act explained the logic of these public dissections: "the crime of murder has been more frequently perpetrated than formerly . . . and . . . it is thereby become necessary that some further terror and peculiar infamy be added to the punishment of death" (Ross and Ross 1979, 109). Outside of these stipulations, which were insufficient for medical schools, the law forbade the anatomical dissection of other cadavers. Surgeons, their students, and several entrepreneurial criminals (known as "resurrectionists" or "body snatchers") then began digging corpses out of fresh graves late at night to deliver or sell them to the medical schools (Johnson 2013, 2; Mitchell et al. 2011, 92–93; Ross and Ross 1979, 110–111).

At first, all stakeholders passively cooperated with the body-snatching practice. British merchants were willing to pay more for good medical care that was dependent on anatomical knowledge acquired during dissections. Surgeons cooperated with the current law because gallows dissections provided them with royal patronage. Anatomists and students needed cadavers to support their training. Private anatomy schools were dependent on tuitions; students would drop out without access to dissections. The emerging forensic medical science further increased the demand for cadavers. Magistrates refused to confront public opinion that resisted any mutilation of the cadaver, and opted not to find new ways to supply cadavers. The law itself did not consider the cadaver as property so, technically, the snatcher was not a thief. Even entrepreneurial sheriffs sometimes sold bodies to medical schools (Magee 2001, 377; Mitchell et al. 2011, 97; Ross and Ross 1979, 110–112).

From Body-Snatching to Murder

The very early grave robbers were surgeons and their students. Next, professional body-snatching gangs entered this illegal exchange and fought over territories and clients. Gang members desecrated other gangs' graveyards and broke into medical schools to mutilate rival gangs' corpses. They cut and sewed the cadavers into parts so that they could sell the parts separately. Modern forensic analysis of some of these cadavers revealed the sewing marks (Johnson 2013, 4; Magee 2001, 378; Mitchell et al. 2011, 91).

Citizens mobilized to protect graves, the cadaver supply went down, and the price went up. The poor organized to protect their cemeteries with spring guns, primitive land mines, cemetery watch clubs, and vigilante justice. The rich purchased iron coffins, put iron-bar cages around graves, and hired armed guards to protect their graveyards (Johnson 2013, 4; Magee 2001, 378; Ross and Ross 1979, 114).

The body snatchers then developed new, creative ways to recruit supply. In one case two snatchers dressed a corpse in a suit and a hat and walked away from a guarded cemetery with their "sick friend." Other snatchers acquired cadavers before burial by conspiring with undertakers to replace the body in the coffin with coal or by removing a cadaver from one room while mourners in another room made burial plans. But this was insufficient to meet supply and prices increased again. Salted and pickled Irish cadavers were imported by sea until dock laborers complained to port authorities about intolerable odors emerging from the containers of concealed cadavers (Magee 2001, 379; Ross and Ross 1979, 117).

Medical personnel did not escape the public's fury. At the Oxford gallows, the mob stoned surgeons' agents. Rumors spread about medical students dissecting convicts who survived hanging. Other rumors suggested that professors were maintaining warehouses of cadavers and keeping vultures to discard remains. A public mob's "dirty murdering anatomists" sentiment turned into a riot in 1832: twenty thousand men looted and burned down the Aberdeen anatomy school (Hurren 2008, 780–781; Johnson 2013, 3–4; Magee 2001, 379; Mitchell et al. 2011, 93; Ross and Ross 1979, 109, 112).

Then came murder. In 1831, two body snatchers confessed that they murdered a child and a woman to provide anatomical specimens. Likewise, two other body snatchers, Burke and Hare of Edinburgh, murdered at least sixteen friendless persons to collect ten pounds per corpse (Johnson 2013, 5; Magee 2001, 379; Mitchell et al. 2011, 92; Ross and Ross 1979, 117–118).

The 1832 Anatomy Law and Its Aftermath

In 1832, the magistrates could no longer look the other way. They began charging students and professors in court for snatching and possession of illegally acquired dissection material. The reputation of the medical profession was tarnished, and surgeons and anatomists could no longer passively support body snatching (Johnson 2013, 4; Magee 2001, 379; Ross and Ross 1979, 114, 118).

The Anatomy Law of 1832 created an incipient contested commodity exchange in cadavers. This law introduced a new cadavers exchange system and imposed a set of restricted commoditization arrangements on the new exchange. It allowed unclaimed bodies in workhouses and hospitals to be transferred to medical schools. Inspectors were appointed to supervise and record the supply of cadavers and the proper burial of remains in consecrated grounds. Only certified medical staff was authorized to conduct dissections. Legal owners of cadavers could refuse anatomical examinations; inmates or patients could also register objections to dissection. Dissection was no longer a criminal offense and medical personnel could not be punished for possessing human organs (Office of the Attorney General 1832).

The 1832 law was partially successful. Murder for cadavers to dissect and body snatching vanished. However, the public still viewed dissections as sacrilegious so cadaver shortage, scandals, and riots continued, though were less frequent. There was no new technology to address the lack of cadavers, so prices remained high and dissected bodies mostly belonged to the unclaimed poor. Agents continued to purchase pauper bodies in secretive transactions. The new exchange system was highly dependent on all stakeholders' good will. For example, the Oxford City coroner's strained relationship with the Oxford University's Anatomy Department, prompted him to disrupt the local cadaver supply system for seventeen years (Hurren 2008, 789, 797, 799, 809; Johnson 2013, 5; Magee 2001, 378; Mitchell et al. 2011, 92). Ethical concerns have only dissipated recently with the invention of a new technology that enables virtual cadaver dissections.

Cadavers Exchange Lessons for PSIE

The cadavers case study provides four lessons for PSIE. First, it illustrates the importance of defining what a "person" is in the context of a contested commodity exchange. In the case of cadavers, does this definition include the person having rights to his body after death? In the PSIE case, does "personhood" include rights over digital data about the virtual self that is stored in governmental databases? We will address the personhood question in chapter 7.

Second, the cadavers case study reminds us that supply will always emerge to meet demand even if acquired unethically and criminally. Bad exchange systems evolve because good people passively support the status quo. Chapter 4 highlighted costs (such as monopolies and waste) of passively accepting the information-sharing status quo. Our governmental information sharing challenge is critical, immediate, and demands bold and creative solutions. The cadavers exchange did not experience a cresting moment (only two hundred years later did the technology of virtual dissections emerge); therefore restricted commoditization arrangements vanquished murder and body snatching but the black market in cadavers lived on for another hundred years. In contrast, a breakthrough technology (e.g., electronic exchange of information goods) has emerged to meet the information sharing shortage in the public sector as demonstrated in chapter 6.

Third, the cadavers case study underscores the argument that a change in public opinion or a breakthrough technology is needed to support a successful new contested commodity exchange. The British cadavers supply challenge was resolved only after 1920 when the public began donating cadavers; the ethical concerns only dissolved more recently, with the invention of virtual dissections.

Finally, the cadavers case study emphasizes the role that the law must play in the design of a contested commodity exchange. The 1832 Anatomy Law addressed only the most urgent problems (i.e., murder and body snatching) but was insufficient to bring about a complete change. PSIE will require the same legal support that the 1832 Anatomy Law provided to the new cadavers exchange. By itself, the law will not overcome bad practices. However, the law can redirect human agents toward a different and better future.

One last important lesson of this chapter concerns the changing nature of the ethical debate regarding contested commodities over time. Initially, trading in certain goods such as cadavers, blood, and sperm was widely perceived as unethical and even punishable by law. However, over time and through public debate, technological breakthroughs, and educational efforts people accepted that these goods could be traded under certain trade restrictions as a means to increase their circulation. In the same way, initial ethical opposition to the public data-trading approach is likely to dissipate as citizens debate the idea and learn about its merits. The next chapter provides theoretical and empirical examples of how such data trade might function.

6   The Public Sector Information Exchange (PSIE)

The chapter first defines the Public Sector Information Exchange (PSIE) concept by drawing on the strengths of the three existing information sharing approaches (coerce, consent, and coax—see chapter 2). Next, the chapter discusses how different countries could build different PSIE programs suited to their particular needs and national culture. An existing Australian supply-chain model (in the policing domain) and a hypothetical American exchange model (in the environmental domain) are described to support this discussion. The American PSIE model is contrasted with existing information sharing technologies to demonstrate the advantage of the incentives-driven PSIE approach over primarily technological solutions to the information sharing challenge. Finally, three clusters of economic, legal, and technical challenges are described and proposals are made to address them. The chapter provides PSIE design solutions to these challenges, leading up to a discussion of the tougher ethical and political challenges in chapter 7.

The Concept of a PSIE

A PSIE program is an institutional arrangement based on the idea that selective incentives can overcome seemingly insurmountable information sharing obstacles. This program aspires to create a new information sharing ecosystem inside the public sector. The PSIE concept utilizes one key idea from each of the three information sharing approaches discussed in chapter 2 while rejecting their less-successful features. In line with the coerce approach, PSIE assumes that agency interests come first. However, PSIE rejects the claim that such interests inevitably lead to a refusal to share information, and demonstrates how trading can propel selfish actors to bring data goods to the exchange. PSIE borrows the coax approach's plea for the institutionalization of standards. However, PSIE highlights the need to use concrete incentives to nudge agencies to cooperate with such standards. Finally, PSIE adopts the belief in human ingenuity from the consent approach while rejecting this approach's naive assumption that altruism is a sufficient basis for improving information sharing.

Agencies' electronic mountains have certain similar features to the archeological mountain that Bliss and MacAlister uncovered at Tel Gezer. Nonetheless, this similarity does not imply that we must adopt a fatalist approach toward the public sector's electronic mountains. Rather, like Bliss at Tel Gezer, PSIE architects will discover that there is enormous vitality and energy buried inside agencies' electronic mountains and that with the right incentives these resources can be harnessed to improve electronic information sharing.

Information sharing is context-specific as explained in chapter 2. Countries will require different PSIE programs to address their unique needs, cultures, and institutions. Culture in particular is an important variable. One study revealed that, in contrast to their Australian colleagues, Taiwanese employees are more willing to share information for the good of the organization even if doing so is potentially disadvantageous for the person concerned (Chow et al. 1999). Therefore, the next two sections highlight two different PSIE programs each tailored to the unique institutional and cultural setting of a specific country: a supply-chain program that effectively overcame information sharing barriers in the Australian policing community, and a proposed trade program for exchanging environmental data in the United States.

A Supply-Chain PSIE Model (Australia)

Political rivalry for available taxpayers' funds characterizes the relationships among the nine police jurisdictions of Australia (six states, two territories, and the federal government). Each state and territory has its own jurisdictional police force and the Australian Federal Police (AFP) constitutes the ninth police force. These agencies mistrust each other, and jointly mistrust federal employees. During the second half of the 1990s a crime wave swept Australia. The criminals manipulated the lack of information sharing across police jurisdictions to their advantage. Several information sharing failures resulted in highly publicized crimes. The public was infuriated and politicians vowed to defeat the "tyranny of distance" (Mobbs 2001, 3). At the same time (1995–1997), the Wood Royal Commission discovered systemic corruption within the New South Wales (NSW) police force (Royal Commission 1997). The NSW government recruited Peter Ryan, a distinguished British policeman, as the NSW police commissioner, to root out corruption.

NSW police hosted the IT infrastructure of an organization called the National Exchange of Policing Information (NEPI). NEPI was overseen by a board on which all police organizations were represented. Police organizations paid for NEPI services annually based on their force size (so NSW paid the highest sum, followed by Queensland and Victoria). By the late 1990s NEPI's mainframes were on the brink of complete failure. The police organizations were embarrassed by their failure to ensure the upgrade of NEPI's operations but did not consider replacing it with a new system (CrimTrac 2002, 2003). They continued to use their own IT systems, which did not converse with each other. Only the facsimile machine was considered a secure method of passing information between jurisdictions.

Ryan was eager to establish intelligence-led police work but he was frustrated by the advice he received, that NEPI's systems were obsolescent. Eventually, in 1998, after lobbying the federal government, he received a pledge from Prime Minister John Howard for the funding required to revamp NEPI. Howard was searching for opportunities to increase federal influence over the states and territories. He asked Ryan how much it would cost to replace NEPI and Ryan responded with the figure of A\$50 million. The promise to revitalize law enforcement and the A\$50 million pledge became a major part of Howard's subsequent, successful reelection campaign.

Data Ownership Fights during CrimTrac's First Years

Shortly after Howard was reelected in October 1998, the federal government and the eight police organizations signed an intergovernmental agreement (IGA) to establish CrimTrac to improve information sharing among the police jurisdictions. The A\$50 million pledge became CrimTrac's initial budget (CrimTrac 2001). During 1999–2000, a small project team from the Commonwealth Attorney-General's Department established CrimTrac. Top priority was given to developing contracts to replace the failing NEPI systems. In January 2001, Mobbs became CrimTrac's inaugural CEO. During the previous seven years, Mobbs had demonstrated vision and managerial skill as PSMA's inaugural CEO, convincing mapping agencies to share their data for incentives (see chapter 4). His recruiters hoped that he would achieve similar success at CrimTrac.

The police organizations initially exhibited resistance to CrimTrac. Mobbs was a federal appointee who had never worn a police uniform. A Board of Management made up of both police commissioners and federal officials supervised CrimTrac. The Board was initially chaired by a Commonwealth representative from the Attorney-General's Department who could veto any expenditure of the A$50 million (although this veto power was never exercised). The Board also included independent nonvoting members with expertise in finance and IT. The Board did not include a police commissioner appointee for every jurisdiction; two voting members represented large jurisdictions and another two represented smaller jurisdictions—a measure deliberately adopted to ensure progress and to compel police commissioners to act cooperatively. Mobbs wrote: "The police jurisdictions were still smarting over the failure of NEPI and some jumped-up civilian like me, even with my successful recent history with PSMA, was not going to be allowed to tell them how to redo their business models overnight. Police are hugely tribal in this country. If you weren't in the tribe, then you had to prove that you were worthy" (Mobbs 2012a).

Police organizations were primarily concerned about the issue of data ownership. Some were convinced that CrimTrac was a thinly disguised federal plot to nationalize their information assets. This was a valid concern, as the IGA declared that the IP rights of *anything* produced jointly with CrimTrac was to be federal property (CrimTrac 2001). Mobbs realized that CrimTrac would not succeed if he insisted on implementing the IGA's data ownership principle verbatim. He wrote: "We had to have debate over data sovereignty and what the terms 'national operational policing data' and 'sharing' in the IGA really meant. It soon became clear that no state or territory police service intended to cede its data to a Commonwealth agency" (Mobbs 2005, 5).

Mobbs became personally frustrated by prolonged data ownership and data sharing struggles. He wrote: "In 2001 CrimTrac was spending an undue amount of time trying to convince senior police officers in some states that CrimTrac, created as a multi-jurisdictional data sharing initiative, held no hidden agendas. We were not about hoarding, altering, or misusing the hard-won policing data stored in obsolescing state or territory databases that existed incommunicado. We were not about 'nationalizing' data held by the policing collective" (Mobbs 2005, 8).

Mobbs worked hard to win the support of the police organizations. He was frugal with the A$50 million budget. The powerful Senate Estimates Committee of the Australian Parliament even asked him to explain why he did *not* plan to spend the entire grant during CrimTrac's first three years of existence, as per the election pledge. Patiently, he commissioned evaluation studies, supervised the design of new IT architecture, and negotiated contracts with external vendors. He smoothed over tension between his two supervisors—the Board of Management and the Minister of Justice. Police commissioners outnumbered federal officials on the Board, so, on several occasions, Mobbs gained the former's cooperation by reminding them that he could report back to his Minister that the A$50 million might be better spent elsewhere. Mobbs also reminded the Minister (who was eager to see a federal gain in publicity for the A$50 million grant) that local policemen are the ones who do the legwork and should therefore be permitted to claim credit for a significant arrest, even if CrimTrac had supported their success.

Mobbs gained initial support by swiftly revitalizing the National Automated Fingerprint Identification System (NAFIS). NAFIS was an ideal first target for several reasons. First, this technology was originally developed with federal funds, so there were no objections to using federal funds to revitalize it. Second, the public accepted fingerprinting as a legitimate policing technology; hence, no privacy concerns accompanied the NAFIS project. Third, the police organizations were eager to replace the failing NAFIS because without an effective system the fingerprints they collected were effectively useless. Fourth, politicians were keen to see Australia regain its status as a leader in this domain. Howard, the Minister, and Mobbs launched the new NAFIS on June 20, 2001. The ceremony emphasized the new NAFIS as CrimTrac's first deliverable. Police commissioners' testimony provides evidence that they were more impressed by NAFIS than by CrimTrac (CrimTrac 2001).

NCHRC's Breakthrough Selective-Incentives Solution

CrimTrac inherited the National Criminal History Record Checking (NCHRC) program, which provided background checks to public sector agencies. A small number of accredited agencies used the information to assess the suitability of persons for purposes such as employing individuals in positions of trust. Police and accredited agencies sent CrimTrac requests to check names against the National Name Index (NNI) of persons of interest to police. If a potential match was identified, the name was referred to the police organization holding the record. CrimTrac then paid this organization a set fee for providing criminal history information (CrimTrac 2003). Each police organization charged a different fee and issued a different type of clearance report. CrimTrac charged client agencies a modest processing fee. In 2001, CrimTrac provided background checks at a loss (CrimTrac 2001). Complicating things further, sometimes police organizations provided the background information directly to accredited agencies including running an NNI query on their behalf.

The police organizations were the key NCHRC clients. They used NCHRC to check if a person held in custody in a given state had been previously convicted in another state. Police organizations paid CrimTrac an annual subscription fee based on a sliding-scale formula: organizations that ran many checks in a given year paid a lower fee per check than other organizations. This arrangement encouraged wasteful use of the service, and smaller police jurisdictions perceived that bigger jurisdictions got a better deal.

The NCHRC background check process was inefficient for several reasons. First, the process was manual and paper based. Second, police organizations did not regard background checks as true "police work" and therefore several jurisdictions used less qualified and lower paid civilian staff for this task. Third, preparing a request that returned a "no hit" was as labor intensive as preparing one that resulted in a "hit." Fourth, administrative delays (such as appeals processes) slowed the release of conviction details from the court, and the subsequent creation of an NNI entry. This occasionally allowed criminals released on parole to exploit the system by passing the background check before an NNI entry was created.

Mobbs wanted to simplify the NCHRC program. Instead of nine separate police organizations dealing with different privacy laws, CrimTrac would aim to do the same work more efficiently, more cheaply, and with faster results. In addition, CrimTrac would deal directly with all accredited agencies so that local uniformed police could be redeployed to more valuable tasks. Mobbs also wanted to ensure that CrimTrac could sustain itself after the A$50 million grant was depleted. Following the 9/11 terror attacks, he understood that the demand for background checks would greatly increase.

Many organizations began mandating an NCHRC check as part of an improved security regime for recruiting new employees.

CrimTrac hired a consultant to model a revised NCHRC service (Crim-Trac 2002), and then modified the service according to feedback from the client agencies and police stakeholders. CrimTrac decided to charge "per person" for an NCHRC check, as opposed to "per name" (a criminal frequently uses multiple names) in order to deliver cost savings to accredited agencies (ibid.). The new NCHRC program had to ensure that CrimTrac would recover all costs including R&D (CrimTrac 2004). Mobbs described his vision: "to offer a truly NATIONAL criminal history checking service via the IT improvements that we were also making." A "no hit" could be returned in minutes, rather than days, as previous, thus enabling an honest applicant to be employed sooner (Mobbs 2012a).

Yet, Mobbs had to convince the police organizations to share their data assets with CrimTrac so that the latter could accomplish the data integration to support this vision. In October 2003, Mobbs proposed a new incentives-driven NCHRC plan. He requested that the police organizations permit CrimTrac to create and manage a central fee-per-check service for accredited agencies. Mobbs appealed to the federal government to allow CrimTrac to retain these fee revenues. In return, CrimTrac could afford to exempt police organizations from paying subscription fees for all CrimTrac services (CrimTrac 2004).

The new formula converted suspicious policemen into incentivized partners and provided CrimTrac with self-sustaining funds. The police organizations acquired three benefits: they no longer needed to pay annual subscription fees, they could reduce overhead costs related to processing NCHRC requests, and they now enjoyed unlimited access to all CrimTrac services. These budget-savings were real and immediate. In Mobbs's words: "THAT gained their attention!" (Mobbs 2012a) (note that NCHRC fee revenues were previously channeled into the revenue coffers of the state governments, so the police commissioners were not concerned that these revenues would be channeled to CrimTrac). CrimTrac could now provide service that was more equitable, demanded less paperwork, was simpler and faster to process, and could provide superior customer support.

Figure 6.1 below visualizes the success of the new NCHRC formula. The red arrows mark the October 2003 date when it was adopted:

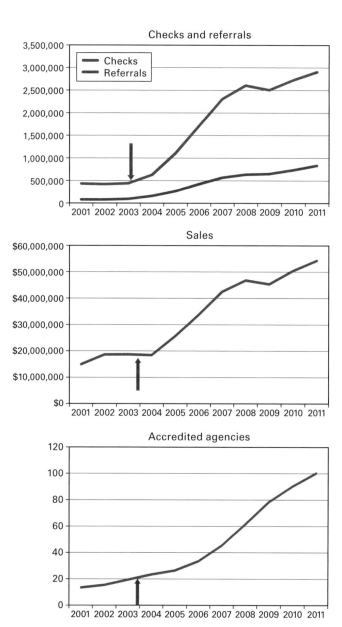

Figure 6.1

CrimTrac: The growth after 2003 of checks and referrals, sales, and accredited agencies.

Source: CrimTrac 2001–2011.

The NCHRC program has been expanding since October 2003. Police organizations have increased their use of CrimTrac's services. New legislation compelled more agencies to use NCHRC. NCHRC revenues allowed CrimTrac to upgrade and maintain existing systems, and to construct new ones. Since 2005, CrimTrac has drawn over 95 percent of its revenues from NCHRC. The agency generates A$50 million *annually* in NCHRC revenues—the same amount as the grant CrimTrac received in 2000 (CrimTrac 2011).

NCHRC History and Contested Commodity Exchange Lessons

NCHRC's history supports the lessons gleaned from the analysis of the thirty contested commodities in chapter 5. First, NCHRC illustrates the cresting moment lesson. NCHRC became the meeting ground between a scarce good (i.e., shared police information) and a new technology (i.e., a centralized database and web interface). However, these two factors alone did not ensure CrimTrac's success; CrimTrac created something out of nothing by ensuring that all stakeholders benefited from the new information-sharing game plan.

Second, NCHRC's history exemplifies the black markets and fraud lesson. Before October 2003, police organizations occasionally engaged in unofficial exchanges to provide background checks. In 2002, as part of audit activities, Mobbs discovered that one police organization failed to declare large volumes of NNI checks that it conducted (allegedly for internal purposes), thus avoiding paying fees. Mobbs informed the relevant commissioner that his senior IT officer responsible for NNI checks was not acting in good faith. The other commissioners reviewed the audit data and demanded a more equitable arrangement (Mobbs 2012a). In October 2003, such unofficial exchanges vanished overnight because police jurisdictions now received NNI checks at no cost. CrimTrac efficiently processed cross-jurisdictional background checks and police organizations could use the NCHRC service for free. Today, a small number of background checks (less than five hundred in three years) are referred to state, territory, and federal police forces, while CrimTrac processes the large-volume clients (in the order of millions of checks per annum).

NCHRC's history also supports the restricted commoditization lesson. CrimTrac applied, from day one, restricted commoditization arrangements related to privacy protection. In its first annual report, CrimTrac highlighted privacy concerns as a "critical area of risk" (CrimTrac 2001,

46–47). CrimTrac then instituted strong privacy protections including inviting external auditors, establishing advisory groups, consulting with privacy commissioners, publishing privacy policy and a code of conduct, and launching an educational website. In 2003, CrimTrac piloted a new Minimum Nationwide Person Profile (MNPP) electronic exchange containing only twenty-six policing data elements to help identify an offender (as opposed to the previous exchange that empowered police officers to view more data elements that were not relevant for identifying the offender) (CrimTrac 2003). In June 2009 the agency added a new CrimTrac Audit Log Integration Facility (CALIF) service that empowered jurisdictional auditors to access the activity logs of key systems (CrimTrac 2010).

Privacy protections governed each NCHRC check. A person subject to an NCHRC check was required to sign an informed consent application. The NCHRC background checking process adhered to complex federal, state, and territorial "spent conviction" legislation that defined which information could be reported, and for how long after a crime was committed. For example, if a person committed a felony in Tasmania ten years ago but Tasmania's spent conviction legislation prohibited reporting back five years after the felony was committed, CrimTrac would not report this criminal activity. Finally, CrimTrac provided information to accredited agencies based on a carefully defined set of categories that included "no exclusion," "partial exclusion," and "complete exclusion"; information ranged from disclosing only court outcomes to disclosing full criminal history. Ultimately it would be the accredited agencies themselves who decided whether or not to employ an applicant—based on the information disclosed by Crim-Trac. These restricted commoditization arrangements existed *before* October 2003. The Australian public understood that CrimTrac had done an outstanding job of protecting privacy; therefore, they trusted and accepted the new NCHRC background checks workflow. NCHRC's history demonstrates that public sector incentives-driven information sharing programs work best if they adopt restricted commoditization arrangements from the outset.

Information Types Not for Trade: DNA and Protecting Children

CrimTrac's history also illustrates why selective incentives are suitable for certain public data types but not others. Fingerprinting (NAFIS) and background checks (NCHRC) were domains where, historically, the public had been supportive of improving inter-jurisdictional data exchange. In contrast, personal privacy concerns characterized the public's attitude toward sharing DNA data and information about people who work with children. CrimTrac wisely steered away from using selective incentives in these domains.

In 2003, CrimTrac planned to deploy a national DNA-matching system. This National Criminal Investigation DNA Database (NCIDD) used web technology to view potential links among DNA records within and among police jurisdictions. Police forensic officers could search results instantly via a secure web browser linked to the central DNA database. The system demonstrated its utility after the Bali bombings (October 12, 2002) by helping families to identify victims. All that remained to deploy NCIDD nationally was to upload all state and territory DNA profiles into the database (CrimTrac 2003).

The intended launch of a national DNA system had already aroused public dismay in 2000 and 2001 (Waters 2006a). The public was alarmed when several state and territory governments adopted legislative initiatives for mandatory DNA testing of persons convicted and jailed for indictable offenses. Supporters of such legislation highlighted how DNA matching can help resolve unsolved crimes. However, television news in late 2001 aired disturbing images of the measures allegedly taken to acquire a DNA sample from prisoners in Victoria; prison dogs and handlers were present and police officers in riot gear seemed to be necessary to obtain the sample from an uncooperative prisoner. One politician declared: "this is worse than George Orwell forecast in his prophetic book, 1984" (Australia League of Rights 2001; Mobbs 2005, 6). Civil rights leaders warned that using DNA testing on prisoners sets a precedent for an attack on the civil rights of the entire population.

CrimTrac adopted unprecedented privacy protections to address these concerns. DNA could be collected only from a crime scene, from a suspect in connection with a crime, a serious offender, a missing person, or an unknown deceased person. NCIDD records were depersonalized, encrypted, transmitted across secure police communication links, decrypted, and stored in a highly secure defense facility. NCIDD records did not contain information about the human subject from which the DNA data was taken (other than gender). CrimTrac itself had no means of identifying individuals or crime scene details; if a database person profile was matched to crime scene DNA the identity of the person associated with the matched profile could only be obtained through direct contact between police organizations who held the original forensic evidence. Two authorized users in each jurisdiction were required to confirm a DNA profile. All activities on NCIDD were logged and audit trailed. NCIDD was the first DNA database that completely automated the destruction of profiles. Private corporations were barred from accessing the NCIDD system. Statistical studies of the racial or ethnic makeup of database records were not allowed. Two external advisory boards made up of scientists, lawyers, end users, and police officials governed NCIDD and two additional groups advised the Australia New Zealand Policing Advisory Agency (ANZPAA) on how to supervise NCIDD. CrimTrac's privacy protections were harsher than those of police jurisdictions. CrimTrac even barred Northern Territory (NT) police from using NCIDD for inter-jurisdictional matching because NT refused to accept the automatic destruction of DNA profiles, and wanted to allow nonauthorized personnel to access the system.

Yet, even these safeguards were insufficient to address privacy concerns in a timely manner. The process of changing state and territory legislation progressed at a snail's pace. In June 2003, there were no DNA profiles in the NCIDD database and CrimTrac stated that "it has taken much longer than anticipated" to make the legislative changes (CrimTrac 2003, 3). A year later, with 50,988 profiles, CrimTrac highlighted "legislative complexities" and admitted that inter-jurisdictional DNA matching is "yet to occur" (CrimTrac 2004, 21). Two years later, with 190,293 profiles loaded, CrimTrac reported that only three states had agreed to inter-jurisdictional DNA matching (CrimTrac 2006a). Finally, on June 28, 2007, all police stakeholders signed a DNA data exchange agreement. The NCIDD system then expanded to accommodate more than 408,000 DNA profiles. Still, selective incentives were never used in the NCIDD program, due to sensitivities over privacy.

The history of the Australian National Child Offender Register (ANCOR) system mirrors that of NCIDD. In the past, in Australia, information sharing failures have led to the abuse and even death of children at the hands of their adult custodians. It was difficult to track and manage convicted child offenders across jurisdictional boundaries if they failed to report regularly as ordered by court. Public investigation committees were appointed to examine cases of child maltreatment (Bamblett, Bath, and Roseby 2010).

CrimTrac inherited the limited NEPI system that provided information about people who work with children to six NSW accredited agencies. CrimTrac was instructed to expand this program into a national system (CrimTrac 2002).

An NCHRC background check provided insufficient information for this purpose, thus potentially leading to the rejection of suitable employees. For example, a minimal background check could reveal that, as a teenager, a man was convicted of engaging in underage sexual intercourse (with his girlfriend who was under sixteen years of age, the age of consent in certain jurisdictions). This information could have resulted in disqualifying this person from working with children for life. Therefore, the background check for people who seek to work with children needed to encompass supplementary information such as court proceedings.

By the end of 2003, CrimTrac was ready to roll out ANCOR nationally, contingent only on changes in state and territory privacy legislation. After years of delay, on November 26, 2009, the Australian Parliament and the eight states and territories signed an ANCOR MoU. This MoU made expanded criminal information available to certain information screening units. These screening units, in turn, were familiar with federal and jurisdictional employment policies and could therefore make an informed decision regarding an applicant's suitability to work with children.

A careful reading of the 2009 MoU reveals the *un*commoditized nature of the ANCOR program. Screening units exerted considerable effort to process an ANCOR check directly. Police jurisdictions directly invoiced, billed, paid, and disputed bills with each other. The processing fees only partially covered the cost of responding to an ANCOR request and fee revenues were channeled to the revenue coffers of each state or territory and not to the police organizations. The number of ANCOR data exchange transactions is miniscule in comparison to the volume of NCHRC transactions (11,543 ANCOR background checks as compared to 2,720,000 NCHRC background checks during the twelve months ending in June 2010).

NCIDD and ANCOR's histories provide support to the last lesson of chapter 5. Despite excellent technology and comprehensive privacy protections, CrimTrac could not commoditize NCIDD and ANCOR data-exchange transactions. Restricted commoditization arrangements cannot overcome heightened ethical concerns; certain public data types must remain outside the scope of the incentives-driven information sharing approach.

An Exchange PSIE Model (USA)

An exchange tradition dominates American politics, society, and the public sector. In *Federalist 51*, Madison recommended to build government on a "multiplicity of interests" and on the principle that "ambition must be made to counteract ambition" (Hamilton, Madison, and Jay [1787] 1961, 322). Tocqueville praised Americans who "put something heroic in their way of trading." He added, "the American is not just working by calculation but is rather obeying an impulse of his nature" (Tocqueville [1840] 1969, 403). Closer to our times, Schultze was puzzled by the ineffective tendency of Washington reformers to adopt command-and-control approaches rather than to rely on the modification of the private incentives that drive governmental work (Schultze 1977). Niskanen recommended changing government officer rewards and injecting competition to make "an adversary process work better" (Niskanen 1975). The National Performance Review campaign of the 1990s bolstered exchange thinking in governmental reform. So, what might an American Public Sector Information Exchange look like?

Constructing a PSIE Program to Exchange Environmental Information

The first PSIE program will address a public goods problem such as clean air, soil, or water that requires numerous agencies to exchange information. National security justifications for not sharing data are not common in a public goods domain such as protecting the environment. Initial funding could empower agencies to develop starter datasets that hold valuable information for other organizations to purchase. Trading would then evolve from horizontal exchange (among federal agencies), to vertical exchange (incorporating state and local agencies). Later on, this information exchange would be expanded to address neighboring environmental problems. The OMB can influence agencies to join in trading, similar to its actions from 1989 to the present day to nudge federal agencies to share credit loan data via the Credit Alert Verification Reporting System (CAIVRS) (U.S. Department of Housing and Urban Development 2013).

Bio-monitoring is one good incipient domain for an environmental PSIE program. Bio-monitoring measures chemicals in individuals' tissues or body fluids in order to provide insight into the population's exposure to chemicals. The 1976 Toxic Substances Control Act (TSCA) empowered the EPA to develop chemical toxin risk assessments; yet this domain is too complex for a single agency to tackle alone (it takes the EPA ten years to complete a new toxin study). The CDC collects data on known chemicals, but has collected data on only 250 chemicals included in the list of its 83,000 known chemicals (with 700 new chemicals added to the list every year). It is difficult for the EPA to complete a risk assessment because bio-monitoring data does not indicate the source, route, or timing of a person's exposure to a given chemical. The GAO includes bio-monitoring in its high-risk series (GAO 2009i, 2009d).

The bio-monitoring domain is suited to introduce a PSIE for several reasons. The law (TSCA, sections 5a, 8a, 8d–e) discourages secrecy in this domain. At the same time, the public cares deeply about exposure to chemicals. Public opinion is affected by chilling media reports on how bio-monitoring data-collection efforts neglect young children. Numerous agencies are active in this domain including: EPA departments (the Office of Pollution Prevention and Toxics (OPPT), the Office of Pesticide Programs (OPP), and the Office of Research and Development (ORD)), federal agencies (USDA, CDC, the National Institutes of Health (NIH), FDA, the Occupational Safety and Health Administration (OSHA), the USFWS, the National Science and Technology Council (NSTC), states (Alaska and California), and a nonprofit organization (the National Academy of Sciences) (GAO 2009d).

The EPA's Integrated Risk Information System (IRIS) is a good starter database to cultivate this data exchange. Figure 6.2 illustrates the proposed exchange.

In the proposed exchange, agencies will accumulate credits by allowing other agencies to access their data. A micropayment engine will aggregate the results of information sharing transactions. Agencies that perform well will then exchange credits for dollars that could be invested in new information products. These dollars will be a small fraction of the $80 billion invested in federal IT annually. Less successful agencies will not suffer penalties, to encourage them to continue trading. Offices within the same agency will also be enabled to exchange information assets with each other through PSIE. The Treasury's Intra-governmental Payment and Collection (IPAC) system that has facilitated the intra-governmental transfer of funds for over a decade now will support this credits system.

To trade, agencies will inscribe their trading algorithms into intelligent software agents that possess the ability to adapt to the behavior of other

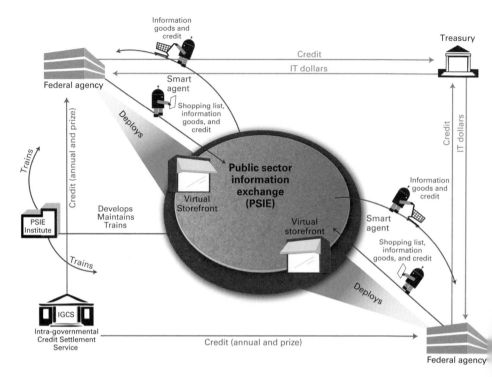

Figure 6.2
How PSIE works.

agents. These agents will know how to find other agents, negotiate a price, sign a contract, and deliver home the purchased information goods. Agents will also know how to simulate trade patterns and how to generate and work with subordinate agents. These agents will thus become sophisticated bargain-hunting electronic nomads that visit the virtual storefronts of other agencies, extract and compare prices for the information goods they seek to purchase, and execute trades (Gazis 1998; Premkumar 2003).

This solution mimics the role of medieval agents. Back then agents were the hands and voices of rich traders and roamed the globe hunting for bargains (Braudel 1992). MIT Media Lab experiments discovered that software-agent-based trading is limited only by the extent to which a trader trusts the software program that serves as the agent during computer simulations (Chavez et al. 1997). Information about medieval agents (humans) and modern agents (software programs) support the same lesson: it takes time to build trust among traders in any type of exchange (human-mediated or software-program-mediated) (ibid.). Therefore, PSIE's early comers are likely to do better in trading than agencies that join later on, as the former will have more time to build up trust.

Algorithms to support automated exchanges exist and are used in niche exchanges such as Google's advertisement bidding business (Clarke 1971; Conitzer and Sandholm 2004; Cramton, Shoham, and Steinberg 2006; Groves 1973; Papadimitriou 2001; Vickrey 1961). A new generation of computer scientists is working to improve these algorithms (Bartal, Gonen, and Nisan 2003; Gonen, Gonen, and Pavlov 2007; Gonen and Lehmann 2000; Gonen and Pavlov 2007; Gonen and Vassilvitskii 2008).

An independent PSIE Institute will develop and host the exchange, train agencies to build virtual storefronts, and guide them in developing pricing algorithms. Broker-hosted exchanges are popular because traders consider a broker, such as the PSIE Institute, to be an honest and fair governor of the exchange. Congress will provide a modest initial grant to the Institute, similar to CrimTrac's initial grant from the Australian government; thereafter, the PSIE Institute will sustain itself by collecting a tiny percentage of the monetary value of information sharing transactions. Analysts from different agencies will help the PSIE Institute to develop the program and ensure that it does not become the exclusive playground of a small number of agencies (Fountain 2007; Geer 1998; Premkumar 2003). Citizens will learn later on about the back-office data-integration revolution that PSIE helped unleash. E-government user interfaces may not alter dramatically after PSIE becomes operational but citizens will benefit from faster responses, improved data quality, and new e-government information services that were not available before the PSIE era.

New information services built on top of an environmental PSIE could empower citizens to mesh together skills, experience, and expertise to create new businesses in this domain. For example, such a service could bring together a Pashto student (one of the two main Afghani languages), an Afghanistan veteran, and a researcher who studies cheap and innovative ways to detect toxins in arid ground. These three individuals could create a startup to provide cheap and innovative toxin detection solutions to Third World countries beginning in Afghanistan. Discovering and developing this opportunity would require the integration of information that is currently buried in the silo databases of more than a dozen agencies. This startup would also address no fewer than five of President Obama's seven mission-oriented priority goals launched in the 2013 budget ("Exports," "Entrepreneurship and Small Business," "Science, Technology, Engineering, and Mathematics Education," "Job Training," and "Veteran Career Training").

The environmental PSIE will grow via trial-and-error experiments. It will be self-regulated via an eBay-style reputation-based system to ensure that cheating does not pay off. Plans to trade in genetic data and nano-materials are based on similar reputational systems (Bowman and Hodge 2008; Parry 2004). A traders' forum will encourage agencies to share best practices. A similar best-practices forum (the International Carbon Action Partnership) was successfully established for countries with cap-and-trade systems to share knowledge. PSIE's audit log will help identify who inside government exchanges environmental data, and when and why they do so (Ellerman and Joskow 2008). New search engines will evolve to support interagency data trading based on the miscellaneous order concept: any topic that is of interest to anyone is available (Mayer-Schönberger and Lazer 2007a; Weinberger 2007).

Over time agencies will learn how to develop new data types for trading such as tertiary information products. These products are based on futures trading and seek to exhaust an inexhaustible series of variables that affect data quality and pricing. For example, within PSIE an agency may find funding to build a new information system by selling another agency the rights to harvest its future clickstreams, with certain ethical limitations regarding the use of such data. A similar option-based system exists in Europe as part of the carbon emissions cap-and-trade system. In the United States, plans are in place for the creation of a futures exchange for cadaveric organs and nitrogen fertilizer pollutions (Appadurai 1986; ECX 2010; Hey, Urban, and Kostel 2005). Scholars have argued that futures exchanges are more effective than punitive measures to address problems such as reducing the use of materials that deplete the ozone layer (the Montreal Protocol) or saving endangered species (e.g., the International Whaling Convention) (Jenkins 1993).

Agencies could even set up their own mini exchanges that tackle complex problems and then develop and sell new information products based on insights gleaned in such exchanges. For example, the FDA can only send an inspection team to the site of a foreign manufacturer, whose drugs are approved for U.S. use, once every thirteen years. There are tens of thousands of such foreign corporations worldwide with complex ties among them that impact the production and quality of a specific drug. This fact severely limits the FDA's capacity to comprehend the global drug market as well as the composition, promise, and potential hazards of a specific drug. Prediction markets that yield payments based on the outcome of uncertain events effectively tackle such problems because they collect knowledge widely dispersed among numerous economic actors to assess the outcome of uncertain events. So, the FDA could establish a predictions exchange on foreign drug manufacturing, to better understand future global trends and to acquire information about the production and qualities of a specific drug. Insights gleaned from prediction exchanges will then be packaged and sold to other agencies in PSIE. Ethical limits will curb trading in such information products. For example, agencies will not be allowed to profit from betting that another agency will fail to build a new IT system (GAO 2009i).

A PSIE program could become a new win-win informational ecosystem for multiple stakeholders. Citizens will benefit from improved public data integration. Politicians will gain votes from delivering better e-government services. A veteran government official proposed that PSIE would appeal to agencies because "no one agency would be seen as the winner" (Moscoe 2011). If PSIE is designed and managed correctly, both monopolistic information-rich agencies and information-poorer agencies (see chapter 4) will discover how it increases the effectiveness and attractiveness of their information assets.

Federal IT vendors too will discover new opportunities to provide emerging technologies and services to empower the new exchange to replace their lost revenues (from older information sharing solutions that PSIE renders obsolete). Agency general counsels are likely to see their workload drop because they will no longer need to develop numerous, separate bilateral information sharing MoUs (see chapter 4). These counsels and their aides are overburdened by information sharing MoU tasks; they may welcome PSIE because it will free them to do higher-value work for their agencies.

Expanding the Environmental PSIE Program

Once bio-monitoring data exchange is established, trading can expand to address a neighboring problem such as the Formerly Used Defense Sites (FUDS) cleanup job. Here too, the law (Comprehensive Environmental Response, Compensation, and Liability Act [CERCLA] 1980) deters secrecy, and there are many agencies involved in the cleanup project. The cleanup challenge is too complex for a single organization to address alone (the U.S. Army Corps of Engineers is responsible for identifying and cleaning up to 31,600 sites). In addition, the public cares about this issue ($18.4 billion have already been spent on FUDS cleanup, and the effort has barely begun). Expanding PSIE to FUDS cleanup data trade makes good sense as it involves several agencies, with the DOD holding permanent responsibility for cleaning emergent contaminants published by the EPA in IRIS (GAO 2009f, 2009h).

As trading agencies learn more about each other's information assets, the PSIE can be further expanded to trade in bio-surveillance data. In August 2007, the DHS established the National Bio-surveillance Integration Center (NBIC) to tackle biological and chemicals threats. Other agencies are active in this effort, including the USDA, DOC, DOD, HHS, DOI, DOJ, DOS, DOT, VA, EPA, the USPS, and state and local agencies. These agencies suspect the inexperienced NBIC. They fear that sharing bio-surveillance data with NBIC might lead to confusion. Here too, data trading will help overcome suspicion (GAO 2009b). Enterprise architects will be chartered to preserve the integrity of the underlying agency systems that participate in PSIE; these architects will help convince agencies to use PSIE to exchange data.

PSIE's success can be measured through its ability to support data exchanges across established information domains. An information domain is a sphere where a certain institution's control over information is unquestionably accepted. Strong forces protect the autonomy of an information domain including constitutional and civil rights, professional paradigms, and the structure of the public expenditure. Information resources are compartmentalized within a given information domain. The PSIE will be successful as soon as trading agencies exchange data across these domains (Bellamy and Taylor 1996).

Comparing PSIE to Other Public Sector Information Sharing Programs

PSIE's promise to improve information sharing is best illustrated in comparison to four other existing information sharing programs as shown in table 6.1. This comparison highlights each program's strengths and weaknesses and the unique PSIE approach.

Enthusiastic social networkers within the intelligence community fueled Intellipedia's initial success. One of the U.S. federal information sharing

Table 6.1
PSIE compared to existing U.S. federal information sharing platforms

Program	Description	Years	Key strength	Key weakness
Intellipedia	The intelligence community's data-sharing application based on the Wikipedia format	2006–present	Easy and fast to launch	Initial excitement dissipated quickly
Diplopedia	Department of State (DOS) information sharing application based on the Wikipedia format	2006–present	Good dissemination of information within DOS	DOS-centric tool (internal)
Environmental Information Exchange Network (EIEN)	Environment Protection Agency (EPA) network that links EPA, state, tribal, and territorial environmental protection agencies, and industry	2004–present	Good tool to collect data from industry and the states	EPA-centric tool (external)
National Information Exchange Model (NIEM)	Joint Department of Justice (DOJ) and Information Sharing Environment (ISE) program to establish standards for interagency data exchange	2005–present	Aspires to replace bilateral interagency data-use arrangements	A "technology first" solution
Public Sector Information Exchange (PSIE)	A proposed data-trading arena to incentivize federal agencies to improve information-exchanges	New program	New federal information sharing ecosystem utilizing a "politics first" approach	Slow to get off the ground

platforms, Intellipedia was cheap, intuitive, and quick to launch; however the early excitement dissipated quickly. Managers opposed the program and employees had to enter the same data twice—once into their operational systems and then into Intellipedia (CIA 2009; Dixon and McNamara 2008; Dizard 2006; Jackson 2009; Zyskowski 2009).

Another such platform is Diplopedia, whose founders tried to address this shortcoming by allowing only DOS employees to publish data in Diplopedia while non-DOS end users could only read it. By so doing, Diplopedia became less helpful to officials outside the DOS (Bronk and Smith 2010; Cohen 2008; Hickey 2010; Johnson 2007). The EPA launched the Emissions Inventory Exchange Network (EIEN) to enable sharing of data that the EPA is required to collect from the chemical industry, but industry reports are sent to state-level agencies. However, EIEN became an information sharing system dominated by the data-gathering needs of a single agency (Garvey and O'Neill 2003; Greene et al. n.d.; Jackson 2008; Miller 2004). The National Information Exchange Model (NIEM) program attempts to eliminate bilateral data-use agreements. NIEM has adopted a "technology first" approach that does not address the political challenges that curtail information sharing (Jackson 2005; Moore 2011; NIEM Program Management Office 2007). In contrast to these four programs, the PSIE program will take off more slowly because it will require legal support. However, only PSIE employs a unique "politics first" approach by accounting for existing bureaucratic politics in its design.

PSIE's Economic Foundations

Information Asymmetry Challenges
In most countries, a handful of information-rich agencies dominate the public sector's information flows. The asymmetry between these few agencies and the many information-poor ones expresses itself in multiple ways. The information-rich adopt technologies more efficiently than the information-poor, exacerbating the gap between them. Information-rich agencies command more valuable information assets than other agencies; therefore, the latter are in a weaker negotiating position with the former. The relationship between the British Prison Service and the British Criminal Justice System (CJS) exemplifies such an uneven relationship. The Prison Service is a net recipient of data received from CJS. The Prison Service has little valuable data for other CJS-subscriber agencies and therefore receives fewer

CJS benefits than other agencies. Information-rich agencies dictate harsh data-access terms to other agencies as evidenced by the history of the CBSV system (see chapter 4). Finally, information-rich agencies design exchanges that institutionalize their information power (Bellamy and Taylor 1996; Clarkson, Jacobsen, and Batcheller 2007; Hart and Saunders 1997; Horowitz 1998; Kamal 2006; Kugler, Neeman, and Vulkan 2006; Prins 2004).

Critics may therefore ask: why create an exchange that is likely to empower the already powerful? Information-rich agencies could abuse PSIE in several ways. PSIE might teach agencies a bad lesson—that everything is a fair game if one can make a profit. This would be especially destructive in the public sector that is required to display higher norms of equity and fairness than the private sector.

Stronger agencies could lobby their congressional appropriation sub-committees to mandate that other agencies provide them with data for free. Information-rich agencies could also wait on the sidelines until information accumulates inside PSIE, then join the exchange, acquire what they need, and defect. They could price their information too high to dissuade others from purchasing it (although the exchange will not tolerate this practice for long, if it is properly constructed). Or, they could overwhelm other agencies by flooding PSIE with meaningless data. Such abusive behavior would demoralize the information-poor and eventually they too would abandon PSIE. Then, the information-richer (due to data they acquired in the short-lived PSIE program) would reestablish a more exploitative information-sharing oligopoly regime than before (Branscomb 1994; Dirks and Ferrin 2001; Flanagin, Monge, and Fulk 2001; Fountain 2007; Fulk et al. 2004; Hart and Saunders 1997; Jackelen 2000; Monge et al. 1998; Parry 2004).

At the end of the nineteenth century, a small group of barons dominated the U.S. railroads, steel manufacturing, and telegraph networks. Antitrust laws were then adopted to ensure that such a monopoly in the private sector would not repeat itself (Mayer-Schonberger and Cukier 2013, 183). In our information age, critics could warn that PSIE is likely to empower a handful of agencies to grow and become the new data barons of the modern economy.

Overcoming Information Asymmetry

In practice, free riding, cheating, and defections are not likely to occur. Abusers will discover that short-term gains are costly because PSIE's trader-reputation system will enable agencies to identify dishonest traders and to

refrain from trading with them. Early traders in PSIE will acquire formative rewards including a better learning curve, thicker connectivity to other
trader-agencies, centrality within the new trading network, and reputation
as experts who can be consulted on technical matters.

A study of the genesis and evolution of a network of forty-eight
law enforcement agencies to combat illegal drug activity revealed that
information-poor agencies benefited more from this network than larger,
information-rich agencies. The smaller information-poor agencies commanded niche expertise, joined the network early on, were more eager and
motivated to learn than bigger organizations, and, jointly, benefited from
their power to organize and from acquiring technical sophistication. Later
on, the CEOs of these smaller founding organizations were widely perceived as the most knowledgeable network members. In contrast, the larger,
inertia-driven information-rich organizations joined the network later, did
not invest significantly in it during its first years, and did not acquire the
same status and benefits as the smaller founding member organizations.
This study also discovered that information resources were concentrated
in the large organizations, but these resources did not generate the greatest
interest among network members (Flanagin, Monge, and Fulk 2001; Vangen
and Huxham 2003). In the same vein, PSIE may actually provide smaller,
information-poorer agencies an advantage over larger, information-richer
agencies because the former would be more motivated to engage in PSIE
transactions early on. Later on, these smaller agencies might discover that
their PSIE expertise is an in-demand organizational resource.

PSIE could be successfully launched without the support of the
information-rich agencies. Only a handful of collaborative relationships is
required for an exchange to take root. Empowered by PSIE-purchased information, smaller agencies will provide better services to citizens, thus setting
an example that the information-richer agencies will emulate later on. Information paternalism will not survive in a PSIE exchange (Bandt 1998; Clarkson, Jacobsen, and Batcheller 2007; Markus and Connolly 1990; Monge
et al. 1998).

Good exchange design decisions are critical to PSIE's success. These decisions include what the unit of trade will be, how to price data, and which
trading techniques to allow. A cross-agency enterprise architecture (EA)
team can create a fair trading game. Key data elements such as the identifier
of each citizen will become nontradable infrastructure components that

support trading. Some data could undergo a "cooling off" period before it becomes tradable in order to eliminate manipulative trading; such a cooling off period was proposed to support transplant organ exchanges (Becker and Elias 2007). Like national health insurance frameworks, trading agencies will sign pacts barring discrimination (Gerards and Janssen 2006).

The PSIE Institute will level the playing field by reducing the cost for joining PSIE for information-poor agencies (Monge et al. 1998). It will invest a small part of PSIE's revenues to prepare weaker agencies for trade (Fountain 2007; Premkumar 2003; Raul 2002). Buyers will develop an understanding of how to piece together data from separate sellers into a valuable mosaic. Each seller will provide one piece of the puzzle that the buyer seeks to complete. Buyers will therefore have the edge in negotiating prices (Braudel 1992). Several information-poor agencies could mesh their data together to bring valuable information products to PSIE. Like medieval peddlers who banded together to sell products to the wealthy, information-poor agencies will discover that, jointly, they can develop data products that the information-rich want to buy.

New agency entrepreneurs will emerge to help their agencies develop data trading strategies. Such entrepreneurs emerged in the emissions exchange domain, after trading commenced. These entrepreneurs will coach their agencies to strike pay-per-view, rental, and licensing deals. They will facilitate the creation of "trading hubs" within PSIE (EU ETS 2010; Premkumar 2003). These entrepreneurs will learn more quickly if permitted to fail and pay the cost of failure. The history of the early stock markets teaches that traders who pay the cost for initial unsuccessful decisions trade better later on (Brown 1995).

PSIE's Legal Foundations

Lobbies and Slow Legislation Challenges

The cadavers case study of chapter 5 revealed the importance of supporting PSIE early on with appropriate legislation. The law sets the boundaries of legitimate agency action. Agencies require strong legal definitions that specify under what circumstances information collected by one agency can be shared with another agency. Therefore, PSIE's success depends on the adoption of a law that explicitly authorizes agencies to buy and sell information assets (Braman 2006; Dawes and Prefontaine 2003; Landsbergen and Wolken 1998; Rainey, Backoff, and Levine 1976). European scholars emphasize that strong information sharing legislation must precede the construction of information sharing technical solutions (Hijmans 2006).

Designing a PSIE Act is hard work. In a two-party system such as the U.S. system, the legislative and executive branches compete to control the bureaucracy, often resulting in lengthy, overly complex information sharing regulations. For example, the EPA possesses two thick volumes of regulations regarding clean air. Federal, state, and local laws clash on topics such as public access, privacy, system integration, and security. One-year budget cycles and technological changes further challenge information sharing laws.

Powerful lobbies aggravate the problem of mobilizing sufficient political support for a historic PSIE Act. After 9/11, prompted by lobbying from the chemical industry, several agencies removed data about hazardous waste sites from their web pages. Some of these actions made good sense. However, commentators pointed out that the chemical industry had tried to keep such information private for years and that the events of 9/11 merely provided them with the pretext to pressure agencies to remove access to information. In a similar way, powerful constituencies that benefit from the current inefficient information-sharing regime in the public sector can foil efforts to pass the PSIE Act (Dawes 1996; Gil-Garcia and Pardo 2005; Rocheleau 2003; Zhang, Dawes, and Sarkis 2005).

If PSIE legislation is slow to emerge, the consequences could be destructive, as demonstrated by the sluggish legislation of transplant organs trading that has cost lives. At the other extreme, hasty legislation can also damage trading. The General Agreement on Tariff Trade's Related Intellectual Property Rights (1994) sought to monitor compensation for the use of genetic materials in creating new drugs. However, the hasty legislative campaign ignored the fact that it is impossible to trace the myriad steps in the development of new drugs, from genome to cure (i.e., who gave what, when, why, and how). Hence, this legislation created a bloated bureaucracy that deepened miscommunication among genetic data traders.

Another challenge concerns PSIE's legal guardians. It is up to them to determine how much freedom to grant to traders and how to handle abuse. An elite network of executives, lawyers, and ethno-botanists hold a monopoly over rulemaking in the genetics data domain. Could PSIE become the exclusive playground of a similar elite group?

Linking PSIE to Existing Legislation

An answer to these challenges must begin with an important observation: in most countries, interagency data trade practices are legal and even applauded. European agencies, as the most important holders of noncopyright factual databases, benefit from an EU legislative act that provides them with the absolute right of protection of these databases (Prins 2004). U.S. jurists can find support for data trading in sixteen congressional acts, presidential directives, and OMB memorandums that encourage agencies to exchange electronic data. The OMB and the Federal CIO Council encourage agencies to document information as assets and to increase the exchange of such assets (Economist 2008).

The U.S. E-Government Act of 2002 (H.R. 2458/S. 803) highlighted the need to create a market-based government. Another U.S. presidential task force recommended a "market-based approach" to e-government (Vann 2005, 150). The OMB's directive A-130 grants agencies a broad mandate for imposing fees on the provision of data to other agencies. Even mundane legislation supports PSIE. The Drivers Privacy Protection Act (1994) sets limits on selling personal information, but exempts agencies from these limits for carrying out their functions (Raul 2002). PSIE is also compatible with exchange-based ideas on how to solve environmental problems (Schoenbrod, Stewart, and Wyman 2010). Most recently, the OMB and the GPRAMA (Government Performance and Results Act Modernization Act) urged agencies to use incentives to improve collaboration and information sharing (Fountain 2013, 106).

Therefore the PSIE Act can draw on an existing legal repository that encourages agencies to share information based on the principles of competition, exchange, and incentives. The Act can raise the priority of the information sharing topic, grant PSIE public legitimacy, secure the confidentiality of shared data, alleviate concerns regarding privacy, and help agencies to develop mutual trust (Dawes 1996; Gil-Garcia, Chengalur-Smith, and Duchessi 2007; Gil-Garcia and Pardo 2005; Lam 2005; Landsbergen and Wolken 2001; Otjacques, Hitzelberger, and Feltz 2007a; Perri 6 et al. 2007; Zhang and Dawes 2006).

The PSIE Act must delineate which agencies own what data products and which data types are nontradable (Constant, Kiesler, and Sproull 1994). The Act can provide a timeline to implement PSIE in phases. Current legislation requires agencies to have a compelling reason to request information from another agency (Wenjing 2011). The PSIE Act must support interagency information browsing without a compelling reason. The real cost of not letting agencies browse information held by other agencies are the expensive and life-threatening information sharing failures discussed in chapter 1. The Act will provide a mechanism for citizens to opt out of certain data exchanges, and will prohibit unjustifiable uses of purchased information goods. The Act must guarantee the exchange's long time frame.

Initially, a voluntary code (VC) agreement among trading agencies can support PSIE. VCs are flexible and well suited to the dynamic data trading domain. A VC regime relies on peer pressure rather than punitive litigation. It takes less time to create a VC regime than to enact a new parliamentary act. However, in the long run, only a formal PSIE Act can ensure the success of interagency data trading. Legislatures can overcome objections to the PSIE Act if they promote it immediately after an information sharing disaster such as Hurricane Katrina. Also, because PSIE promises to save billions of dollars by eliminating unnecessary bilateral information-sharing projects, legislatures will do well to promote the Act during a time of economic crisis (Bowman and Hodge 2008; OCA 2007; Fountain 2007).

The Initial Funding: PSIE and the GPRAMA

The U.S. Congress can fund an initial PSIE pilot through the GPRAMA. The original GPRA (1993) was agency-centric requiring individual agencies to set goals, measures, and progress reports. In stark contrast, the latest GPRAMA (2010) emphasizes government-wide priority goals and cross-agency coordination to accomplish these goals. GPRAMA-related work commenced in February 2014. Research on the GPRAMA is still scant but one pioneering GPRAMA study revealed that Congress did not pay enough attention to the tools required to support GPRAMA (Fountain 2013).

A complementary GPRAMA-PSIE Act would provide agencies with the means to discover other agency's datasets and mesh agencies' informational resources into virtual repositories to address the complex and extensive inter-agency problems discussed in chapter 1. A GPRAMA-PSIE Act could stipulate the initial grant to kickstart PSIE and help agencies build new cross-agency dashboards and scoreboards in domains such as cybersecurity, sustainability, real property, improper payments, data center consolidation, closing skill gaps, strategic sourcing, and OD.

These seven domains were each separately identified as critical priority domains in President Obama's 2013 budget. Currently, agencies are unmotivated to integrate their data to generate the type of dashboards and scoreboards that are required to support the GPRAMA goals. This Act contains no specific suggestions to prompt agencies to share data. PSIE credits could provide the humble, initial prompting to motivate agencies to genuinely support the vision and goals of GPRAMA.

PSIE's Technical Foundations

PSIE is a government-to-government (G2G) program that falls under the broader category of e-government programs. G2G refers to a category of internal public sector information and communication systems. G2G empowers agencies to communicate effectively with each other and provides the engine for e-government (Dawes and Cook 2006; Reddick 2005). Scholars propose that e-government today is stalling partially because the back-office G2G engines cannot integrate information from different agencies (Accenture 2001, 2004; Kim and Kim 2003; Reddick 2005). The U.S. eGov initiatives of 2001–2003 tackled this problem and the programs met most of their funded objectives. However, these initiatives lost momentum later on as goals and priorities changed. Federal IT chiefs are likely to raise several technical concerns about PSIE as a G2G and e-government program.

Cost, Design, Expertise, Visibility, and Security Challenges

IT chiefs could be concerned about PSIE's disruptive data extraction operations that might consume critical technical manpower, lead to increased data access requests, and drain resources. IT chiefs already consider information sharing to be a resource drain. They are concerned about having to pay to maintain their data in redundant formats so that it can be shared with other agencies. They are likely to reject the claim that selective incentives would compensate them for their investment in PSIE that would include maintaining data in various different formats (Bajaj and Ram 2003; Dawes 1996; Hart and Saunders 1997; Landsbergen and Wolken 1998).

PSIE requires knowledge about the design of a multi-dimensional combinatorial electronic exchange. This automated exchange will support bidding on the three types of information goods defined in chapter 4 (primary data, secondary information, and information services) and two types of information delivery mechanisms ("browse data" and "download data"). To support trading with credits, PSIE's algorithms will support traders with budgets. The algorithms will need to motivate trading agencies to report the true quality and freshness of their information goods. A cross-agency EA team can provide good solutions to these challenges. Solutions to most of these challenges already exist so team members will mostly evaluate, test, and adopt the ones most fitting to support the PSIE model chosen for implementation (i.e., supply chain or exchange).

IT chiefs may warn that IT expertise to design PSIE does not exist in the public sector. One survey discovered that federal software developers refuse to fix problems unless instructed to do so by regulations. This same survey exposed the fact that federal software developers are rewarded with bonuses for fixing bugs that they themselves created (this type of behavior also exists in the private sector) (Greenberg 2012a). Complaints regarding public sector IT capacity appear frequently in e-government literature; it seems public IT chiefs believe that they can only play catch up with the private sector but cannnot lead the pack (although public sector IT chiefs are neither chartered to lead the pack nor staffed to do so). R&D is best pursued by the private sector. IT chiefs could suggest that within such a software development environment the prospects of designing PSIE well are slim (Gil-Garcia and Pardo 2005; Lam 2005; Landsbergen and Wolken 1998; Mahler and Regan 2003; Zhang, Dawes, and Sarkis 2005).

IT chiefs may dislike the fact that PSIE empowers outsiders to look into their databases, and possibly discover poorly managed data. PSIE would also facilitate the entry of new players into the information sharing arena, to the possible chagrin of the current data monopolist agencies (Macher, Mowery, and Simcoe 2002). The failure of the European Telecommunications Standards Institute to establish a standard for mobile commerce demonstrates how old players can foil a new technical standardization program (Lembke 2002).

Finally, IT chiefs might be concerned that hackers may exploit data security vulnerabilities in the PSIE network. Hackers have managed to steal sensitive data from organizations such as the International Monetary Fund (IMF), the Pentagon, Lockheed Martin, the Los Alamos National Laboratory, and the UN (Eaton 2011; Perlrot 2011; Poulsen 2011; Riley and Rastello 2011). Surveys reveal that since 9/11 the American public is increasingly concerned about the hacker threat (Kim and Kim 2003).

Designing a Successful PSIE Program

To address these challenges, PSIE architects must convince IT chiefs that PSIE will reduce IT cost in two ways. First, PSIE will render obsolete existing bilateral information-sharing projects, thus releasing technologists to work on more critical projects. PSIE will also empower government officials to execute data-exchange tasks that were previously only executed by software developers, similarly making technologists available to work on other projects. Second, PSIE architects will demonstrate how PSIE can be erected by using existing software. For example, opportunities exist to reuse the software that banks use to reconcile numerous interbank transactions in near-real time. PSIE could even help IT chiefs to convert their departments from cost centers into revenue generators. With PSIE, IT chiefs will claim credit for converting arcane databases into assets and new revenue streams.

PSIE architects must also emphasize that the proposed exchange will rely on an intermediary network-centric service that will translate requests from buyers and submit them to each agency in its native language (Bonometti, Smith, and White 1998). Rather than fight a hopeless rearguard battle to impose a standard on reluctant agencies, initially PSIE will not require agencies to alter their internal computing infrastructure immediately. This message will help convince IT chiefs that the required initial PSIE investment will not be demanding. However, over the long run and as PSIE becomes more established and successful, IT chiefs will need to invest more in changing some features of their legacy systems (ibid.; Sarkar, Butler, and Steinfield 1995).

A core PSIE requirement is that system analysts from different agencies will jointly design PSIE and serve as the EA team for this project. Prototype software can be built early on to ensure that PSIE does not become the exclusive domain of one vendor. PSIE architects should pay special attention to usability. Thousands of small agencies will use PSIE. These agencies will participate in PSIE if—and only if—they can interact with the system easily. Ease of use also includes the topics of data discovery and the removal of legal and technical hurdles before trading commences (Akbulut 2003; Kim and Lee 2006; Newcomer and Sharon 1991). The cross-agency EA team that oversees the process of designing and building PSIE will also provide sound measures to protect the integrity of the data from attacks from external hackers. The process of converting the PSIE architectural plans into working software will be delegated to the private sector to encourage technological innovation. IT chiefs already know that solutions exist for seemingly insurmountable information sharing problems. With the proper incentives, they will develop these solutions and put them to work.

Finally, PSIE architects can remind IT chiefs that the public sector has played a leading role in important technological revolutions. Faced with insurmountable problems, U.S. federal agencies have twice reinvented computer technology. In 1890, the Census launched a competition to automate the processing of census surveys that led to the invention of the computer (Austrian 1982). In the late 1960s, a Defense Advanced Research Projects Agency (DARPA) project led to the invention of the Internet with a project designed to ensure the survivability of communication systems after a nuclear strike led to the invention of the Internet (Belfiore 2009). Today, as the public sector must tackle poor information sharing mechanisms that cost lives and billions of dollars, PSIE could become the third most significant public sector computer innovation in history. To do so, IT chiefs will need to confront one more important concern: develop a solution to empower one agency to understand the data definitions of another.

Developing Common Data Definitions: The deNovis Case Study

PSIE requires a data-exchange standard known as semantic interoperability; it mandates that an agency's computer system *understands* information received from another computer system. Agencies maintain the lower-level syntactic interoperability that exchanges data in a compatible format. A GAO report demonstrated how agencies use fifty-six different Sensitive But Unclassified (SBU) designations. There are no guidelines for using these designations, leaving government officials to tag documents with their choice of SBU term. Sometimes, an agency employs multiple SBU terms to express the same meaning. At other times, different agencies employ the same SBU term to express different meanings. If such confusion surrounds the use of a single word, what are the prospects that an agency will understand the complete language of another agency? (GAO 2006a). Citizens suffer when agencies lack semantic interoperability. For example, the environment becomes polluted when agencies do not share a common concept of "hazardous waste." Different statutory definitions further aggravate this problem. Homeless children in America do not always receive life-saving services because HUD and the HHS use different definitions of the term "homelessness" (Lam 2005; Landsbergen and Wolken 1998; Pardo and Tayi 2007; GAO 2006a; GAO 2011l; Zhang, Dawes, and Sarkis 2005).

Yet, solutions to address this challenge exist (Bajaj and Ram 2003; Pardo and Tayi 2007). Computational linguistics teams have made great strides in dividing and conquering language in various domains. Consider, for example, how European citizens execute library searches in their native language but retrieve data in any available language (Levergood, Farrenkopf, and Frasnelli 2008). Likewise, people today can communicate meaningfully with computers to set up travel plans or study for a test (Jurafsky and Martin 2008). Automating specific domains of human language is a thriving IT subject.

The U.S. government supports efforts to construct ontologies to bridge the semantic differences among agencies. The history of deNovis, a start-up company created to address the rising administrative cost of health care provision in the United States, provides encouragement that such an approach can succeed. Federal healthcare programs (including Medicare and Medicaid) cover 115 million U.S. citizens, making the federal government the world's largest financer of health care (GAO 2003a, 2005a, 2009e; Connolly 2003; Leonhardt 2009). One problem specific to healthcare is the adjudication of insurance claims. About 60 percent of insurance claims are manually adjudicated. In 2003 alone, the federal government spent an estimated $250 billion on this adjudication. The HHS relies on private sector initiatives to solve this problem (GAO 2003a, 2006b, 2009e).

In December 2000, deNovis (originally called "eHealthDirect") was established to tackle this issue. deNovis created a new English-like language (dubbed Health Insurance Contract Language or HICL). Health insurance claims that ran through the deNovis system were matched to the HICL versions of payer and provider contracts. The system then made payment decisions. The system proved capable of handling complex health care situations, ranging from a simple physician office visit to multi-hospitalization liver transplant cases. deNovis's technology was revolutionary: the company's engineers developed a singular vocabulary and set of grammatical rules drawn from the medical jargon of approximately two hundred health insurance companies. It succeeded in rendering multiple, hard-to-comprehend medical bureaucratic languages into simple, common English documents, informing medical providers and patients how much a specific medical treatment would cost, and explaining to both patients and providers how each provider's fees and each patient's benefits were calculated. This technology also empowered health insurers to combat fraudulent claims and to more quickly customize medical plans.

DeNovis raised funds from leading venture capitalists ($125 million). Its technology won awards and drew new clients. In 2002, Empire Blue Cross and Blue Shield of New York signed an agreement with deNovis valued at $1.3 billion over a period of ten years. Tufts Health Plan (THP) also decided to invest heavily in deNovis's technology. Then, in 2003, deNovis defeated forty-one competitors and signed a $100 million contract with the Centers for Medicare & Medicaid Services (CMS) to replace its core claims adjudication system handling claims valued at $1 billion a day for 80 million Medicare patients. This would have led to state and private sector medical insurance companies becoming deNovis's clients, as they too relied on CMS claims adjudication (Business Wire 2002, 2003; Connolly 2003; Healy 2004).

On October 22, 2004, deNovis collapsed. The failure resulted from wasteful financial practices. Despite its downfall, deNovis's technology succeeded in automating portions of the complex U.S. bureaucratic medical language. DeNovis's innovative solution lives on. Another company purchased deNovis's abandoned patent applications (Bergeron et al. 2003a; Bergeron et al. 2003b; Bergeron et al. 2003c; Bergeron et al. 2003d; Health Edge 2009). The claims adjudication process remains inefficient and expensive (GAO 2010d). Other organizations are developing deNovis-like solutions to improve the process (GAO 2009e; HCLS 2013).

deNovis demonstrated that it is possible to "divide and conquer" the data definitions of different organizations. Federal IT officials already believe that the harmonization of data definitions across agencies is the third most critical step required to develop cross-agency collaboration (following appropriations and authorizations) (Fountain 2013, 105). These officials explain that the U.S. government cannot track its budgetary goals without standardizing data definitions across agencies. Technologies such as those developed by deNovis already exist to empower agencies to keep their individual data definitions while exchanging data based on common definitions.

However, the fundamental problem here is politics rather than technology. Agencies are accustomed to think about "data-as-control" rather than "data-as-assets"; therefore agencies default to a "this data cannot be made public" argument (Fountain 2013, 57). Yet, PSIE is not a typical technology that seeks to harmonize data definitions across agencies. PSIE is primarily an innovation in bureaucratic politics. It seeks to provide agencies with just enough incentives to nudge them to engage each other more seriously in a discussion (followed by a resolution) of how to exchange data.

PSIE does not aspire to build strong, shared data definitions or compel agencies to abandon their standalone data dictionaries. Nor does PSIE aspire to build weak, shared data definitions that will compel agencies to negotiate separate data definitions for every new information sharing project. The concept of PSIE does not even promote a specific information sharing technology. Rather, PSIE aspires to incentivize senior agency officials to walk the extra mile toward the goal of improving interagency information sharing.

7 Four PSIE Challenges

Thus far, this book has emphasized information as a commodity. But information is primarily a constitutive force in society that shapes our social and material reality including guiding, controlling, and rearranging all economic activity. As a constitutive force, information has constitutional roles and an empirical impact on society (Braman 2006, 19). We must consider tensions and trade-offs between the idea of information as a commodity and the concept of information as a constitutive force. Four challenges to PSIE are addressed in this chapter: (1) the democracy challenge, (2) the privacy challenge, (3) the data ownership and intellectual property (IP) challenge, and (4) the freedom of information (FOI) challenge. Will a PSIE program damage democratic values such as active citizenship? Will this program degrade citizens' privacy? Might the PSIE concept clash with the ideas of IP and FOI?

A debate about PSIE's rewards and risks is a debate about information policy. Information policy refers to all laws and policies affecting the creation, processing, flows, and use of information including information sharing (Braman 2006, 77). Unlike the legal, economic, and technical challenges addressed in chapter 6 there are no simple technical solutions for the information policy dilemmas raised in the pages that follow. Rather, each challenge presents a compelling reason to reflect carefully and debate the inherent trade-offs between competing values and goods. Privacy and transparency concerns might lead some to refuse consideration of any sacrifices to improve information sharing. Others may opt to give PSIE a chance in order to avoid information sharing calamities such as the ones discussed in chapter 1. Readers are asked to reflect upon these uneasy ethical choices and to consider each one carefully. Rewards from a PSIE program must be carefully weighed against the risks associated with the implementation of this concept.

The Democracy Challenge

The "democracy challenge" demands that key political goods such as active citizenship, political control of the bureaucracy, and separation of powers be produced, exchanged, and enjoyed outside of market relations (Anderson 1993; Satz 2010). Sandel remains concerned about the penetration of marketplace logic into other domains of human activity including political institutions such as the U.S. Congress. He proposes that marketplace reasoning "empties public life of moral argument" (Sandel 2012, 13).

Other scholars provided empirical evidence in support of Sandel's arguments. In a recent article in the prestigious *Science* journal, two scholars presented controlled experimental evidence to support the claim that market interactions tend to lower moral values. The scholars also demonstrated that the appeal to morality has only a limited impact for alleviating negative market externalities. They concluded that markets erode moral value and proposed to consider carefully whether a market solution is appropriate or not (Armin and Szech 2013, 710). Another scholar has suggested that governmental information sharing does not belong to the "regime of management" but rather to the "regime of justice and legitimacy" (Wenjing 2011, 365). According to this argument, government officials must free data to strengthen citizens' control over government; the process of commoditizing public information debases the ideals of active citizenship and free public debate (Gilder 1992; Prins 2004).

A related issue is PSIE's impact on the egalitarian ethos of the state. The concern here is that underprivileged social groups might be disadvantaged because agencies would exchange too little or too much information about them. Critics might ask: Would agencies exclusively collect and exchange data about affluent citizens, because other agencies are more interested in purchasing such data? Consequently, will affluent citizens become more visible and important than poorer ones in public policy planning? Or PSIE could embolden an efficient bureaucracy unwilling to take instructions from politicians, which would undercut the principle of political control over the bureaucracy (Wenjing 2011). Parliaments outside the United States fear that information sharing programs might create an efficient and less controllable bureaucracy (Luna-Reyes, Gil-Garcia, and Cruz 2007).

Addressing the Democracy Challenge

The democracy critique ignores the fact that, today, most governmental databases are sealed data graveyards that almost no one knows about or cares about (in corporate IT, this phenomenon is known as "security by obscurity"). Democratic ideals—as embodied in e-government services that empower citizens to know more about government and to enable better interactions with the public sector—cannot thrive in these graveyards. The PSIE program will give agencies an incentive to rediscover neglected data and to utilize it. Public information can only empower citizens if agencies resolve data quality problems, extract new insights from linked data, and, then, exchange information with other agencies effectively. Then (and not before such back-office data integration occurs) citizens will begin enjoying improved e-government services.

The democratic ideal depends in part on the effectiveness of the day-to-day interactions between citizens and their governments. PSIE will improve such interactions and will therefore contribute to the democratic ideal. The difficulty is that citizens will not easily recognize the value of PSIE until it is operational and successful, but will be asked, via taxes, to pay up front the cost of building PSIE. This problem plagues all infrastructure improvement projects whose initial costs appear very high and whose future benefits cannot be known in advance.

Elected politicians will continue to inject values into the bureaucracy after PSIE becomes a reality, and senior government officers will instruct subordinates to search for information in PSIE to support a political agenda. For example, a newly elected "environment-friendly President" or "development-oriented President" will cause government officials to search PSIE for different information.

Most important to understand is that scholars like Sandel incorrectly portray a world where pure "markets" collide with pure "morality." Yet, as demonstrated in chapter 6, there are different kinds of markets including contested commodity exchanges designed to impose restricted commoditization arrangements on some goods and services. Scholars have highlighted this important idea arguing that the manner in which goods are traded, rather than their content, provides public legitimacy and moral support for the exchange (such as the cadavers exchange) (Anteby 2010).

The public debate about PSIE and its virtues and moral risk can contribute to the egalitarian and participatory democracy vision. The divide between exchange rationale and civic ideals widens if the public is excluded from foundational debates. For example, a divide exists between American corporations that secretly extract human cells to generate biotech products and the public's view that celebrates the integrity of the human body (Andrews and Nelkin 1998). In contrast, Icelandic, Estonian, and British citizens were actively involved in debates regarding the construction of genetic data exchanges. These debates contributed to civic mindedness, and narrowed the gap between public opinion and exchange practice (Anderlik and Rothstein 2001). The debate in Iceland in particular serves as a fascinating example of how a commoditization debate can reinvigorate democratic ideals.

Case Study: The Icelandic Genome-Commoditization Debate

Origins of the Icelandic Health Sector Database Law In the late 1990s, genome research opened up possibilities to produce new treatments for diseases. To isolate the genetic origins of diseases, a homogenous population was required. Iceland's population of about 275,000 constituted an ideal sample because it has remained isolated from outside genetic influences for centuries (Philipkoski 1999). Iceland also meticulously maintains genealogical and health records (Lemonick 2006).

Dr. Kari Stefansson realized the economic potential of the Icelandic population for genome research. He cofounded deCODE Genetics in his native city of Reykjavik, as a Delaware company. He planned to create a database holding linked genetic, medical, and genealogical data about as many Icelanders as possible and then sell access to this database to drug corporations (known in Iceland as the Biogenetics Project) (Lemonick 2006). On December 17, 1998, the Icelandic Parliament adopted the Health Sector Database Law (known as the "Database Law") empowering a private company to construct an electronic database of the country's genetic, health, and genealogical records. This law specified under what conditions medical records could be combined with genetic and genealogical data, including for deceased persons (Pálsson and Harðardóttir 2002). The Parliament granted deCODE an exclusive twelve-year license to build the database and to analyze the data, exclusive rights to commercial exploitation of the database for those twelve years, and permission to access government-held medical records (Chadwick 1999; Lemonick 2006).

At first, thousands of Icelanders donated blood to the company while buying company stock, whose price climbed to a high of $65 a share. However, shares collapsed in the late 1990s when the high-tech bubble burst, leaving deCODE close to bankruptcy. Hoffman-La Roche then purchased deCODE. Simultaneously, Icelanders began to feel uneasy knowing their personal medical files were being used by a private foreign firm (Lemonick 2006). The failure of the deCODE initiative and the deNovis failure (see chapter 6) serve as reminders of the reasons why legislatures are often reluctant to support financially entrepreneurial, joint public-private information sharing endeavors.

The Icelandic Genome-Commoditization Debate and Outcome   Extensive public debate regarding the database took place between April 1998 and November 2003, when the Icelandic Supreme Court consolidated the legislative settlement (Gertz 2004). The scope of the debate was impressive. The Icelandic press published hundreds of articles about the Biogenetics Project (one newspaper published 569 op-eds and articles in just over two years), and television programs explained the issues to the public. Icelanders passionately debated the Biogenetics Project in town meetings, through long-winded parliamentary debates, in shopping centers and cafés, and around dinner tables. Icelanders also closely followed extensive world press and television coverage regarding the database under construction (Pálsson and Harðardóttir 2002).

Proponents and opponents of the Database Law primarily debated medical ethics versus commercial interest (Chadwick 1999). Writers, scholars, and the general public were the main participants in this debate; politicians and lobbyists played a lesser role. Proponents of the law emphasized the economic opportunities the database provided; they highlighted Iceland's urgent need to create new sources of revenue to replace the declining fishing industry. Opponents emphasized ethical concerns, particularly those of consent, privacy, data ownership, and control. Specifically, they objected to the institution of a "broad consent" clause that empowered deCODE to resell data without renewed consent from its human subject. They argued

Figure 7.1
Taking it to the biobank.
Source: Harris 2006. Permission to print granted by artist Richard Grote.

that this clause compromised the patient's autonomy. They also objected to deCODE's monopoly over Iceland's genetic information (Philipkoski 1999).

Figure 7.1 captures the spirit of the vigorous Icelandic debate representing both proponent ("go to the bank with your genes!") and opponent ("how could you go to the bank with your genes?!") viewpoints. Figure 7.1 also aptly illustrates this chapter's primary argument: there is no absolute "right" or "wrong" in an ethical debate about exchanges like the Icelandic Biogenetics Project or PSIE. Rather, citizens must vigorously debate the pros and cons of such exchanges and decide for themselves whether and how to strike a new balance between important values.

Equally important, the passionate Icelandic debate forced Parliament to adopt restricted commoditization and selective incentives to convince Icelanders to support the Database Law. The Parliament changed the proposed law four times during the debate, each time adding more privacy protection clauses and extracting more economic benefits for Iceland. In August 2001, deCODE struck a deal with the Icelandic Medical Association. Citizens could opt out from being included automatically in the deCODE database, and deCODE agreed to delete personal data about people who decided to opt out after such inclusion (Pálsson and HarÐardóttir 2002). By 2002, 7 percent of the population chose to be removed from the database (Kaiser 2002). It was also agreed that two different governmental boards would encrypt the data (Philipkoski 1999). In 2003, a citizen sued deCODE for refusing to remove her deceased father's medical records from the database. Iceland's Supreme Court ruled in her favor (Lemonick 2006). Following this case, Hoffman-LaRoche agreed that in return for their data Icelanders would receive free access to the database and free use of medicines produced utilizing it. By 2006 the database contained information about 100,000 Icelanders (ibid.).

Iceland was the first country to adopt a biobank, a biorepository that stores biological samples for use in research. Other countries and regions followed including Estonia, Latvia, the UK, Quebec City in Canada, and the State of Wisconsin in the United States. Officials in these jurisdictions were wary of running into the same public controversy that Iceland faced (Kaiser 2002, 1161). Yet, these officials avoided engaging public debate and so missed the main lesson of the Icelandic experience: the commoditization of public data is an opportunity to reinvigorate the democratic ideal of an active citizenship. The PSIE debate is also an opportunity to engage citizens and empower them to shape the debate's outcome. The impressive scope and depth of the Icelandic debate also demonstrate that engaged and informed citizens can propel politicians to enforce restricted commoditization arrangements on a new contested commodity exchange.

The Privacy Challenge

Ethicists might be concerned about a PSIE program that empowers agencies to link disparate data and violate citizens' privacy. Ethicists are already alarmed because traditional privacy protection mechanisms are becoming obsolete in our Big Data era. Techniques such as individual notice and consent, allowing citizens to opt out from data collection programs, and anonymity cannot protect citizens' privacy when data is harvested to support secondary uses unanticipated at the time when the data was generated (Mayer-Schönberger and Cukier 2013, 156).

Ethicists will therefore become even more alarmed about a PSIE program that empowers agencies to link huge quantities of disparate data and explore the results for any purpose. Data that previously resided within the computer systems of a single agency would transition easily into other agencies' systems. More data about citizens would be collected with no opportunities for citizens to opt out from such collection efforts. Agencies would have new incentives to store everything. Agencies could then penetrate more deeply into private lives. Most of the time, citizens would not even be aware of data collection efforts or know why agencies suddenly are so knowledgeable about their lives.

The information state already knows a great deal about individuals while individuals know less about the state. The state's increasing reliance on electronic dossiers and statistical portraits of citizens threatens civil liberties (Braman 2006). Today, agencies are sensitive to this argument and therefore demand that the legislature affirms their authority to share specific information with other agencies (Dawes 1996). PSIE, ethicists might suggest, would empower agencies to dispense with such legalities and to probe more deeply into citizens' private affairs without their prior consent. The U.S. Congress is concerned about this danger and is constantly searching for new ways to protect citizens' privacy from IT changes that have occurred since the U.S. Privacy Act was passed in 1974 (GAO 2012i).

Sometimes, politicians even boast about information sharing failures as evidence that they are willing to pay any price to protect privacy. During the 1990s, dangerous criminals returned to the street because British agencies insisted on preserving data in paper format and would not share these records with other agencies. Rather than fix this abysmal condition, politicians highlighted it as a symbol of their determination to protect at all costs the ideals of limited government, individual rights, and privacy. This example illustrates the clash between the absolutist claim for privacy and PSIE's pragmatic approach: sacrifice minimal privacy rights to improve information sharing (Bellamy and Taylor 1996).

Zealous privacy-protection supporters mistrust the law to protect against privacy violations. They demonstrate how legal privacy protection exemptions often exacerbate privacy violations. The U.S. Privacy Act of 1974 (see also chapter 4) exempts interagency data exchanges from privacy protections if these exchanges are part of agencies' "routine uses" (GAO 2008a), meaning "for a purpose which is compatible with the purpose for which it was collected" (Wenjing 2011, 365). Agencies must declare why they collect a certain piece of data and cannot use it for other purposes without permission. European agencies also transact in data using "routine use" exemptions. In PSIE, agencies will frequently employ the "routine use" concept. The right to privacy is therefore more likely to be violated (Braman 2006).

Addressing the Privacy Challenge

Privacy must be weighed against values such as free speech, crime prevention, and governmental efficiency. A dynamic tension exists between citizens as individuals who value privacy and citizens as sovereigns who yearn for an efficient government. As citizens, we wish to minimize the amount of personal information that agencies possess. However we are also *citoyens*: citizens who are active participants in the political life of their community and the carriers of the tradition of political rights. As *citoyens*, members of the collective sovereign, we demand that agencies process information efficiently (Mayer-Schönberger and Lazer 2007b).

An improvement to information sharing always involves a privacy sacrifice because information becomes available to circulate. This citizen-*citoyen* dilemma resembles a pendulum clock that swings in the direction of either governmental efficiency or privacy protection. Since 9/11 Americans have felt such swings between the demand to share information to protect the homeland and the urge to defend civil liberties (Dizard 2002). British citizens also experience such swings between sharing too much or too little data in the health and social care domains (Perri 6 et al. 2007). Scholars noted the same phenomenon in Australia, Hong Kong, and New Zealand (Lam 2005).

Several reasons support information sharing over privacy concerns. First, much governmental data is not personal information. For example, governments collect and store huge amounts of data that sensors and machines generate about the environment. Privacy restrictions do not apply to such data (Mayer-Schönberger and Cukier 2013, 152). Second, citizens place life before privacy, and effective information sharing often makes the difference between life and death, as exemplified by the events of 9/11 and other case studies of information sharing failure discussed in chapter 1.

Third, agencies often employ privacy concerns when they do not wish to share information for less noble reasons (Perri et al. 2007). Fourth, legislatures often approve more sharing as exemplified by the growing number of U.S. agencies that have received permission to exchange data with the IRS in recent years (GAO 2011k). A transparent PSIE program could end private bilateral information-sharing arrangements, which are slow, tedious, and almost impossible to monitor. Last, and perhaps most important, PSIE will have strong mechanisms to monitor its privacy-violation risks. Ultimately, transparency is the best privacy protection because it exposes inaccurate and incomplete data. Once information is gathered by agencies, the only true privacy protection is to increase transparency about what is stored and who can access it. PSIE will provide agencies with a better view and understanding of what data other agencies collect, store, and use. This will lead to better and more honest preventive measures against the misuse of data. The current information sharing regime (described in chapter 4) is not monitored. An unmonitored risk is far more dangerous than one that is transparent to all.

Countries outside the United States are also searching for breakthrough legal pathways to improve information sharing without damaging privacy. Recently, a New Zealand public commission searched for an innovative legal solution to transform the self-interested bureaucratic perspective and compel agencies to integrate information more effectively and provide better e-government services to citizens. The commission stated that a narrow, agency-specific view of the activity for which information was originally collected works against subsequent sharing of the information with another agency. Agencies were encouraged to take a "whole-of-government" viewpoint. This new approach encourages agencies to state broad purposes whenever they collect information from the public. Agencies are to explain the goals of collecting information to citizens in a way that does not compromise their ability, later on, to share information with other agencies to advance programs that benefit the individuals concerned. The commission recommended amending the existing Privacy Act of 1993 to support this idea, but warned agencies to avoid making the impression that information provided to one agency would automatically become available to all other agencies (Law Commission 2011).

A PSIE program will comply with existing privacy protection mechanisms including the U.S. Privacy Act (1974), the U.S. Computer Matching and Privacy Protection Act (1988), privacy advocates, ombudsmen, internal privacy review boards, and data protection commissioners. The PSIE Act discussed in chapter 6 will emphasize that PSIE's data exchanges are subject to these traditional privacy protection mechanisms. Old habits will continue to protect privacy after PSIE becomes operational. Government officials will continue to print an obscene volume of nontradable paper documents (Lexmark 2009). The most significant safeguard will remain citizens' deep mistrust and fear of a strong government (Cate 1997).

Existing privacy protections will be augmented by new proactive protections that only an electronic exchange like PSIE can provide. Data will be scattered across decentralized databases rather than stored in a central location. The process of browsing data will require accessing data located on the computer systems of dozens of agencies. It will therefore be easier to detect privacy abuses, as the privacy guardians of many agencies will have a commercial stake in closely tracking such transactions. PSIE will increase the number of watchful eyes inside government that keep track of how data elements travel across government. At the same time, each pair of watchful eyes will only guard the data assets of its own agency. Thus, there will be more proactive privacy guardians but fewer opportunities for the guardians themselves to invade citizens' privacy.

PSIE will also reduce the number of humans involved in data exchanges. Current information-gathering processes often involve numerous human actors. Thirteen DOS officials are involved in thirty-nine steps to issue a passport (GAO 2002). With PSIE, there will be fewer opportunities for humans to invade privacy, because automatic software agents will exchange data. With fewer humans involved, PSIE will also reduce errors in data transfer processes. This, in turn, will reduce the risks and costs associated with inadvertent propagation of inaccurate data.

PSIE's restricted commoditization arrangements will make it easier to remove some data assets from the exchange or to require the consent of data-subjects to trade information about them. These arrangements could also ensure that some data elements will not be tradable after a certain period of time. PSIE will encourage agencies to trade in large volumes of data. Trading in large-volume data frequently improves privacy because it diverts resources to the statistical analysis of data about groups and away from investigating individual cases.

Agencies will have new incentives to develop more privacy protections. For example, agencies could improve privacy protection by offering cheaper prices for browsing data rather than downloading it. This pricing incentive to browse data will cause agencies to refrain from duplicating datasets. This will mean fewer ill-secured databases and increased privacy protection within the government data domain.

PSIE's enterprise architects will harness metadata to create new privacy protections that only an automated data exchange can provide. Metadata is data about other data used to describe informational activities, including information about who used what data when and for what purposes. PSIE will empower investigators to detect abuse using new metadata tools such as sending citizens an automatic email that an inter-agency data transaction about them just took place (Parycek and Sachs 2010; Raul 2002). In short, PSIE could become a good example of how Big Data can monitor itself to detect misuses of Big Data. PSIE's enterprise architects will also forbid the use of predictive analytics to judge and punish people before they have acted. This use of PSIE to support a "dictatorship of data" negates the presumption of innocence until proven guilty and our concepts of justice, moral choice, and free will (Mayer-Schönberger and Cukier 2013, 151).

An important final privacy protection will be to construct a representative body of experts and laypersons to serve as PSIE enterprise architects. These architects will hold agencies accountable for their use of data exchanged via PSIE. The burden of responsibility for misusing the data will transition from its original producers to the agency officials who purchase the data for secondary uses. PSIE architects will have the skills and experience required to examine the algorithms that agencies create to integrate data from different sources. These guardians will have the mandate to impose sanctions on abusers (Mayer-Schonberger and Cukier 2013, 180–182).

The Data Ownership/IP Challenge

The Coase theorem argues that once property rights are defined, market transactions can take place and market efficiency can be accomplished (Coase 1960). Scholars might argue that all public data must be freely available to anyone; therefore agencies cannot assert ownership over the information assets they produce. However, agencies view themselves as owners of their information and are increasingly concerned about data ownership challenges (Dawes and Prefontaine 2003; Lam 2005). Yet, it is not clear if the information sharing contracts (e.g., MoUs) that agencies sign with each other today are enforceable contracts; it is not possible for one agency to sue another because government cannot sue itself (Pollock, Newbery, and Bently 2008, 108). So, on what legal grounds might agencies claim ownership of the information assets they will exchange in PSIE?

Addressing the Data Ownership/IP Challenge

We must first acknowledge the inherent tension between the public nature of agencies' data, and agencies' ownership claim over the same data. Assigning too much weight to the "all public data belongs to the people" argument will cause agencies to find ways to avoid sharing their data (as in the OD case described in chapter 3). Agencies' database gardens will remain sealed to outsiders. Conversely, overemphasizing agencies' data ownership might hurt numerous weaker actors within and outside government who need access to the data and cannot afford to purchase it. An effective solution requires a new balance between existing competing values.

We can design a unique public information commons to support PSIE. Different types of information commons already exist to address different needs (Samuelson 2006, 2011). Today there is a proliferation of legal pathways through which individuals can retain ownership over information while making it accessible to wider crowds. Nonprofit organizations have developed techniques that empower individuals to use existing copyright law to shape licenses to copyrighted materials to maximize public access (Braman 2006). In PSIE, agencies can enjoy data ownership rights in an *internal* information commons. These rights will not apply to their relationships with private organizations. European scholars have suggested that the creation of a new type of creative commons might convince agencies to comply with OD (Van Den Broek et al. 2011).

Additional means exist to help agencies acquire ownership over their information assets. The U.S. Congress can expand the Bayh-Dole Act (1980) to protect agencies' data ownership rights. Today, this act encourages universities to own patents, obtain copyrights, or maintain trade secrets. Europeans can extend legal frameworks that empower agencies to sell data to outsiders. Agencies could also use this book's information service concept (defined in chapter 4) to support their data ownership rights. U.S. IP Law recognizes modern databases as engines of invention. Agencies already use this argument to claim ownership over their databases' contents. Several scholars have suggested that this trend would damage the FOI cause (Prins 2004). Yet, this trend is a legal opportunity to support the construction of a unique internal public information commons as demonstrated by the Dutch RINIS case study that follows.

Case Study: The Dutch RINIS Project

The Dutch Routing of (Inter)National Information Streams (RINIS) project exemplifies how agencies can create an internal public information commons. In the mid-1990s, a Dutch citizen could register in one agency to receive unemployment benefits while being registered as employed in another agency, and not fear detection. The CEOs of three large, Netherlands welfare agencies discussed how to eliminate such fraud. This resulted in the invention of RINIS, which was initially established as an arena for the exchange of social welfare data among agencies. RINIS's creators asked a simple question: who owns data elements about Dutch residents? A 1995 study revealed that every data element was "claimed" by a specific agency. An RINIS law then codified which agencies own specific data elements. By this law, agencies retain legal powers to update their data elements. Organizations are required to sign agreements specifying the terms for accessing other organizations' data elements. RINIS placed bureaucratic politics first by demanding to know—for each data element—which agency is its authentic owner. For example, the Citizens Registration Office was the authentic owner of residents' date of birth, while the Job Center was the owner of residents' job seeking history (Bekkers 2000; Homburg 1999; Huijboom and Hoogwout 2004; OECD 2007; Snellen 2002; Zuurmond 1998).

Every RINIS feature reflects the requirement that an agency retain ownership over its data. The RINIS Institute, established in 2003, was created to facilitate data exchanges rather than to integrate data. This institute neither owns computing assets nor stores data. Agencies are divided into sectors such as "national health service" or "municipal social security." Each sector is responsible for the execution of a specific social welfare function, and each sector has a central verification office where an RINIS computer server is installed. Agencies install referral indices on these servers. Thereafter, the servers automate requests from one agency to access the data of another agency. A resident may apply to receive a social security allowance via the municipal social security agency. This agency can then receive answers to questions such as "where does the resident live?" (Citizen Registration Office owns the answer to this question), or "what was the resident's last reported income?" (Inland Revenue Office owns the answer).

RINIS's "politics first" strategy was successful. It became impossible to obtain a welfare benefit on false grounds. The program empowered agencies to handle more cases more quickly. Additional agencies signed on. In 2004, participant organizations had already exchanged 56.5 million messages as compared to 200,000 such messages that were exchanged during RINIS's first year. The Organisation for Economic Co-operation and Development (OECD) recognized RINIS as a "best-practice system" for electronic data exchanges. RINIS's fraud detection mission was expanded. In 2005, the Dutch government announced plans to use the program to handle all electronic data exchanges (Huijboom and Hoogwout 2004; OECD 2007; Snellen 2002). RINIS's success is impressive because it built technology suited to existing public sector behavior, rather than developing "pie in the sky" technologies that ignore the political nature of agencies. PSIE closely follows the RINIS politics-first approach but adds a selective incentives component that RINIS never adopted.

The Freedom of Information Challenge

Citizens who receive free information from databases such as the SEC's Electronic Data Gathering, Analysis and Retrieval (EDGAR) system would be outraged if agencies shut down these resources so that they could trade the data for profit with other agencies. Critics could highlight a seeming contradiction between the proposed PSIE (where data is for sale) and FOI (which dictates that agencies' data is a public good). Most democracies stipulate FOI laws. The United States has a long tradition of protecting citizens' rights to receive public data for free (Braman 2006). The U.S. Congress vigilantly protects the FOI claim. In 1996, Congress passed the Electronic Freedom of Information Act to expand the 1974 Freedom of Information Act to cover electronic records. FOI is embedded in the constitution of several countries including Sweden, Finland, and Belgium (Prins 2004). The concern is that PSIE might encourage agencies to become less supportive of FOI because they would want to profit from trading data.

Addressing the FOI Challenge

To avoid any negative impact on FOI, agencies could trade certain information with each other while granting citizens free access to other information. Similar arrangements already exist in the private sector. The three U.S.

credit bureaus grant free access to some data while selling other identity theft protection products. PSIE's expansion could yield similarly creative solutions. Citizens might provide timely personal data in return for credit that could be applied to reduce fees (such as a passport renewal fee). Agencies would provide such discounts because PSIE gives them an incentive to gather high-quality fresh data then package and sell it to other agencies. Citizens would also benefit from receiving better-integrated and therefore more useful information for free from the e-government portals of different agencies. So, PSIE could actually complement FOI by helping agencies to provide citizens with larger volumes of meaningful information. The evolution of other contested commodity exchanges for hair, blood, sperm, medical services, and memorial services further demonstrates that exchanges increase easy access to contested commodities (Cooper and Culyer 1968; Fader 2010; Tharp 2003; Tomes 2003; Sheumaker 2003).

The GAO recently accused agencies of not disclosing their more valuable data via FOIA channels. GAO staffers suggested that agencies know what information to deposit or not to deposit in their electronic FOIA libraries (GAO 2012k). This is another opportunity for PSIE to complement FOI laws. FOI laws provide transparency via an individualistic, reactive, delayed, emergency-oriented, history-driven, confrontational, judicial, do-it-yourself, and costly (in terms of expertise required) mechanism (Kreimer 2008). PSIE will complement FOI laws by providing an aggregated, proactive, immediate, future-oriented, nonconfrontational, business-like, agency-driven, and cost-effective mechanism to increase interagency sharing of the vast data that FOI laws never touch. FOI laws work because there is a scarcity of information sharing between government and citizens. PSIE will work because there is a scarcity of information sharing inside government.

Addressing Ethical and Political Challenges

Jointly, the four PSIE challenges discussed in this chapter are the core ethical and political arguments against implementing the proposed PSIE. Programs that fail to properly address such ethical challenges can be terminated quickly. DARPA's FutureMAP program that aimed to create a commodity-based exchange to trade in predictions about political events including terrorism is an extreme case that illustrates such quick termination (Meirowitz and Tucker 2004). U.S. representatives viewed this program as an attempt to "trade in death" and described it as "irresponsible and outrageous," "repugnant," "grotesque," and "sick" (Sandel 2012, 150). On July 28, 2003, Congress terminated FutureMAP one day after learning of its existence, making it perhaps the shortest-lived federal pilot program in American history (Seife 2003; Weigle 2007). This chapter has explained how to address similar ethical and political concerns *before* unleashing PSIE. The next, concluding chapter 8 proposes a concrete, political plan of action for implementing a PSIE pilot program.

8 A Political Strategy to Promote PSIE

In 1985, Stuart Brand suggested that a key trade-off of the coming information age would be the balance between "information wanting to be free" and "information wanting to be expensive" (Brand and Herron 1985). Brand explained that information wants to be free because the cost of providing it is getting lower. At the same time, information wants to be expensive because it is so valuable.

Today, agencies face the same dilemma: how to strike a balance between the "free" and "expensive" features of their information assets. Agencies can free information to reinvigorate democracy and boost the economy. At the same time, as organizations, agencies own the most valuable information assets in the state and want to secure ownership over these assets and benefit from them. Like Brand in 1985, agencies seek a path to "square the circle"—release information assets to promote the greater good while remaining their owners and beneficiaries.

For more than two decades now, the existing information sharing approaches (called "coerce," "consent," and "coordinate" in chapter 2) have failed to nudge agencies to share information. This book proposes an innovative, incentives-driven approach to help agencies develop a new path to reconcile the "free" and "expensive" features of their information assets. This chapter provides practical advice to politicians, senior public officials, IT consultants, and citizens on how to turn this approach from theory into reality. The concluding section returns to the book's foundational "Bliss and Tel Gezer" metaphor to highlight why people rather than technology are the key to addressing the public sector's information sharing crisis.

The Promise of PSIE

The popular consent approach (open data in its current political form as explained in chapter 3) informs citizens that public data must be "free." Yet, OD does not provide agencies with incentives to share their valuable data. Most agencies therefore have adopted a passive-aggressive stance toward this program and have released little or no valuable data. In other contested commodity domains described in chapter 6, scholars have similarly discovered that attempts to eliminate incentives in the name of altruism result in waste and inefficiency (Mahoney 2000).

The coerce approach too has failed to provide a satisfactory information sharing solution. Agencies command sufficient means to passively resist legal efforts to coerce them to exchange information with no compensation. Agencies also easily bypass weak coordination efforts to nudge them to share information, again, with no compensation (see chapter 2). Decades of futile information sharing attempts must come to an end. Politicians, senior public officials, and citizens must ask: are we better off commanding agencies to share data and then spending years and billions of dollars on failed enforcement efforts? Are we spending taxpayer funds wisely by mandating that self-interested agencies share information for the greater common good only to discover, time and again, that these agencies find a way to evade these mandates?

In current data exchange practices we find an indication of how information sharing might be improved. Agencies agree to exchange valuable information if they receive something in return. Nonetheless, current exchange practices are cumbersome and wasteful. Agencies frequently fail to find useful data held by other agencies. Existing information sharing arrangements also empower information-rich organizations to exploit poorer ones.

By manipulating the self-interested behavior of agencies, a PSIE program will inject immediacy into the dormant life of public sector data, creating new supply zones in response to new demand. Agencies will discover that unlocking their databases pays off. Information trading will also blur established information domains because exchanges are flexible and create instant competition that removes information sharing barriers. A pricing mechanism is the most effective means to encourage agencies to share information.

Rather than reeducate public sector officials to support the greater common good, the incentives approach expands interagency, calculus-based trust. This approach encourages agencies to think about information sharing as a long-term exchange game where the trader's reputation is critical. A PSIE program could also inject life into existing technical solutions such as NIEM because agencies will now understand that it pays to share.

Higher volumes of data trade will propel agencies to make more data accessible to other agencies. Taxpayers will save money because a PSIE program will render obsolete other expensive projects to build bilateral information sharing solutions, will eradicate fraud, and will eliminate duplicative information sharing programs. Lives will be saved by the increased sharing of public data. Over time, an information trading community of agencies will emerge based on high standards of reciprocity.

Researchers must study four additional questions. First, what is included in the definitions of a "governmental record" and a "public sector dataset"? These concepts as defined in the U.S. Privacy Act (1974) are arcane in an age when agencies acquire data from social networking channels (GAO 2010b). Second, which data types will be suitable for PSIE trade? Chapters 5 and 6 provided some guidelines and examples to address this question. However, related questions are yet to be addressed including: Should the criteria for selecting public data types for trade be based on the data's inherent features, on the data's intended use, or on the data-use intentions of the buyer? Where do we draw the line between public data types suited to be freed via OD web portals and other types that are suited to exchange? The most challenging task here is to reap the advantages of the exchange approach while keeping exchange activities confined to goods proper to this approach (Anderson 1993).

Third, how will PSIE's success change the public sector? Which agencies will benefit most from the proposed new information ecosystem? Which skills will become obsolete and which skills will prosper in this new data mosaic environment? Agencies that do well in PSIE may no longer need to be the most technically proficient ones. Rather they will need to be visionary and adaptable, and be able to understand how to mesh together purchased and in-house data to convert visions into reality.

Finally, how will PSIE change the balance of power among the public, private, and nonprofit sectors? In the nineteenth century, the British built centers of analysis, such as the Royal Botanical Gardens at the Kew, where colonial botanical materials were analyzed. The knowledge gained was distributed throughout the empire resulting in the creation or destruction of local economies (Parry 2004). Will PSIE empower agencies to gain power at the expense of private corporations (Mayer-Schönberger and Lazer 2007a)? Governments already use IT to encroach on civic domains such as scientific research (although, despite this, agencies still lag far behind private sector corporations in IT sophistication) (Braman 2006). Will PSIE's success amplify such undesirable trends?

Implementing PSIE in the United States

In the United States the legislative tide has changed course, moving away from funding standalone agency programs and toward funding programs that mandate close interagency collaboration. The GPRAMA is the most important legislation pointing in this new direction.

The first round of GPRAMA milestones are scheduled for 2014. Therefore not much is known about this Act's actual impact. It takes many years of consistent cooperation to build successful interagency collaboration (including improved information sharing) as demonstrated by the Partnership for Sustainable Communities joint effort of HUD, the DOT, and the EPA (Fountain 2013, 80, 84, 87). Therefore the empirical impact of the GPRAMA on changing agencies' behavior will remain unknown for some time.

One GPRAMA research report suggested that this Act mandates important changes in agencies' behavior without providing the authority, resources, or tools to support this change (Fountain 2013, 54). A PSIE program could provide some of these missing elements. For example, the GPRAMA is silent on how two or more agencies would "establish mutually reinforcing or joint strategies" or "establish compatible policies, procedures and others means" (Fountain 2013, 42). The GPRAMA also does not provide a mechanism for agencies to calculate the costs and benefits of their new collaboration. PSIE's metadata and incentives would help drive agencies to share more valuable information and to empirically measure some of the costs and benefits of doing so. Implementing a humble PSIE program to improve interagency information sharing could be a good first step to convert the GPRAMA's goals into reality. A cadre of open-minded reformists already exists in the federal sector, eager to implement a bold new experiment like PSIE (Kelman 2004).

Cross-agency collaboration including information sharing costs money and a PSIE program too will require funding (Fountain 2013, 45). A PSIE pilot program could start as a small project to improve information sharing within a single large agency. U.S. federal IT leaders command sufficient authority and budgets to fund such a pilot. These IT leaders are disturbed by new unfunded OD rules that they must comply with (Biddick and Kash 2013, 7). They may welcome a bold new initiative that demonstrates a more effective, incentives-driven way to improve information sharing.

Within a single agency, one deputy assistant secretary can implement a PSIE pilot program as a tool to help headquarters and field offices more easily discover each other's datasets. It will be easier to implement the first PSIE program in a single large agency where critical issues such as funding, authority, and accountability are clearly defined (Fountain 2013, 57, 59). Later on, PSIE could grow outside this first agency to help improve information sharing across agencies.

Extending PSIE to Countries Outside the United States

Scholars sometimes envy countries where a single federal agency can allegedly create and enforce a unified information sharing approach (Fountain 2013, 64). But many countries suffer from the same acute information sharing crisis that haunts the U.S. public sector. A few countries have dared to develop original information sharing solutions that display some (though not all) of PSIE's features. These programs include the Dutch RINIS program (see chapter 7), the Australian PSMA and CrimTrac institutions (see chapters 4 and 6), and the important debate in Iceland over the national health database (see chapter 7). Still, such programs are rare. Many countries can benefit from the proposed PSIE approach tailored appropriately to their unique national culture and needs.

A PSIE program is not suitable for small, authoritarian, or poorly developed countries. The intimate relationships among agencies in small countries are sufficient to support information sharing. Authoritarian governments effectively coerce agencies to share information, as demonstrated by several Chinese information sharing projects (Wenjing 2011; Yu 2007). The widening information divide between the "have now" and "have later" countries makes the latter unlikely candidates to adopt a PSIE program that requires sophisticated and expensive IT infrastructure (Evans and Yen 2006;

Garson 2005a; Luna-Reyes, Gil-Garcia, and Cruz 2007; Norris 2001; Shulman, Thrane, and Shelley 2005; Yu 2006).

Large, developed, and democratic countries can benefit from a PSIE program. These countries are endowed with rich computing infrastructure as well as social and civil freedoms. Developed countries invest more resources in e-government than underdeveloped countries and information sharing is a necessary precondition for improving e-government programs. The benefits of implementing innovative information sharing programs will be most significant in countries where officials and politicians are prepared to discuss competing ethical arguments regarding the value of such programs. Programs like PSIE are most likely to succeed in countries where citizens are public-spirited, understand the benefits and cost of implementing these programs, and are vigorous in terms of setting restrictions on the process of commoditizing public data. The United States, the EU member states, India, Brazil, Canada, and Australia are good incipient candidates for a PSIE program.

Insights for Politicians

If politicians continue to accept the current abysmal public sector information-sharing status quo, there will be more lives lost and billions of dollars wasted every year. Researchers have noted the dire consequences of information sharing failures in the domain of governmental scientific data (Wood et al. 2010, 11). But the public sector's information sharing crisis is wider and more pervasive than this domain alone.

Politicians would do well to choose an appropriate election cycle in which to promote the PSIE concept (Gil-Garcia and Pardo 2005). The current election cycles marked by tight budgets and information sharing failures are an opportunity to promote the PSIE idea. An outrageous information sharing fiasco like Hurricane Katrina can be the catalyst for developing the first PSIE program (Landsbergen and Wolken 1998). This program will encounter opposition. Some voters might be suspicious of a program that clashes with an absolutist demand for privacy (as occurred when the civil rights movement opposed the U.S. Patriot Act after 9/11). Some inertia-driven public officials might argue that they can improve information sharing without PSIE. Information-rich agencies may fear PSIE's impact. Conversely, information-weak agencies are likely to support a plan to level the interagency information-sharing playing field. Politicians will need to work hard to aggregate the support of many diverse actors.

Wise politicians will recruit support for PSIE among senior public officials who crave an original, creative information-sharing regime. Politicians must identify such officials and provide them with an opportunity and authorization to criticize the current information sharing regime and take action. PSIE will constitute the reform opportunity that public sector officials are waiting to pursue (Kelman 2004). Politicians must expand the ranks of PSIE supporters to include privacy advocate groups, U.S. congressional legislatures, and the media. The goal will be to promote PSIE and the PSIE Act (Bajaj and Ram 2003).

PSIE will need time and patience to bloom. Several of the most successful information sharing programs in the history of the U.S. federal government took many years before they matured. For example, the most successful program for reducing veteran homelessness in the United States is the HUD-VA Supportive Housing rental voucher program. Today the two large departments monitor veteran homelessness and report to Congress with one voice. However, it took more than two decades to develop this program including its shared data definitions (Fountain 2013, 71).

Legislatures can provide a framework for PSIE's growth. In the United States, a PSIE Congressional Act could specify which agencies own which data, what the guidelines are for owning information products, and what types of data are nontradable. In certain domains (such as standard welfare data exchanges between the federal government and the fifty states) efficient information sharing arrangements already exist. Over the past decade, the SSA has invested $5 billion to improve its computer systems and the capability of these systems to share information with other federal and state agencies (Gallagher 2009; GAO 2012n). Congress could divert the PSIE program to support domains in greater need of information sharing improvement (such as the environmental domain as discussed in chapter 6).

A PSIE Act could preemptively restrict government intervention to articulating principles, enacting minimal regulations, and adjudicating disputes that PSIE cannot handle on its own, facilitating discussion and reducing administrative costs. Contested commodity exchanges have proven to be flexible if permitted to operate with minimal interference. Therefore, the PSIE Act must guarantee that the legislature itself will not rig the fair information trading game. Fearing such interference, experts have conditioned the expansion of a U.S. cap-and-trade greenhouse gases program on Congress's willingness to make a legal commitment not to intervene in the exchange (GAO 2010a). Congress must also guarantee PSIE a long future, to allow it time to grow.

Several scholars have suggested that American politicians can coerce agencies to follow their commands (Balla and Wright 2001; Bawn 1995; Epstein and O'Halloran 1999; Huber and Shipan 2002; McCubbins, Noll, and Weingast 1987; Yackee and Yackee 2006; Zegart 2004). The OD case study (discussed in chapter 3) does not support this argument. Officials effectively employed IT tools to appear as if they were in compliance with information sharing instructions while in fact not complying at all. Therefore, politicians will do well to provide incentives to public officials to support a PSIE program.

Observations for Public Sector Officials

The histories of successful collaborative IT projects demonstrate that political sponsors paved the way to these successes (Dawes and Prefontaine 2003; Kamal 2006; Kamal and Themistocleous 2006; Luna-Reyes, Gil-Garcia, and Cruz 2007). Senior public sector officials must partner with politicians endowed with the rare qualities of vision and persistence. Over time, it will become easier to find supportive politicians as PSIE yields initial results and gains popularity.

Markets are successful if they are compatible with people's natural tendencies (Ariely 2010). Officials will adjust quickly to PSIE's information trading regime because it extends competitive bureaucratic practices into a new domain. Senior officials will win the support of lower-ranking officials by presenting PSIE as an incremental information-sharing solution for current failing information-sharing practices. Carrots will work better than sticks to generate support for PSIE. Coerced officials will derail even carefully designed information sharing reforms (Iacovou, Benbasat, and Dexter 1995).

A sequence of small steps to introduce PSIE will generate a self-enforcing change cycle and deepen officials' commitment to PSIE. Officials who lay the groundwork with such small steps will find it easier to take larger ones (Kelman 2004). Officials must postpone judgment regarding PSIE's success. In another U.S. collaborative program (the International Trade Data

System) observers prematurely announced failure only to discover that this project became successful later on (Garson 2005a).

Officials can prepare for PSIE in four ways. First, senior public sector officials must develop a deeper understanding of the potential value of their information assets. The most successful information trading agencies will comprehend which information will interest buyer agencies. Second, officials can invest in BI expertise to harvest insights from their data. Such insights will command prime prices in PSIE. For example, an agency could create an effective scoring index to assist with the problem of overseeing less regulated financial markets, and profit from selling the index to other agencies (GAO 2009i). Third, officials must organize their existing information-sharing programs inventory. Some projects must be terminated. Other technology-first programs such as NIEM could become the technical foundation for a politics-first program such as PSIE. Finally and most important, U.S. senior public officials possess sufficient power and means to experiment with and pilot PSIE-like initiatives even before politicians budget a full-scale PSIE program (Fountain 2013, 108). Public officials must be bold and endowed with the "spirit of experimentation." The best PSIE program will emerge from such trial and error experiments (Fountain 2013, 87).

Advice for Technologists

PSIE technologists must "think big, start small, and scale fast." They can help politicians and officials to find a domain where technical interoperability exists, so that data trading can begin more quickly. Technologists can also keep the PSIE program nimble, frugal, and flexible; top IT performers are often tightfisted while lavish IT spenders rarely post the best results (Carr 2003). Technologists must borrow ideas, concepts, and code from existing programs. They must also integrate scientific and private sector technologies to support the PSIE framework. For example, a Dartmouth College group has already developed an automated negotiations information-sharing system called SCENS. Another research group has already built a prototype of a negotiating software agent (Kraus and Lehmann 1995; Makedon, Ye, and Zhao 2003). Borrowing technical ideas from such projects will enable PSIE architects to build the PSIE framework cheaply and efficiently. PSIE architects can offer prize money to contenders who solve tough semantic challenges. These architects must not attempt to solve all problems. Exchanges, on their own, are efficient problem solvers.

PSIE technologists must quickly create a program pilot. The empirical results of a pilot could overcome skepticism (Yuan et al. 2005). For example, the pilot can simulate trade to examine whether trading blocks emerge in PSIE, and then tweak the PSIE design to address this danger. If the pilot enjoys early success, it might alarm key stakeholders that benefit from the current information-sharing status quo. Nevertheless, the best support for PSIE is the empirical results of a successful program pilot. Technologists must be ready to swiftly expand such programs. Information-sharing program pilots for pressing problems evolve quickly, as evidenced by the twenty-three-month history of the United States Patent and Trademark Office (USPTO)'s Peer-to-Patent program (Noveck 2009).

Technologists can also help politicians measure PSIE's success. To do so, they must partner with officials who are frustrated by current data-exchange routines. These officials will share performance data demonstrating that information is found more quickly and more efficiently in PSIE. PSIE's ultimate measure of success will be the creation and growth of a large community of trading agencies that find useful information in PSIE daily and routinely (Carr 2003; Fulk et al. 2004; Kamal 2006).

Most important, technologists must adopt a humble approach to the task of building PSIE. The PSIE program can employ a similar concept to Google's Deep Web project, in which Google plans to query databases hidden beneath the web's surface in order to index their content (Madhavan et al. 2008; Madhavan et al. 2009). However, PSIE technologists must emphasize the importance of incentivizing all agencies to exchange data, as opposed to Google's approach of indexing databases even if their creators are not cooperative. PSIE technologists will fail unless they can convince all trading agencies that they stand to gain from this new exchange.

Lessons for Citizens

Taxpayers must remember that the current monopolistic interagency information-sharing regime is wasteful and inefficient. Information monopolies inside the public sector are responsible for the failure of e-government programs. PSIE will save taxpayer funds because it will eliminate other information sharing projects. The current U.S. federal IT Dashboard displays no fewer than 636 information-sharing projects. The American federal government invests about $80 billion annually in IT, some of it wasted on failing information sharing projects. Many such projects will no longer be needed once PSIE is operational (Garson 2005b; GAO 2010f; Vann 2005). PSIE is an opportunity for citizens to better their relationship with government. Information will be more accessible and cheaper. Eventually citizens may also enjoy more direct control over their privacy rights with schemes such as Laudon's privacy rights trading exchange (that allows agencies and individuals to trade in privacy rights over information that individuals currently publish on the web free of charge) (Braman 2006; Laudon 1996).

Citizens must pay close attention to the horrific consequences of decades-long public sector information-sharing failures, and demand a resolution to this crisis. Sometimes, agencies mask their inertia as a concern for citizens' privacy. Citizens must demand more action and fewer excuses. The spirited Icelandic database debate (see chapter 7) demonstrates that citizens can become involved in a foundational debate regarding the commoditization of public data and can influence the outcome of this debate.

Information Sharing Lessons from Tel Gezer

In 1902, Frederick Jones Bliss was invited to deliver the prestigious Ely lectures at Union Theological Seminary in New York, his alma mater. Bliss chose the topic of the development of Palestine archeological exploration and his lectures became the cornerstone for this emerging new field. Bliss delivered eight lectures on this topic in 1903. Above all, his lectures celebrated the theme of information sharing among past, present, and future explorers of different periods, ethnicities, and nationalities. Bliss presented his own career as a continuation of a historic trajectory that began with ancient Egyptian explorers. Humbly, he minimized his own role in the field (Hallote 2006, 153–154).

Bliss was the great information-sharing architect of archeological exploration because he developed ingenious ways to incentivize antagonistic stakeholders to talk to each other and share information. Bliss incentivized the Ottoman authorities by helping them build a new museum in Jerusalem to display ancient objects. He used his good relationship with the Ottomans to acquire digging permits for PEF explorers and American Schools of Oriental Research (ASOR) explorers. He diplomatically reconciled dissenting political opinions among Western explorers and facilitated the sharing of information (Hallote 2006).

Bliss also incentivized local explorers by being the first Westerner to write their legacy into the history of excavating Palestine and by inviting them to take the leading role in exploring their country's archeology. He perfected the *bakhshish* system to encourage local *fellahin* workers to find and submit valuable objects for a small monetary bonus (depending on the value of the object). He invented new incentives by becoming the first explorer to employ local women, thus providing subsistence to an entire local village. In gratitude, the local diggers developed interest in his project, shared information with him, displayed courage and skills in the mining tasks Bliss assigned to them, and followed him from site to site. In his diary, Bliss wrote: "Our honest dealing was an astonishment to them and they responded in kind" (Bliss 1894, 179).

Information sharing dominated Bliss's archeological innovations. His breakthrough stratigraphic techniques celebrated to this day empowered mute objects of one civilization to exchange information with the objects of another civilization buried in the same tel. In the new information eco-system that Bliss created around the tel, the present provided clues about the past and the past informed the present.

Ultimately, Bliss succeeded because he understood that information sharing is about nudging people to talk to each other, across geographies, across time, and across national origins. At the end of his first book, Bliss asked all those interested in his work to remember "how much they owe to the loyal labor of the descendants of the old peoples whose cities we have examined" (Bliss 1894, 183).

Bliss concluded the description of his later archeological expedition with a telling anecdote. Several months after he finished digging in the area of Zakariya, Bliss's brother came to visit him. At the time, the digging site was unimpressive as the excavation trenches were filled with dirt (so the locals could plant crops). But Bliss and his brother descended to the nearby village to meet Bliss's former employees. In a most unusual passage, Bliss describes what transpired:

On descending from the *tels* into the village we found an impression of our work, gratifying because it was an impression on human hearts. Our welcome from the work-people, men and women, boys and girls, culminated at the village of Zakariya. No longer did our coming mean gain, good wages, and delectable Bakhshish. We were simply old friends, honored guests bringing nothing, receiving unbounded hospitality. . . . Cordial were the greetings, hearty the inquiries for Mr. Macalister and Yusif, many the humorous reminiscences of past events. I returned to Jerusalem cheered with the thought that at least from the point of view of our relations with the people our campaign had been a success. (Bliss and Macalister 1902, 11)

Bliss remains the ultimate information-sharing architect because he placed people and the relationships among people above all else.

In an identical manner, any information sharing solution begins and ends with people and the willingness of people to share with each other. Minor and small incentives can nudge public officials to engage each other in a more creative discussion about removing information sharing obstacles. To these incentives we must add the other qualities that Bliss displayed: passion for the cause, humanity, humility, mutual respect, ingenuity, and eagerness to learn from others. The public sector information-sharing technologies that we will build on these foundations over the next decade will remain fragile. Yet the new public sector information-sharing ecosystem will endure because it will be based on people rather than on technology.

Appendix: Abbreviations

ABS	Australian Bureau of Statistics (Australia)
AFC	Arkansas Forestry Commission (USA)
AFP	Australian Federal Police (Australia)
ANCOR	Australian National Child Offender Register (Australia)
ANZPAA	Australia New Zealand Policing Advisory Agency (Australia–New Zealand)
AOUSC	Administrative Office of the U.S. Courts (USA)
ASIAS	Aviation Safety Information Analysis and Sharing (USA)
ASOR	American Schools of Oriental Research (USA)
AUSLIG	Australian Land Information Group (Australia)
BBC	British Broadcasting Commission (Britain)
BI	business intelligence
BLM	Bureau of Land Management (USA)
BoA	Bank of America (USA)
BOEMRE	Bureau of Ocean Energy Management, Regulation and Enforcement (USA)
BP	British Petroleum (Britain)
CAIVRS	Credit Alert Verification Reporting System (USA)
CALIF	CrimTrac Audit Log Integration Facility (Australia)
CAP	Cross-Agency Priority (USA)
CBP	Customs and Border Protection (USA)
CBSV	Consent Based Social Security Number Verification Service (USA)
CCDF	Child Care and Development Fund (USA)
CDC	Centers for Disease Control and Prevention (USA)
Census	U.S. Census Bureau (USA)
CEO	chief executive officer
CERCLA	Comprehensive Environmental Response, Compensation, and Liability Act (USA)
CFTC	Commodity Futures Trading Commission (USA)
CIA	Central Intelligence Agency (USA)
CIO	chief information officer

CJS	Criminal Justice System (Britain)
CMS	Centers for Medicare & Medicaid Services (USA)
COINS	Combined Online Information System (Britain)
COBOL	COmmon Business Oriented Language
CRS	Congressional Research Service (USA)
CTO	chief technology officer
DARPA	Defense Advanced Research Projects Agency (USA)
DCDB	Digital Cadastral Database (Australia)
DHS	Department of Homeland Security (USA)
DMF	Death Master File (USA)
DMV	Department of Motor Vehicles (USA)
DOC	Department of Commerce (USA)
DOD	Department of Defense (USA)
DOE	Department of Energy (USA)
DOI	Department of the Interior (USA)
DOJ	Department of Justice (USA)
DOS	Department of State (USA)
DOT	Department of Transportation (USA)
EA	enterprise architecture
EC	European Commission
ED	Department of Education (USA)
EDGAR	Electronic Data Gathering, Analysis and Retrieval (USA)
EHR	Electronic Health Record (USA)
EIEN	Emissions Inventory Exchange Network (USA)
EOP	Executive Office of the President (USA)
EPA	U.S. Environmental Protection Agency (USA)
EU	European Union
FAA	Federal Aviation Administration (USA)
FBI	Federal Bureau of Investigation (USA)
FCC	Federal Communications Commission (USA)
FCEN	Financial Crimes Enforcement Network (USA)
FCS	Future Combat Systems (USA)
FDA	Food and Drug Administration (USA)
FEMA	Federal Emergency Management Agency (USA)
FERC	Federal Energy Regulatory Commission (USA)
FHA	Federal Housing Administration (USA)
FOI	freedom of information
FOIA	Freedom of Information Act (USA)
FTE	full-time equivalent
FUDS	Formerly Used Defense Sites (USA)
G2G	government-to-government
GAO	Government Accountability Office (USA)
GCPR	Government Computer-based Patient Record (USA)

GIS   geographic information system
GPRAMA   Government Performance and Results Act Modernization Act (USA)
GSA   General Services Administration (USA)
HHS   Department of Health and Human Services (USA)
HICL   Health Insurance Contract Language (USA)
HIPAA   Health Insurance Portability and Accountability Act (USA)
HSIN   Homeland Security Information System (USA)
HSOC   Homeland Security Operations Center (USA)
HUD   Department of Housing and Urban Development (USA)
IAEA   International Atomic Energy Agency
IAS   Integrated Acquisition System (USA)
ICTs   information and communication technologies
iEHR   integrated Electronic Health Record (USA)
IGA   intergovernmental agreement
IMF   International Monetary Fund
INS   Immigration and Naturalization Service (USA)
IP   intellectual property
IPAC   Intra-Governmental Payment and Collection (USA)
IRIS   Integrated Risk Information System (USA)
IRS   Internal Revenue Service (USA)
ISE   Information Sharing Environment (USA)
IT   information technology
LIC   Land Information Centre (Australia)
LOC   Library of Congress (USA)
MNPP   Minimum Nationwide Person Profile (Australia)
MoU   Memorandum of Understanding (USA)
NACWA   National Association of Clean Water Agencies (USA)
NAFIS   National Automated Fingerprint Identification System (Australia)
NARA   National Archives and Records Administration (USA)
NASA   National Aeronautics and Space Administration (USA)
NBIC   National Bio-surveillance Integration Center (USA)
NCHRC   National Criminal History Record Checking (Australia)
NCIDD   National Criminal Investigation DNA Database (Australia)
NDWAC   National Drinking Water Advisory Council (USA)
NEPI   National Exchange of Policing Information (Australia)
NHS   National Health Service (Britain)
NIH   National Institutes of Health (USA)
NISA   Nuclear and Industrial Safety Agency (Japan)
NMCA   national mapping cadastral agency
NNI   National Name Index (Australia)
NOAA   National Oceanic and Atmospheric Administration (USA)
NRC   Nuclear Regulatory Commission (USA)
NRT   National Response Team (USA)

NSA	National Security Agency (USA)
NSR	New Source Review (USA)
NSTC	National Science and Technology Council (USA)
NSW	New South Wales (Australia)
NT	Northern Territory (Australia)
NTIS	National Technical Information Service (USA)
NWS	National Weather System (USA)
OD	open data
ODNI	Office of the Drector of National Intelligence (USA)
OECD	Organisation for Economic Co-operation and Development
OFR	Office of Financial Research (USA)
OGD	Open Government Directive (USA)
OGPL	Open Government Platform
OMB	Office of Management and Budget (USA)
OPM	Office of Personnel Management (USA)
OPP	Office of Pesticide Programs (USA)
OPPT	Office of Pollution Prevention and Toxics (USA)
ORD	Office of Research and Development (USA)
OS	open source
OSHA	Occupational Safety and Health Administration (USA)
OSRI	Oil Spill Recovery Institute (USA)
OTC	over-the-counter
PEF	Palestine Exploration Fund (Britain)
PHMSA	Pipeline and Hazardous Materials Safety Administration (USA)
PMIS	public management information systems
PM-ISE	Program Manager of the Information Sharing Environment (USA)
PR	public relations
PSIE	Public Sector Information Exchange
PSMA	Public Sector Mapping Agencies (Australia)
QA	quality assurance
R&D	research and development
RA Svy	Royal Australian Survey Corps (Australia)
RAE	Royal Australian Engineers (Australia)
RINIS	Routing of (Inter)National Information Streams (Holland)
RISS	Regional Information Sharing System (USA)
RTI	right to information
ROSD	Reduced Output Spatial Dataset (Australia)
SACWIS	Statewide Automated Child Welfare Information Systems (USA)
SAR	suspicious activity report
SBA	Small Business Administration (USA)
SBU	Sensitive But Unclassified (USA)
SEC	Securities and Exchange Commission (USA)
SOS	Science-on-Sphere (USA)

SPEEDI	System for Prediction of Environment Emergency Dose Information (Japan)
SRB	solid rocket booster
SSA	Social Security Administration (USA)
SSN	Social Security Number (USA)
TANF	Temporary Assistance for Needy Families (USA)
TEPCO	Tokyo Electric Power Company (Japan)
THP	Tufts Health Plan (USA)
TRI	Toxics Release Inventory (USA)
TSC	Terrorist Screening Center (USA)
TSCA	Toxic Substances Control Act (USA)
TTIC	Terrorist Threat Integration Center (USA)
UK	United Kingdom
UN	United Nations
USBR	U.S. Bureau of Reclamation (USA)
USCIS	U.S. Citizenship and Immigration Services (USA)
USDA	U.S. Department of Agriculture (USA)
USFWS	U.S. Fish and Wildlife Service (USA)
USGS	U.S. Geological Survey (USA)
USNPS	U.S. National Park Service (USA)
USPS	U.S. Postal Service (USA)
USPTO	United States Patent and Trademark Office (USA)
VA	Department of Veteran Affairs (USA)
VAR	value-added reseller
VC	voluntary code
WWI	World War I
WWII	World War II

Notes

1   The Information Sharing Crisis that Does Not Go Away

1. The seven agencies are the U.S. Bureau of Ocean Energy Management, Regulation and Enforcement (BOEMRE), U.S. Environmental Protection Agency (EPA), U.S. National Aeronautics and Space Administration (NASA), U.S. National Oceanic and Atmospheric Administration (NOAA), U.S. National Response Team (NRT), Oil Spill Recovery Institute (OSRI), and Pipeline and Hazardous Materials Safety Administration (PHMSA).

4   How Data Trade Opens Agencies' Closed Doors

1. In 1996, RA Svy was reabsorbed into the Royal Australian Engineers (RAE) from whose ranks it had been created back in 1915. Thereafter, Australia has had nine federal, state, and territory mapping agencies.

References

Accenture. 2001. *eGovernment Leadership: Rhetoric vs Reality—Closing the Gap*. Dublin: Accenture. http://www.epractice.eu/files/media/media_846.pdf (accessed December 10, 2011).

Accenture. 2004. *eGovernment Leadership: High Performance, Maximum Value*. Dublin: Accenture. http://access-to-law.com/elaw/readings/gove_egov_value.pdf (accessed October 23, 2013).

Adams, Rachel. 2005. "'Going to Canada': The Politics and Poetics of Northern Exodus." *Yale Journal of Criticism* 18 (2): 409–433.

Agnew, Jean-Christophe. 2003. "The Give-and-Take of Consumer Culture." In *Commodifying Everything: Relationships of the Market*, ed. S. Strasser, 11–41. New York: Routledge.

Akbulut, Asli Yagmur. 2003. "An Investigation of the Factors that Influence Electronic Information Sharing between State and Local Agencies." PhD diss., Louisiana State University.

Akhavan, P., M. Jafari, and M. Fathian. 2006. "Critical Success Factors of Knowledge Management Systems: A Multi-Case Analysis." *European Business Review* 18 (2): 97–113.

Akiyama, Nobumasa, Heigo Sato, Kaoru Naito, Yosuke Naoi, and Tadahiro Katsuta. 2012. *The Fukushima Nuclear Accident and Crisis Management—Lessons for Japan-U.S. Alliance Cooperation*. Tokyo: The Sasakawa Peace Foundation. http://www.spf.org/jpus/img/investigation/book_fukushima.pdf (accessed October 25, 2013).

Alavi, Maryam, and Dorothy E. Leidner. 2001. "Review: Knowledge Management and Knowledge Management Systems: Conceptual Foundations and Research Issues." *Management Information Systems Quarterly* 25 (1): 107–136.

Ammirati, Sean. 2011. "Infographic: Data Deluge—8 Zettabytes of Data by 2015." *ReadWrite.com*. http://www.dzone.com/links/infographic_data_deluge_8_zettabytes_of_data_by_2.html (accessed January 20, 2014).

Anderlik, Mary R., and Mark A. Rothstein. 2001. "Privacy and Confidentiality of Genetic Information: What Rules for the New Science?" *Annual Review of Genomics and Human Genetics* 2:401–433.

Anderson, Chris. 2008. "The End of Theory: The Data Deluge Makes the Scientific Method Obsolete?" *Wired*, June 23. http://www.wired.com/science/discoveries/magazine/16-07/pb_theory (accessed January 20, 2014).

Anderson, Elizabeth. 1993. *Value in Ethics and Economics*. Cambridge, MA: Harvard University Press.

Andrews, Lori, and Dorothy Nelkin. 1998. "Whose Body Is It Anyway? Disputes over Body Tissue in a Biotechnology Age." *Lancet* 351:53–57.

Anteby, Michel. 2010. "Markets, Morals, and Practices of Trade: Jurisdictional Disputes in the U.S. Commerce in Cadavers." *Administrative Science Quarterly* 55 (4): 606–638.

Appadurai, Arjun. 1986. "Introduction: Commodities and the Politics of Value." In *The Social Life of Things: Commodities in Cultural Perspective*, ed. A. Appadurai, 3–64. Cambridge: Cambridge University Press.

Appleyard, Melissa M. 1996. "How Does Knowledge Flow? Interfirm Patterns in the Semiconductor Industry." *Strategic Management Journal* 17:137–154.

Ardichvill, A., V. Page, and T. Wentling. 2003. "Motivation and Barriers to Participation in Virtual Knowledge Sharing Communities of Practice." *Journal of Knowledge Management* 7 (1): 64–77.

Argote, Linda, and Paul Ingram. 2000. "Knowledge Transfer: A Basis for Competitive Advantage in Firms." *Organizational Behavior and Human Decision Processes* 82 (1): 150–169.

Ariely, Dan. 2010. *The Upside of Irrationality: The Unexpected Benefits of Defying Logic at Work and at Home*. New York: HarperCollins.

Arkansas Forestry Commission (AFC), United States Department of Agriculture (USDA), Arkansas Natural Resources Conservation Service (NRCS), Arkansas Forestry Association (AFA), and American Tree Farm System (ATFS). 2011. *Memorandum of Understanding between the Arkansas Forestry Commission, and the United States Department of Agriculture Natural Resources Conservation Service and the Arkansas Forestry Association, American Tree Farm System*. Washington, DC: Natural Resources Conservation Service.

Australia League of Rights. 2001. "On Target." Last modified May 11. http://www.alor.org/Volume37/Vol37No17.htm (accessed January 20, 2014).

Austrian, Geoffrey D. 1982. *Herman Hollerith, Forgotten Giant of Information Processing*. New York: Columbia University Press.

Avanade. 2012. "Global Survey: Is Big Data Producing Big Returns?" Seattle, WA: Avanade. http://www.avanade.com/Documents/Research and Insights/avanade-big-data-executive-summary-2012.pdf (accessed August 25, 2013).

Ayers, Ian. 2007. *Super Crunchers: Why Thinking-by-Numbers Is the New Way to Be Smart*. New York: Bantam Books.

Bajaj, A., and S. Ram. 2003. "IAIS: A Methodology to Enable Inter-Agency Information Sharing in E-Government." *Journal of Database Management* 14 (4): 59–80.

Balla, Steven J., and John R. Wright. 2001. "Interest Groups, Advisory Committees, and Congressional Control of the Bureaucracy." *American Journal of Political Science* 45 (4): 799–812.

Bamblett, M., H. Bath, and R. Roseby. 2010. "Growing Them Strong, Together: Promoting the Safety and Wellbeing of the Northern Territory's Children." Summary Report, Board of Inquiry into the Child Protection System in the Northern Territory 2010. Northern Territory Government, Darwin.

Bandt, William D. 1998. "The Digital Utility: Premonitions of the Future of the Last Great Monopoly." In *The Future of the Electronic Marketplace*, ed. D. Leebaert, 115–143. Cambridge, MA: MIT Press.

Bannister, Frank, and Regina Connolly. 2011. "The Trouble with Transparency: A Critical Review of Openness in e-Government." *Policy & Internet* 8 (3): 1–30.

Bartal, Y., Rica Gonen, and Noam Nisan. 2003. "Incentive Compatible Multi-Unit Combinatorial Auctions." In *Proceedings of the Theoretical Aspects of Rationality and Knowledge (TARK)*, ed. M. Tennenholtz, 72–87. New York: ACM.

Barton, Mike. 2012. "Webcast (Thursday): Obama Goes Big on Big Data." *Wired*, March 27. http://www.wired.com/insights/2012/03/obama-big-data (accessed January 20, 2014).

Barzelay, Michael, and Linda Kaboolian. 1990. "Structural Metaphors and Public Management Education." *Journal of Policy Analysis and Management* 9 (4): 599–610.

Bass, Gary, Danielle Brian, Meredith Fuchs, Ari Schwartz, Patrice McDermott, Ellen Miller, and Anne Weismann. 2010. "Letter Encouraging the Administration to Improve Its Open Government Efforts." Last modified February 3. http://www.pogo.org/our-work/letters/2010/gs-og-20100203.html?print=t (accessed January 20, 2014).

Basu, Arnab K., Nancy H. Chau, and Ulrike Grote. 2006. "Guaranteed Manufactured Without Child Labor: The Economics of Consumer Boycotts, Social Labeling and Trade Sanctions." *Review of Development Economics* 10 (3): 466–491.

Basu, Kaushik. 1999. "Child Labor: Cause, Consequence, and Cure, with Remarks on International Labor Standards." *Journal of Economic Literature* 37 (3): 1083–1119.

Basu, Kaushik, and Pham Hoang Van. 1998. "The Economics of Child Labor." *American Economic Review* 88 (3): 412–427.

Bates, Jo. 2012. "This Is What Modern Deregulation Looks Like": Co-optation and Contestation in the Shaping of the UK's Open Government Data Initiative." *Journal of Community Informatics* 8 (2). http://ci-journal.net/index.php/ciej/article/view/845/916 (accessed March 12, 2014).

Bauerlein, Valerie. 2011. "How to Measure a Storm's Fury One Breakfast at a Time." *Wall Street Journal*, September 1. http://online.wsj.com/article/SB1000142405311190 4716604576542460736605364.html (accessed January 20, 2014).

Bawn, Kathleen. 1995. "Political Control versus Expertise: Congressional Choices About Administrative Procedures." *American Political Science Review* 89 (1): 62–73.

Bayly, C. A. 1986. "The Origins of Swadeshi (Home Industry): Cloth and Indian Society, 1700-1930." In *The Social Life of Things: Commodities in Cultural Perspective*, ed. A. Appadurai, 285–322. Cambridge: Cambridge University Press.

BBC News. 2013. "NHS IT System One of 'Worst Fiascos Ever,' Say MPs." Last modified September 18. http://www.bbc.co.uk/news/uk-politics-24130684 (accessed January 20, 2014).

Beath, Cynthia Mathis. 1991. "Supporting the Information Technology Champion." *Management Information Systems Quarterly* 15 (3): 355–372.

Becker, Gary S., and Julio Jorge Elias. 2007. "Introducing Incentives in the Market for Live and Cadaveric Organ Donations." *Journal of Economic Perspectives* 21 (3): 3–24.

Bekkers, V. J. J. M. 2000. "Information and Communication Technology and the Redefinition of the Functional and Normative Boundaries of Government." In *Governance In Modern Society*, ed. O. Van Heffen, 257–278. Dordrecht: Kluwer Academic Publishers.

Belfiore, Michael. 2009. *The Department of Mad Scientists: How DARPA Is Remaking Our World, from the Internet to Artificial Limbs.* New York: Harper-Collins Publishers.

Bellamy, Christine, and John Taylor. 1996. "New Information and Communications Technologies and Institutional Change: The Case of the UK Criminal Justice System." *International Journal of Public Sector Management* 9 (4): 51–69.

Bergeron, Heather Ellen, Chris Easton, Kunjan Jhaveri, Andrew Kennedy, James Kennedy, Jayant Pai, Alon Peled, Simone Lemos Pringle, Benjamin Sprecher, and John Trustman. 2003a. "Processing Transactions Using a Structured Natural Language." Last modified September 5. http://appft1.uspto.gov/netacgi/nph-Parser?Sect1=PTO1 &Sect2=HITOFF&d=PG01&p=1&u=/netahtml/PTO/srchnum.html&r=1&f=G&l=50 &s1=20050033583.PGNR.&OS=DN/20050033583&RS=DN/20050033583 (accessed January 21, 2014).

Bergeron, Heather Ellen, Chris Easton, Kunjan Jhaveri, James Kennedy, Eugene Krylov, John Morris, Simone Lemos Pringle, Benjamin Sprecher, John Trustman, and Andre Yoshida. 2003b. "Processing Transactions Using a Semantic Network." Last modified September 5. http://appft1.uspto.gov/netacgi/nph-Parser?Sect1=PTO1 &Sect2=HITOFF&d=PG01&p=1&u=/netahtml/PTO/srchnum.html&r=1&f=G&l=50 &s1=20050010428.PGNR.&OS=DN/20050010428&RS=DN/20050010428 (accessed January 21, 2014).

Bergeron, Heather Ellen, Chris Easton, Kunjan Jhaveri, James Kennedy, Eugene Krylov, Simone Lemos Pringle, Benjamin Sprecher, John Trustman, and Andre Yoshida. 2003c. "Configuring a Semantic Network to Process Transactions." Last modified September 5. http://appft1.uspto.gov/netacgi/nph-Parser?Sect1=PTO1&Sec t2=HITOFF&d=PG01&p=1&u=/netahtml/PTO/srchnum.html&r=1&f=G&l=50 &s1=20050010394.PGNR.&OS=DN/20050010394&RS=DN/20050010394 (accessed January 21, 2014).

Bergeron, Heather Ellen, Chris Easton, Andrew Kennedy, James Kennedy, Doug Koen, Eugene Krylov, John Morris, Jayant Pai, Alon Peled, Simone Lemos Pringle, John Trustman, Lyubomir Vujisic, and Andre Yoshida. 2003d. "Processing Health Care Transactions Using a Semantic Network." Last modified October 7. http:// appft1.uspto.gov/netacgi/nph-Parser?Sect1=PTO1&Sect2=HITOFF&d=PG01&p=1 &u=/netahtml/PTO/srchnum.html&r=1&f=G&l=50&s1=20060173672.PGNR.&OS =DN/20060173672&RS=DN/20060173672 (accessed January 21, 2014).

Berkes, Howard. 2013. "Amid Data Controversy, NSA Builds Its Biggest Data Farm." Last modified June 10. http://www.npr.org/2013/06/10/190160772/amid -data-controversy-nsa-builds-its-biggest-data-farm (accessed January 21, 2014).

Berners-Lee, Tim. 2010. "The Year Open Data Went Worldwide." Last modi- fied in March. http://www.ted.com/talks/tim_berners_lee_the_year_open_data_went _worldwide.html (accessed January 21, 2014).

Berners-Lee, Tim. 2012. "Sir Tim Berners-Lee: Raw Data, Now!" *Wired*. Last modified November 9. http://www.wired.co.uk/news/archive/2012-11/09/raw-data (accessed January 21, 2014).

The Bichard Inquiry. 2004. *The Bichard Inquiry Report*. HC653. London: HMSO.

Biddick, Michael, and Wyatt Kash. 2013. *2014 Federal Government IT Priorities*. Washington, DC: Information Week Reports. http://reports.informationweek.com/ abstract/104/11175/Government/Research:-2014-Federal-Government-IT-Priorities .html?cid=nl_analyt_iwkrnwsl201309024&wc=4 (accessed September 25, 2013).

Bingham, Lisa Blomgren, and Susanna Foxworthy. 2012. "Collaborative Governance and Collaborating Online: The Open Government Initiative in the United States." Paper presented at the Converging and Conflicting Trends in the Public Administra- tion of the U.S., Europe, and Germany, The German Research Institute for Public

Administration Speyer (GRIP), and the School of Public and Environmental Affairs (SPEA) of Indiana University, July 19 and 20.

Blackley, Michelle. 2003. "'Eggs for Sale': The Latest Controversy in Reproductive Technology: Couples Are Paying Lofty Fees to Egg Donors with the Perfect Combination of Brains and Beauty." *USA Today*, July. http://www.thefreelibrary.com/%22Eggs+for+sale%22:+the+latest+controversy+in+reproductive+technology:…-a0104971305 (accessed February 21, 2011).

Bliss, Frederick Jones. 1894. *A Mound of Many Cities or Tell El Hesy Excavated*. London: A. P. Watt and Son.

Bliss, Frederick Jones, and R. A. Stewart Macalister. 1902. *Excavations in Palestine During the Years 1898–1900*. London: Palestine Exploration Fund.

Bollier, David. 2010. "The Promise and Peril of Big Data." The Aspen Institute. http://www.aspeninstitute.org/publications/promise-peril-big-data (accessed January 22, 2014).

Bonometti, Robert J., Raymond W. Smith, and Patrick E. White. 1998. "The Walls Coming Down: Interoperatbility Opens the Electronic City." In *The Future of the Electronic Marketplace*, ed. D. Leebaert, 265–301. Cambridge, MA: MIT Press.

Bowman, Diana, and Graeme Hodge. 2008. "A Big Regulatory Tool-Box for a Small Technology." *NanoEthics* 2 (2): 193–207.

Boyd, Danah, and Kate Crawford. 2012. "Critical Questions for Big Data." *Information Communication and Society* 15 (5): 662–679.

Bozeman, Barry. 1987. *All Organizations Are Public*. San Francisco, CA: Jossey-Bass Inc. Publishers.

Bozeman, Barry, and Stuart Bretschneider. 1986. "Public Management Information Systems: Theory and Prescription." *Public Administration Review* 46:475–487.

Braman, Sandra. 2006. *Change of State—Information, Policy, and Power*. Cambridge, MA: MIT Press.

Brand, Stewart, and Matt Herron. 1985. "'Keep Designing': How the Information Economy Is Being Created and Shaped by the Hacker Ethic." *Whole Earth Review* (May): 44.

Branscomb, Anne Wells. 1994. *Who Owns Information? From Privacy to Public Access*. New York: Basic Books.

Braudel, Fernand. 1992. *Civilization and Capitalism, 15th–18th Century: The Wheels of Commerce*. Berkeley: University of California Press.

Bright, Martin, Antony Barnett, Burhan Wazir, Tony Thompson, Peter Beaumont, Stuart Jeffries, Ed Vulliamy, Kate Connolly, Giles Tremlett, and Rory Carroll. 2001.

"The Secret War—Part 2." *The Observer*, September 30. http://www.guardian.co.uk/world/2001/sep/30/terrorism.afghanistan7 (accessed November 4, 2013).

Bronk, Chris, and Tiffany Smith. 2010. "Diplopedia Imagined: Building State's Diplomacy Wiki." Paper presented at the 2010 International Symposium on Collaborative Technologies and Systems, Chicago, IL, May 17–21.

Brown, J. Robert, Jr. 1995. "Order from Disorder: The Development of the Russian Securities Markets." *University of Pennsylvania Journal of Internatonal Business Law* 15 (4): 509–558.

Burkert, Herbert. 2004. "The Mechanics of Public Sector Information." In *Public Sector Information in the Digital Age: Between Markets, Public Management and Citizens' Rights*, ed. G. Aichholzer and H. Burkert, 3–19. Northhampton, MA: Edward Elgar.

Business Wire. 2002. "deNovis Named Rookie of the Year Finalist in MIT Sloan eBusiness Awards." *Business Wire*, February 21. http://wires.vlex.com/vid/denovis-rookie-mit-sloan-ebusiness-54402732 (accessed January 21, 2014).

Business Wire. 2003. "deNovis Transaction Software Selected by Federal Agency for Overhaul of National Medicare Program." *Business Wire*, February 5. http://www.thefreelibrary.com/deNovis+Transaction+Software+Selected+by+Federal+Agency+for+Overhaul...-a097255446 (accessed January 21, 2014).

Campbell, Archie. 1995. *Bernardo Investigation Review—Summary*. Ontario, Canada: Solicitor General.

Capaccio, Tony. 2006. "Pentagon Takes Minimal Cut Out of Boeing Program." *Seattle PI*, January 24. http://www.seattlepi.com/business/article/Pentagon-takes-minimal-cut-out-of-Boeing-program-1193748.php (accessed January 21, 2014).

Caribbean Information Society Portal. 2010. "Haiti and Beyond: Getting it Right in Crisis Information Management." Last modified in March. http://ict4peace.org/haiti-and-beyond-getting-it-right-in-crisis-information-management (accessed January 21, 2014).

Carr, David F., and Edward Cone. 2002. "The Ugly History of Tool Development at the FAA." Last modified April 9. http://www.baselinemag.com/c/a/Projects-Processes/The-Ugly-History-of-Tool-Development-at-the-FAA (accessed January 21, 2014).

Carr, Nicholas. 2003. IT Doesn't Matter. *Harvard Business Review* 81 (5): 41–49.

Cate, Fred H. 1997. *Privacy in the Information Age*. Washington, DC: Brookings Institution Press.

Central Intelligence Agency (CIA). 2009. "Intellipedia Celebrates Third Anniversary with a Successful Challenge." Last modified April 29. https://www.cia.gov/news-information/featured-story-archive/intellipedia-celebrates-third-anniversary.html (accessed January 21, 2014).

Chadwick, Ruth. 1999. "The Icelandic Database: Do Modern Times Need Modern Sagas?" *British Medical Journal* 319 (7207): 441–444.

Chavez, A., D. Dreilinger, R. Guttman, and P. Maes. 1997. "A Real-Life Experiment in Creating an Agent Marketplace." In *Software Agents and Soft Computing: Towards Enhancing Machine Intelligence*, ed. H. S. Nwana and N. Azarmi, 160–179. Berlin, Heidelberg: Springer.

Chin, Michelle L. 2004. "Administrative Renewal: Reorganization Commissions in the 20th Century." *Presidential Studies Quarterly* 34 (3): 704–706.

Chow, Chee W., Graeme L. Harrison, Jill L. McKinnon, and Anne Wu. 1999. "Cultural Influences on Informal Information Sharing in Chinese and Anglo-American Organizations: an Exploratory Study." *Accounting, Organizations and Society* 24:561–582.

Clarke, Edward H. 1971. "Multipart Pricing of Public Goods." *Public Choice* 11 (1): 17–33.

Clarkson, Gavin, Trond E. Jacobsen, and Archer L. Batcheller. 2007. "Information Asymmetry and Information Sharing." *Government Information Quarterly* 24:827–839.

Coase, Roland. 1960. "The Problem of Social Cost." *Journal of Law & Economics* 3:1–44.

Coglianese, Cary. 2009. "The Transparency President? The Obama Administration and Open Government." *Governance: An International Journal of Policy and Administration* 22 (4): 529–544.

Cohen, Lloyd R. 1989. "Increasing the Supply of Transplant Organs: The Virtues of a Futures Market." *George Washington Law Review* 58 (1): 11–52.

Cohen, Noam. 2008. "An Internal Wiki that's Not Classified." *New York Times*, August 4. http://www.nytimes.com/2008/08/04/business/media/04link.html?pagewanted =print (accessed November 3, 2013).

Cole, Roland J. 2012. "Some Observations on the Practice of Open Data as Opposed to Its Promise." *Journal of Community Informatics* 8 (2). http://ci-journal.net/index .php/ciej/article/view/920/917 (accessed March 11, 2014).

Columbia Accident Investigation Board. 2003. *Report*. Vol. 1. Washington, DC: U.S. Government Printing Office.

Committee on Continued Review of the Tax Systems Modernization of the Internal Revenue Service, Commission on Physical Sciences Mathematics and Applications, and National Research Council. 1996. "Continued Review of the Tax Systems Modernization of the Internal Revenue Service." Washington, DC: National Academies Press. http://www.nap.edu/openbook.php?record_id=10771 (accessed September 24, 2013).

Conitzer, Vincent, and Tuomas Sandholm. 2004. "Self-Interested Automated Mechanism Design and Implications for Optimal Combinatorial Auctions." Paper presented at the 5th ACM conference on electronic commerce, New York, May 17–20.

Connolly, Allison. 2003. "Startup deNovis Secures $50M Deal, Charts Course." *Boston Business Journal* 23 (8): 7.

Constant, D., S. Kiesler, and L. Sproull. 1994. "What's Mine Is Ours, or Is It: A Study of Attitudes about Information Sharing." *Information Systems Research* 5 (4): 400–421.

Cooper, Michael H., and Anthony J. Culyer. 1968. *The Price of Blood: An Economic Study of the Charitable and Commercial Principles.* Norwich: The Soman-Wherry Press. http://trove.nla.gov.au/work/21088182?q&versionId=45833703 (accessed October 23, 2013).

Cramton, Peter, Yoav Shoham, and Richard Steinberg. 2006. *Combinatorial Auctions.* Cambridge, MA: MIT Press.

Crespi, Gregory S. 1994. "Overcoming the Legal Obstacles to the Creation of a Futures Market in Bodily Organs." *Ohio State Law Journal* 55 (1): 1–78.

CrimTrac. 2001. *Annual Report 2000–2001.* Canberra: Commonwealth of Australia.

CrimTrac. 2002. *Annual Report 2001–2002.* Canberra: Commonwealth of Australia.

CrimTrac. 2003. *Annual Report 2002–2003.* Canberra: Commonwealth of Australia.

CrimTrac. 2004. *Annual Report 2003–2004.* Canberra: Commonwealth of Australia.

CrimTrac. 2005. *Annual Report 2004–2005.* Canberra: Commonwealth of Australia.

CrimTrac. 2006a. *Annual Report 2005–2006.* Canberra: Commonwealth of Australia.

CrimTrac. 2006b. *Memorandum of Understanding: Between New South Wales Police, Victoria Police, Queensland Police, Western Australia Police, South Australia Police, Northern Territory Police, Tasmania Police, ACT Policing, Australian Federal Police and The CrimTrac Agency.* Canberra: Commonwealth of Australia.

CrimTrac. 2007. *Annual Report 2006–2007.* Canberra: Commonwealth of Australia.

CrimTrac. 2008. *Annual Report 2007–2008.* Canberra: Commonwealth of Australia.

CrimTrac. 2009. *Annual Report 2008–2009.* Canberra: Commonwealth of Australia.

CrimTrac. 2010. *Annual Report 2009–2010.* Canberra: Commonwealth of Australia.

CrimTrac. 2011. *Annual Report 2010–2011.* Canberra: Commonwealth of Australia.

Culnan, Mary J., and Pamela K. Armstrong. 1999. "Information Privacy Concerns, Procedural Fairness, and Impersonal Trust: An Empirical Investigation." *Organization Science* 10 (1): 104–115.

Danko, Stephen. 2011. "Changes to the Public Death Master File (DMF) and the Social Security Death Index (SSDI)." *Steve's Genealogy Blog*, November 1. http://stephendanko.com/blog/15164 (accessed January 21, 2014).

Data.Gov. 2010. "Open Government Directive Agency Datasets." Last modified November 2, 2013. http://www.data.gov (accessed January 21, 2014).

Davenport, Thomas H., and Laurence Prusak. 1998. *Working Knowledge—How Organizations Manage What They Know*. Boston, MA: Harvard Business School Press.

Davenport, William H. 1986. "Two Kinds of Value in the Eastern Solomon Islands Among the Muria Gonds." In *The Social Life of Things: Commodities in Cultural Perspective*, ed. A. Appadurai, 95–109. Cambridge: Cambridge University Press.

Davis, Shelley. 1997. *Unbridled Power—Inside the Secret Culture of the IRS*. New York: Harper Business.

Dawes, Sharon S. 1996. "Interagency Information Sharing: Expected Benefits, Manageable Risks." *Journal of Policy Analysis and Management* 15 (3): 377–394.

Dawes, Sharon S., and Meghan E. Cook. 2006. "Intergovernmental Digital Government through G2G Relationships and Applications." In *Encyclopedia of Digital Government*, ed. A.-V. Anttiroiko and M. Malkia, 1114–1119. Hershey, PA: IGI Global.

Dawes, Sharon S., and Lise Prefontaine. 2003. "Understanding New Models of Collaboration for Delivering Government Services." *Communications of the ACM* 46 (1): 40–42.

De Ville de Goyet, Claude, Juan Pablo Sarmiento, and François Grünewald. 2011. Health Response to the Earthquake in Haiti January 2010: Lessons to Be Learned for the Next Massive Sudden-Onset Disaster. Washington, DC: Pan American Health Organization (PAHO), Regional Office of the World Health Organization.

Dean, Jeffrey, and Sanjay Ghemawat. 2008. "MapReduce: Simplified Data Processing on Large Clusters." *Communications of the ACM—50th Anniversary Issue: 1958–2008* 51 (1): 107–113.

Dever, William G. 1967. "Excavations at Gezer." *Biblical Archaeologist* 30:47–62.

Dever, William G. 1998. *Gezer—A Crossroad in Ancient Israel*. Tel Aviv: Hakibbutz Hameuchad Publishing House, Israel Exploration Society, and Israel Antiquities Authority.

Dever, William G. 1971. "Further Excavations at Gezer." *Biblical Archaeologist* 34 (4): 94–132.

Dever, William G. 1973. "The Gezer Fortifications and the 'High Place': An Illustration of Stratigraphic Methods and Problems." *Palestine Exploration Quarterly* 105: 61–70.

Dirks, K. T., and D. L. Ferrin. 2001. "The Role of Trust in Organizational Settings." *Organization Science* 12:450–467.

Dixon, Michael. 2010. "The Evolution of Data Automation, and Its Importance to the Australian Spatial Data Infrastructure." In *Proceedings of the FIG Congress 2010: Facing the Challenges—Building the Capacity*, ed. R. Staiger. Sydney: FIG.

Dixon, Nancy M., and Laura A. McNamara. 2008. *Our Experience with Intellipedia: An Ethnographic Study at the Defense Intelligence Agency*. Maxwell AFB, AL: Air University. http://conversation-matters.typepad.com/Intellipedia_Study.pdf (accessed October 23, 2013).

Dizard, Wilson P. 2002. "White House Promotes Data Sharing." *GCN*, August 23. http://gcn.com/articles/2002/08/23/white-house-promotes-data-sharing.aspx (accessed January 21, 2014).

Dizard, Wilson P. 2005. "DHS, NASA Sign Interagency Technology Pact." *GCN*, December 7. http://gcn.com/articles/2005/12/07/dhs-nasa-sign-interagency -technology-pact.aspx?sc_lang=en (accessed January 21, 2014).

Dizard, Wilson P. 2006. "Spy Agencies Adapt Social Software, Federated Search Tools." *GCN*, September 22. http://gcn.com/Articles/2006/09/22/Spy-agencies -adapt-social-software-federated-search-tools.aspx?Page=1 (accessed March 12, 2014).

Drucker, Peter Ferdinand. 2006. *Classic Drucker*. Boston, MA: Harvard Business School Publishing Company.

Dyer, J. H., and W. Chu. 2003. "The Role of Trustworthiness in Reducing Transaction Costs and Improving Performance: Empirical Evidence from the United States, Japan, and Korea." *Organization Science* 14 (1): 57–68.

Eaton, Kit. 2011. "How Hackers Stole 24,000 Files from the Pentagon." Last modified July 15. http://www.fastcompany.com/1767327/how-hackers-stole-24000-files -pentagon (accessed January 21, 2014).

Economist. 2008. "The Electronic Bureaucrat." *The Economist*, February 16.

Economist. 2010a. "The Data Deluge." *The Economist*, February 27.

Economist. 2010b. "Of Governments and Geeks." *The Economist*, February 6.

Economist. 2012. "The Best Disinfectant: Hopes of 'Open Government' Under Barack Obama Have Been Only Partly Fulfilled." *The Economist*, May 26.

ECX. 2013. "European Climate Exchange." Last modified November 2. https://www .tradingtechnologies.com/connectivity/europe/ecx/ (accessed January 21, 2014).

Ellerman, Denny, and Paul L. Joskow. 2008. *The European Union's Emissions Trading System in Perspective*. http://www.c2es.org/docUploads/EU-ETS-In-Perspective-Report .pdf (accessed January 21, 2014).

Epstein, David, and Sharyn O'Halloran. 1999. *Delegating Powers: A Transaction Cost Politics Approach to Policy Making under Separate Powers.* Cambridge: Cambridge University Press.

Erkkila, Tero. 2012. *Government Transparency—Impacts and Unintended Consequences.* London: Palgrave Macmillan.

European Commission (EC). 2013. "The EU Endorses a New PSI Directive." Brussels: European Commission. http://www.epsiplatform.eu/content/eu-endorses-new-psi-directive (accessed January 20, 2014).

EU ETS. 2013. "The EU Emissions Trading System." Last modified November 2. http://ec.europa.eu/clima/policies/ets/index_en.htm (accessed January 21, 2014).

Evans, A. M., and A. Campos. 2013. "Open Government Initiatives: Challenges of Citizen Participation." *Journal of Policy Analysis and Management* 32 (1): 172–185.

Evans, Donna, and David C. Yen. 2006. "E-Government: Evolving Relationship of Citizens and Government, Domestic, and International Development." *Government Information Quarterly* 23:207–235.

Ewusi-Mensah, Kweku. 2003. *Software Development Failures: Anatomy of Abandoned Projects.* Cambridge, MA: MIT Press.

Fader, Sonia. 2014. "Sperm Banking: A Reproductive Resource." Last modified November 2. http://www.cryobank.com/Learning-Center/Sperm-Banking-101/Sperm-Banking-History (accessed January 21, 2014).

Falk, Armin, and Nora Szech. 2013. "Morals and Markets." *Science* 340 (6133): 707–711.

Fawcett, Stanley E., Cynthia Wallin, Chad Allred, and Gregory Magnan. 2009. "Supply Chain Information-Sharing: Benchmarking a Proven Path." *Benchmarking: An International Journal* 16 (2): 222–246.

Federal Bureau of Investigation (FBI). 2007. *FBI Hijackers Timeline Report.* Washington, DC: Federal Bureau of Investigation.

Federal Computer Week. 2011. "DOD, VA Recalibrate the Model for Health Records." *FCW,* November 30. http://fcw.com/microsites/2011/insights-health-it/02-dod-va-ehrs.aspx?s=fcwdaily_201211 (accessed January 21, 2014).

Fioretti, Marco. 2012. "Open Data: Emerging Trends, Issues and Best Practices—A Research Project about Openness of Public Data in EU Local Administration." Pisa: Laboratory of Economics and Management of Scuola Superiore Saint Anna. http://www.lem.sssup.it/WPLem/odos/odos_2.html (accessed August 13, 2013).

Fisher, Andrew B. 2003. "Marketing Community: State Reform of Indian Village Property and Expenditure in Colonial Mexico, 1775–1810." In *Commodifying Everything: Relationships of the Market,* ed. S. Strasser, 215–234. New York: Routledge.

Flanagin, A. J., P. Monge, and J. Fulk. 2001. "The Value of Formative Investment in Organizational Federations." *Human Communication Research* 27 (1): 69–93.

Florini, Ann M. 2004. "Behind Closed Doors: Governmental Transparency Gives Way to Secrecy." *Harvard International Review* 26 (1): 18–21.

Foley, John. 2011. "Pentagon Unveils Enterprise IT Strategy." *InformationWeek Government*, December 15. http://www.informationweek.com/regulations/pentagon -unveils-enterprise-it-strategy/d/d-id/1101872? (accessed January 21, 2014).

Fountain, Jane E. 2007. "Challenges to Organizational Change: Multi-Level Integrated Information Structures (MIIS)." In *Governance and Information Technology: From Electronic Government to Information Government*, ed. V. Mayer-Schönberger and D. Lazer, 63–93. Cambridge, MA: MIT Press.

Fountain, Jane E. 2013. *The GPRA Modernization Act Of 2010: Examining Constraints to, and Providing Tools for, Cross-Agency Collaboration*. Amherst, MA: Administrative Conference of the United States. http://www.acus.gov/report/gpra-modernization -act-2010-examining-constraints-and-providing-tools-cross-agency (accessed October 3, 2013).

Frederickson, George H. 1971. "Organization Theory and New Public Administration." In *Towards a New Public Administration: The Minnowbrook Perspective*, ed. F. E. Marini, 309–331. Scranton, PA: Chandler Publishing Company.

Fulk, Janet, Rebecca Heino, Andrew J. Flanagin, Peter R. Monge, and François Bar. 2004. "A Test of the Individual Action Model for Organizational Information Commons." *Organization Science* 15 (5): 569–585.

Interbrand. 2014. *Best Global Brands 2013*. New York: Interbrand. http://www .interbrand.com/en/best-global-brands/2013/Best-Global-Brands-2013.aspx (accessed January 20, 2014).

Gallagher, Michael. 2009. *Statement of the Deputy Commissioner for Budget Finance and Management Joint Oversight Hearing on the Recovery Act Project to Replace the Social Security Administration's National Computer Center*. Washington, DC: U.S. Government Printing Office. http://www.ssa.gov/legislation/testimony_121509.html (accessed January 21, 2014).

Gantz, John, and David Reinsel. 2010. *The Digital Universe Decade—Are You Ready?* Framingham, MA: IDC. http://www.emc.com/collateral/analyst-reports/idc-digital -universe-are-you-ready.pdf (accessed August 25, 2013).

Gantz, John, and David Reinsel. 2011. *Extracting Value from Chaos*. Framingham, MA: IDC. http://www.emc.com/collateral/analyst-reports/idc-extracting-value-from -chaos-ar.pdf (accessed August 25, 2013).

Gantz, John, and David Reinsel. 2012. *The Digital Universe in 2020: Big Data, Bigger Digital Shadows, and Biggest Growth in the Far East*. Framingham, MA: IDC. http:// idcdocserv.com/1414 (accessed October 23, 2013).

Garnett, James L., and Alexander Kouzmin. 2007. "Communicating throughout Katrina: Competing and Complementary Conceptual Lenses on Crisis Communication." *Public Administration Review* 67, Special Issue: 171–188.

Garson, David. 2005a. "Information Systems, Politics, and Government: Leading Theoretical Perspectives." In *Handbook of Public Information Systems*, ed. G. D. Garson, 665–688. Boca Raton, FL: Marcel Dekker.

Garson, David. 2005b. "Public Information Systems in the 21st Century." In *Handbook of Public Information Systems*, ed. G. D. Garson, 3–10. Boca Raton, FL: Marcel Dekker.

Garvey, Pat, and Molly O'Neill. 2003. *Environmental Information Exchange Network*. Washington, DC: Environmental Protection Agency.

Gates Foundation. 2013. "Increasing Interoperability of Social Good Data: Grand Challenges Explorations Round 11." Last modified in March. http://www .grandchallenges.org/Explorations/Topics/Pages/SocialDataInteroperability _Round11.aspx (accessed January 21, 2014).

Gazis, Denos. 1998. "PASHAs: Advanced Intelligent Agents in the Service of Electronic Commerce." In *The Future of the Electronic Marketplace*, ed. D. Leebaert, 145–173. Cambridge, MA: MIT Press.

Geary, Patrick. 1986. "Sacred Commodities: The Circulation of Medieval Relics." In *The Social Life of Things: Commodities in Cultural Perspective*, ed. A. Appadurai, 169–194. Cambridge: Cambridge University Press.

Geer, Daniel D., Jr. 1998. "Unseen Guardians, Invisible Treasures." In *The Future of the Electronic Marketplace*, ed. D. Leebaert, 241–261. Cambridge, MA: MIT Press.

Gelman, Robert. 2004. "The Foundations of United States Government Information Dissemination Policy." In *Public Sector Information in the Digital Age: Between Markets, Public Management and Citizens' Rights*, ed. G. Aichholzer and H. Burkert, 123–136. Northhampton, MA: Edward Elgar.

Gerards, Janneke H., and Heleen L. Janssen. 2006. "Regulation of Genetic and Other Health Information in a Comparative Perspective." *European Journal of Health Law* 13:339–398.

Gerth, Karl. 2003. "Commodifying Chinese Nationalism: MSG and the Flavor of Patriotic Production." In *Commodifying Everything: Relationships of the Market*, ed. S. Strasser, 235–258. New York: Routledge.

Gertz, Renate. 2004. "An Analysis of the Icelandic Supreme Court Judgement on the Health Sector Database Act." *SCRIPT-ed* 1 (2): 241–258.

Gil-Garcia, J. R., I. Chengalur-Smith, and P. Duchessi. 2007. "Collaborative E-Government: Impediments and Benefits of Information-Sharing Projects in the Public Sector." *European Journal of Information Systems* 16 (2): 121–133.

Gil-Garcia, J. R., and T. A. Pardo. 2005. "E-Government Success Factors: Mapping Practical Tools to Theoretical Foundations." *Government Information Quarterly* 22:187–216.

Gilder, George. 1992. *Life after Television—The Coming Transformation of Media and American Life*. New York: W. W. Norton & Company.

Ginsberg, Wendy R. 2011. "The Obama Administration's Open Government Initiative: Issues for Congress." R41361. Washington, DC: Congressional Research Service. http://www.fas.org/sgp/crs/secrecy/R41361.pdf (accessed January 21, 2014).

Gonen, Mira, Rica Gonen, and Elan Pavlov. 2007. "Generalized Trade Reduction Mechanisms." In *Proceedings of the 8th ACM Conference on Electronic Commerce*, ed. J. MacKie-Mason, D. Parkes and P. Resnick, 20–29. San Diego, CA: ACM.

Gonen, Rica, and Daniel Lehmann. 2000. "Optimal Solutions for Multi-Unit Combinatorial Auctions: Branch and Bound Heuristics." In *Proceedings of the 2nd ACM Conference on Electronic Commerce*, ed. A. Jhingran, J. MacKie Mason, and D. Tygar, 13–20. Minneapolis, MI: ACM.

Gonen, Rica, and Elan Pavlov. 2007. "An Adaptive Sponsored Search Mechanism Delta-Gain Truthful in Valuation, Time, and Budget." In *Proceedings of the Third International Workshop on Internet and Network Economics (WINE 2007)*, ed. D. F. Xiaotie and G. Chung, 341–346. San Diego, CA: Springer-Verlag.

Gonen, Rica, and Sergei Vassilvitskii. 2008. "Sponsored Search Auctions with Reserve Prices: Going Beyond Separability." In *Proceedings of the 4th International Workshop on Internet and Network Economics*, ed. C. Papadimitriou and S. Zhang, 597–608. Shanghai: Springer-Verlag.

Grant, Don. 2012a. Legal Challenges Regarding the Foundation of PSMA (correspondence), Australia, October 2–3.

Grant, Don. 2012b. PPP Models vs. the PSMA Model (correspondence), Australia, November 3–16.

Greenberg, Andy. 2012a. "Study Confirms the Government Produces the Buggiest Software." *Forbes* (March): 13.

Greenberg, Douglas. 2012b. "How the IRS Selects Returns for Audit." *SFGate*, June 11. http://blog.sfgate.com/dgreenberg/2012/06/11/how-the-irs-selects-returns-for-audit (accessed January 21, 2014).

Greene, Mary E., Michael N. Beaulac, Molly O'Neill, and Janice Bryant. 2014. *Environmental Information Exchange Network: Improving Environmental Results*. Washington, DC: Environmental Information Exchange Network. http://www.exchangenetwork.net/benefits/successstories.pdf (accessed March 12, 2014).

Groves, Theodore. 1973. "Incentives in Teams." *Econometrica* 41 (4): 617–631.

Grupe, Fritz H. 1995. "Commercializing Public Information: A Critical Issue for Governmental IS Professionals." *Information & Management* 28 (4): 229–241.

Hall, Joseph Lorenzo. 2003. "Columbia and Challenger: Organizational Failure at NASA." *Space Policy* 19:239–247.

Hallote, Rachel. 2006. *Bible, Map, and Spade—The American Palestine Exploration Society, Frederick Jones Bliss, and the Forgotten Story of Early American Biblical Archaeology.* Piscataway, NJ: Gorgias Press.

Halonen, Antti. 2012. *Being Open about Data: Analysis of the UK Open Data Policies and Applicability of Open Data.* London: The Finnish Institute in London. http://finnish-institute.org.uk/images/stories/pdf2012/being open about data.pdf (accessed August 13, 2013).

Hamilton, Alexander, James Madison, and John Jay. [1787] 1961. *The Federalist Papers. Reprint, New York.* New York: Penguin Books.

Hamilton, Lee H. 2005. "Prepared Statement of Lee H. Hamilton Former Vice Chair, National Commission on Terrorist Attacks upon the United States before the Subcommittee on Intelligence, Information Sharing, and Terrorism Risk Assessment Committee on Homeland Security, U.S. House of Representatives—Federal Support for Homeland Security Information Sharing: The Role of the Information Sharing Program Manager." Washington, DC: U.S. Government Printing Office.

Hara, Noriko, Paul Solomon, Seung-Lye Kim, and Diane H. Sonnenwald. 2003. "An Emerging View of Scientific Collaboration: Scientists' Perspectives on Collaboration and Factors that Impact Collaboration." *Journal of the American Society for Information Science and Technology* 54 (10): 952–965.

Hardgrove, Anne. 2003. "The Politics of Ghee Adulteration and Its Public Resolution in Calcutta, c. 1917." In *Commodifying Everything: Relationships of the Market*, ed. S. Strasser, 191–213. New York: Routledge.

Harper, Jim. 2010. "Grading Agencies' High-Value Data Sets." Last modified February 5. http://www.cato-at-liberty.org/grading-agencies-high-value-data-sets (accessed January 21, 2014).

Harper, Jim. 2011. "Government Spending Transparency: 'Needs Improvement' Is Understatement." Last modified December 14. http://www.cato.org/blog/government-spending-transparency-needs-improvement-understatement (accessed January 21, 2014).

Harper, Jim. 2012. "Grading the Government's Data Publication Practices." *Policy Analysis* 711:1–43.

Harris, Catherine. 2006. "Taking It to the Biobank." *Momentum* (Fall). http://whsc.emory.edu/_pubs/momentum/2006fall/biobank.html (accessed January 21, 2014).

Harris, Derrick. 2013. "On Big Data, the Boston Marathon and Civil Liberties." *Gigaom*, April 17. http://gigaom.com/2013/04/17/on-big-data-the-boston-marathon-and-civil-liberties (accessed January 21, 2014).

Harris, Paul. 2012. "US Data Whistleblower: 'It's a Violation of Everybody's Constitutional Rights.'" Last modified September 15. http://www.theguardian.com/technology/2012/sep/15/data-whistleblower-constitutional-rights (accessed January 21, 2014).

Hart, Paul, and Carol Saunders. 1997. "Power and Trust: Critical Factors in the Adoption and Use of Electronic Data Interchange." *Organization Science* 8 (1): 23–42.

Hattotuwa, Sanjana, and Daniel Stauffacher. 2010. "Haiti and Beyond: Getting It Right in Crisis Information Management." Genève: The ICT4Peace Foundation. http://ict4peace.org/haiti-and-beyond-getting-it-right-in-crisis-information-management (accessed September 7, 2013).

Head, Tom. 2013. "Prostitution: An Illustrated History and Timeline." Last modified November 4. http://civilliberty.about.com/od/gendersexuality/tp/History-of-Prostitution.htm (accessed January 21, 2014).

The Health Committee. 2003. *The Victoria Climbié Inquiry Report*. HC570. London: HMSO.

Health Edge. 2009. "Home Page." Last modified November 3. http://www.healthedge.com (accessed January 21, 2014).

Healy, Beth. 2004. "Lexington Software Firm Shuts Down." *The Boston Globe*, October 23. http://www.boston.com/business/technology/articles/2004/10/23/lexington_software_firm_shuts_down (accessed November 4, 2013).

Hendler, Clint. 2009. "FOIA after the Open Government Directive." *Columbia Journalism Review*. Last modified December 8. http://www.cjr.org/campaign_desk/foia_after_the_open_government.php (accessed January 21, 2014).

Hendler, Clint. 2010. "Report Card: Obama's Marks at Transparency U." Last modified January 5. http://www.cjr.org/transparency/report_card.php (accessed January 21, 2014).

Hey, Donald L., Laura S. Urban, and Jill A. Kostel. 2005. "Nutrient Farming: The Business of Environmental Management." *Ecological Engineering* 24 (4): 279–287.

Hickey, Kathleen. 2010. "State Department Social Network in the Works." *GCN*, April 27. http://gcn.com/articles/2010/04/27/statebook-social-network.aspx (accessed January 21, 2014).

Hijmans, Hielke. 2006. "The Third Pillar in Practice: Coping with Inadequacies: Information Sharing between Member States." Paper presented at the Netherlands Association for European Law (NVER), Netherlands, November 24.

Hilgartner, Stephen. 2000. *Science on Stage: Expert Advice as Public Drama*. Stanford, CA: Stanford University Press.

Holden, Stephen H., and Patricia D. Fletcher. 2005. "The Virtual Value Chain and E-Government Partnership: Nonmonetary Agreements in the IRS E-Files Program." In *Handbook of Public Information Systems*, ed. G. D. Garson, 369–387. Boca Raton, FL: Marcel Dekker.

Holder, Eric. 2009. "Memorandum for Heads of Executive Departments and Agencies: The Freedom of Information Act." Last modified March 19. http://www.usdoj .gov/ag/foia-memo-march2009.pdf (accessed January 21, 2014).

Holmes, Martin. 2009. *A Concise History of PSMA Australia Limited: From Collaboration to Success 1992–2005*. Australia: PSMA Australia Limited. http://www.psma.com.au/ psma/wp-content/uploads/ACONCISEHISTORYOFPSMAAUSTRALIALIMITED.pdf (accessed November 3, 2013).

Homburg, Vincentius Martinus Franciscus. 1999. "The Political Economy of Information Management: A Theoretical and Empirical Analysis of Decision Making Regarding Interorganizational Information Systems." PhD diss., University of Groningen.

Horner, Christopher C. 2012. *The Liberal War on Transparency: Confessions of a Freedom of Information "Criminal."* New York: Threshold Editions.

Horowitz, Edward D. 1998. "The Ascent of Content." In *The Future of the Electronic Marketplace*, ed. D. Leebaert, 91–112. Cambridge, MA: MIT Press.

Huber, John D., and Charles R. Shipan. 2002. *Deliberate Discretion: The Institutional Foundations of Bureaucratic Autonomy*. Cambridge: Cambridge University Press.

Huijboom, Noor, and Marcel Hoogwout. 2004. "Trust in e-Government Cooperation." In *Electronic Government*, ed. R. Traunmüller, 332–335. Heidelberg: Springer.

Huijboom, Noor, and Tijs Van den Broek. 2011. "Open Data: An International Comparison of Strategies." *European Journal of ePractice* 12:1–13.

Hurren, Elizabeth T. 2008. "Whose Body Is It Anyway? Trading the Dead Poor, Coroner's Disputes, and the Business of Anatomy at Oxford University, 1885–1929." *Bulletin of the History of Medicine* 82 (4): 775–818.

Iacovou, Charalambos L., Izak Benbasat, and Albert S. Dexter. 1995. "Electronic Data Interchange and Small Organizations: Adoption and Impact of Technology. " *Management Information Systems Quarterly* 19 (4): 465–485.

Internal Revenue Service (IRS). 2009. *Internal Revenue Service 2009 Data Book*. Washington, DC: U.S. Government Printing Office. http://www.irs.gov/pub/irs-soi/ 09databk.pdf (accessed October 23, 2013).

Internal Revenue Service (IRS). 2014. IRS Homepage. http://www.irs.gov (accessed March 5, 2014).

Issa, Darrell Edward. 2012. "The Future of the Federal IT shop." Paper presented at the Nextgov—Forging the Future of Government through People and Technology Conference, Washington, DC, December 3.

Ito, Aki, and Alisa Odenheimer. 2012. "Your 119 Billion Google Searches Now a Central Bank Tool." *Bloomberg*, August 14. http://www.bloomberg.com/news/print/2012-08-02/your-119-billion-google-searches-now-a-central-bank-tool.html (accessed January 21, 2014).

Iverson, Joel O., and Robert D. McPhee. 2002. "Knowledge Management in Communities of Practice." *Management Communication Quarterly* 16 (2): 259–266.

Jackelen, George. 2000. "The Need for a Useful Lessons Learned Database." *Crosstalk: The Journal of Defense Software Engineering* 13 (1): 29–30.

Jackson, Joab. 2005. "Niem Releases First Draft of Info-Sharing Specs." *GCN*, October 13. http://gcn.com/articles/2005/10/13/niem-releases-first-draft-of-infosharing-specs.aspx (accessed January 21, 2014).

Jackson, Joab. 2008. "EPA the Web 2.0 Way." *GCN*, January 29. http://gcn.com/Articles/2008/01/29/Molly-ONeill--EPA-the-Web-20-way.aspx (accessed January 21, 2014).

Jackson, Joab. 2009. "Intellipedia Suffers Midlife Crisis." *GCN*, February 18. http://gcn.com/articles/2009/02/18/intellipedia.aspx (accessed January 21, 2014).

Jacobs, Jane. 1992. *Systems of Survival—A Dialogue on the Moral Foundations of Commerce and Politics*. New York: Random House.

Janssen, Katleen. 2012. "Open Government Data and the Right to Information: Opportunities and Obstacles." *Journal of Community Informatics* 8 (2): 1–15.

Janssen, Marijn, Yannis Charalabidis, and Anneke Zuiderwijk. 2012. "Benefits, Adoption Barriers and Myths of Open Data and Open Government." *Information Systems Management* 29 (4): 258–268.

Jarvenpaa, S. L., and D. S. Staples. 2001. "Exploring Perceptions of Organizational Ownership of Information and Expertise." *Journal of Management Information Systems* 18 (1): 151–183.

Jaschik, Scott. 2007. "The Facebook Style in Finding Applicants." *Inside Higher Ed*, September 28. http://www.insidehighered.com/news/2007/09/28/nacac (accessed January 21, 2014).

Jenkins, Leesteffy. 1993. "Trade Sanctions: Effective Enforcement Tools." *Review of European Community & International Environmental Law* 2 (4): 362–369.

Jian, G., and L. W. Jeffres. 2006. "Understanding Employees' Willingness to Contribute to Shared Electronic Databases: A Three-Dimensional Framework." *Communication Research* 33 (4): 242–261.

Johnson, D. R. 2013. "Introductory Anatomy." Last modified November 3. http://www.leeds.ac.uk/chb/lectures/anatomy1.html (accessed January 21, 2014).

Johnson, Eric M. 2007. "Diplopedia: Knowledge Sharing Through an Enterprise Wiki at the U.S. Department of State." Paper presented at the EPA Environmental Information Symposium, November 14.

Joia, Luiz Antonio. 2004. "Developing Government-to-Government Enterprises in Brazil: A Heuristic Model Drawn from Multiple Case Studies." *International Journal of Information Management* 24 (2): 147–166.

Jolly, David. 2010. "Stolen Bank Data Involved Thousands of Clients, HSBC Says." *New York Times*, March 12. http://query.nytimes.com/gst/fullpage.html?res=9B01E0 DE133BF931A25750C0A9669D8B63 (accessed November 4, 2013).

June, Laura. 2011. "Obama Administration Moves Forward with Unique Internet ID for All Americans, Commerce Department to Head System Up." Last modified January 9. http://www.engadget.com/2011/01/09/obama-administration-moves-forward -with-unique-internet-id-for-a/ (accessed January 21, 2014).

Jung, Stephen M. 2012. Interview with Stephen Jung, Assistant General Counsel, Securities and Exchange Commission (SEC), Washington, DC (phone interview), May 4.

Jurafsky, Daniel, and James H. Martin. 2008. *Speech and Language Processing—An Introduction to Natural Language Processing, Computational Linguistics, and Speech Recognition*. 2nd ed. Upper Saddle River, NJ: Pearson Prentice Hall.

Kaiser, Jocelyn. 2002. "Population Databases Boom from Iceland to the U.S." *Science* 298:1158–1161.

Kamal, Muhammad Mustafa. 2006. "IT Innovation Adoption in the Government Sector: Identifying the Critical Success Factors." *Journal of Enterprise Information Management* 19 (2): 192–222.

Kamal, Muhammad Mustafa, and Marinos Themistocleous. 2006. "A Conceptual Model for EAI Adoption in an E-Government Environment." Paper presented at the European and Mediterranean Conference on Information Systems (EMCIS), Costa Blanca, Alicante, Spain, July 6–7.

Kapucu, Naim, and Montgomery Van Wart. 2008. "Making Matters Worse: An Anatomy of Leadership Failures in Managing Catastrophic Events." *Administration & Society* 40 (7): 711–740.

Kaserman, David. 2002. "Markets for Organs: Myths and Misconceptions." *Journal of Contemporary Health Law and Policy* 18:567–582."

Kelman, Steven. 2004. *Changing Big Government Organizations: Easier than Meets the Eye?* Cambridge, MA: John F. Kennedy School of Government Harvard University. http://www.econbiz.de/en/search/detailed-view/doc/all/changing-big-government -organizations-easier-than-meets-the-eye-kelman-steven/10002197350/?no_cache=1 (accessed October 22, 2013).

Kelman, Steven. 2009. Successfully Executing Ambitious Strategies in Government: An Empirical Analysis. Cambridge, MA: John F. Kennedy School of Government Harvard University. http://papers.ssrn.com/sol3/papers.cfm?abstract_id=1380432 (accessed October 22, 2013).

Kim, Soonhee, and Donghwan Kim. 2003. "South Korean Public Officials' Perceptions of Values, Failure, and Consequences of Failure in E-Government Leadership." *Public Performance & Management Review* 26 (4): 360–375.

Kim, Soonhee, and Hyangsoo Lee. 2006. "The Impact of Organizational Context and Information Technology on Employee Knowledge-Sharing Capabilities." *Public Administration Review* 66 (3): 370–385.

Kim, W. Chan, and Renée Mauborgne. 1998. "Procedural Justice, Strategic Decision Making, and the Knowledge Economy." *Strategic Management Journal* 19 (4): 323–338.

Klein, Alec. 2007. "The Army's $200 Billion Makeover: March to Modernize Proves Ambitious and Controversial." *Washington Post*, December 7. http://www .washingtonpost.com/wp-dyn/content/article/2007/12/06/AR2007120602836_pf .html (accessed November 4, 2013).

Kling, Rob. 1980. "Social Analyses of Computing: Theoretical Orientations in Recent Empirical Research." *Computing Surveys* 2 (4): 61–110.

Kling, Rob, and Suzanne Iacono. 1984. "The Control of Information Systems Development after Implementation." *Communications of the ACM* 27 (12): 1218–1226.

Kolekofski, Keith E., Jr., and Alan R. Heminger. 2003. "Beliefs and Attitudes Affecting Intentions to Share Information in an Organizational Setting." *Information & Management* 40:521–532.

Koman, Richard. 2007. "IRS CIO Holds out Hope for Modernization by Holding onto COBOL Systems." *ZDNet*, April 12. http://www.zdnet.com/blog/government/ irs-cio-holds-out-hope-for-modernization-by-holding-onto-cobol-systems/3072 (accessed January 21, 2014).

Kopytoff, Igor. 1986. "The Cultural Biography of Things: Commoditization as Process." In *The Social Life of Things: Commodities in Cultural Perspective*, ed. A. Appadurai, 64–93. Cambridge: Cambridge University Press.

Kraemer, Kenneth L., and John L. King. 1986. "Computing in Public Organizations." *Public Administration Review* 46:488–496.

Kraus, Sarit, and Daniel Lehmann. 1995. "Designing and Building a Negotiating Automated Agent." *Computational Intelligence* 11 (1): 132–171.

Krause, George A., and James W. Douglas. 2005. "Institutional Design versus Reputational Effects on Bureaucratic Performance: Evidence from US Government Macroeconomic and Fiscal Projections." *Journal of Public Administration: Research and Theory* 15 (2): 281–306.

Kreimer, Seth. 2008. "The Freedom of Information Act and the Ecology of Transparency." *University of Pennsylvania Journal of Constitutional Law* 10:1011–1080.

Kugler, Tamar, Zvika Neeman, and Nir Vulkan. 2006. "Markets versus Negotiations: An Experimental Investigation." *Economic Behavior* 56:121–134.

Kundra, Vivek. 2011. "From Data to Apps: Putting Government Information to Work for You." Last modified May 20. http://www.whitehouse.gov/blog/2011/05/20/ data-apps-putting-government-information-work-you (accessed January 21, 2014).

Lakhani, Karim R., Robert D. Austin, and Yumi Yi. 2010. "Data.gov." Cambridge MA: Harvard Business School Press. http://hbr.org/product/data-gov/an/610075 -PDF-ENG (accessed October 23, 2013).

Lam, W. 2005. "Barriers to e-Government Integration." *Journal of Enterprise Information Management* 18 (5/6): 511–530.

Landler, Mark. 2008. "Liechtenstein Issues Warrant for Tax Informant." *New York Times*, March 13. http://www.nytimes.com/2008/03/13/business/worldbusiness/ 13tax.html (accessed November 2, 2013).

Landsbergen, D. J., and G. J. Wolken. 1998. "Eliminating Legal and Policy Barriers to Interoperable Government Systems." Washington, DC: Ohio Supercomputer Center, ECLIPS program.

Landsbergen, D. J., and G. J. Wolken. 2001. "Realizing the Promise: Government Information Systems and the Fourth Generation of Information Technology." *Public Administration Review* 61 (2): 206–220.

Laudon, Kenneth C. 1996. "Markets and Privacy." *Communications of the ACM* 39 (9): 92–104.

Law Commission. 2011. *Review of the Privacy Act 1993: Review of the Law of Privacy Stage 4*. NZLC R123. Wellington, New Zealand: Law Commission.

Lawrence, Vanessa. 2011. "Investigation into the Spatial Capability of Australia." Last modified October 29. http://apo.org.au/research/investigation-spatial-capability -australia (accessed January 21, 2014).

Lazer, D., and C. B. Maria. 2004. "Information Sharing in E-Government Projects: Managing Novelty and Cross-Agency Cooperation." Arlington, VA: IBM Endowment for the Business of Government. http://www.innovations.harvard.edu/showdoc.html?id=4852 (accessed October 24, 2013).

Le Billon, Philippe. 2006. "Fatal Transactions: Conflict Diamonds and the (Anti) Terrorist Consumer." *Antipode* 38 (4): 778–801.

Leebaert, Derek. 1998. "Present at the Creation." In *The Future of the Electronic Marketplace*, ed. D. Leebaert, 1–33. Cambridge, MA: MIT Press.

Lembke, J. 2002. "Mobile Commerce and the Creation of a Marketplace." *Info—The Journal of Policy, Regulation and Strategy for Telecommunications* 4:50–56.

Lemonick, Michael D. 2006. "The Iceland Experiment." *Time*, February 20. http://content.time.com/time/magazine/article/0,9171,1158968,00.html (accessed January 21, 2014).

Leonhardt, David. 2009. "Real Challenge to Health Bill: Selling Reform." *New York Times*, July 21. http://www.nytimes.com/2009/07/22/business/economy/22leonhardt.html (accessed November 1, 2013).

Levergood, Barbara, Stefan Farrenkopf, and Elisabeth Frasnelli. 2008. "The Specification of the Language of the Field and Interoperability: Cross-language Access to Catalogues and Online Libraries (CACAO)." In *Proceedings of the International Conference on Dublin Core and Metadata Applications (Metadata for Semantic and Social Applications)*, ed. J. Greenberg and W. Klas, 191–196. Berlin: Universitätsverlag Göttingen.

Lexmark. 2009. *2009 Government Printing Report—A Closer Look at Costs, Habits, Policies, and Opportunities for Savings*. Lexington, KY: Lexmark. http://www.govexec.com/pdfs/051209rb1.pdf (accessed November 2, 2013).

Li, S., and B. Lin. 2006. "Accessing Information Sharing and Information Quality in Supply Chain Management." *Decision Support Systems* 42 (3): 1641–1656.

Library of Congress. 2013. "Web Archiving FAQs." Last modified November 3. http://www.loc.gochiviv/webarng/faq.html (accessed January 21, 2014).

Lipowicz, Alice. 2011a. "The Secret Effort to Fix USAJobs." *FCW*, November 15. http://fcw.com/articles/2011/11/15/fedcio-vanroekel-and-swat-team-helping-with-usajobs-recovery.aspx (accessed January 21, 2014).

Lipowicz, Alice. 2011b. "USAJobs on Brink of Becoming a Political Issue." *FCW*, October 28. http://fcw.com/Articles/2011/10/28/USAJobs-on-brink-of-becoming-a-political-issue.aspx (accessed January 21, 2014).

Littlewood, Nick, Sarah MacDonald, and Gerry Stanley. 2010. "The Benefits of the PSMA Australia Data Network." In *Proceedings of the FIG Congress 2010: Facing the Challenges—Building the Capacity*, ed. R. Staiger. Sydney: FIG.

Longo, Justin. 2011. "OpenData: Digital-Era Governance Thoroughbred or New Public Management Trojan Horse?" Public Policy and Governance Review 2 (2): 38–52.

Lovins, Amory. 2011. "Soft Energy Paths for the 21st Century." Snowmass, CO: Rocky Mountain Institute (RMI). http://www.rmi.org/Knowledge-Center/Library/ 2011-09_GaikoSoftEnergyPaths (accessed November 4, 2013).

Lukensmeyer, Carolyn J., Joseph P. Goldman, and David Stern. 2011. *Assessing Public Participation in an Open Government Era: A Review of Federal Agency Plans*. Washington, DC: IBM Center for the Business of Government.

Luna-Reyes, Luis F., J. Ramon Gil-Garcia, and Cinthia Betiny Cruz. 2007. "Collaborative Digital Government in Mexico: Some Lessons from Federal Web-Based Interorganizational Information Integration Initiatives." *Government Information Quarterly* 24 (4): 808–826.

Macalister, R. A. Stewart. 1912. The Excavation of Gezer, 1902–1905 and 1907– 1909—Volume 1. London: John Murray.

Machado, Maira Rocha. 2007. "Financial Regulation and International Criminal Policy: The Anti-money Laundering System in Brazil and Argentina." Paper presented at the Law and Society Association Annual Conference—IRC Transnational Transformations of the State, TBA, Berlin, Germany, July 25.

Macher, Jeffrey T., David C. Mowery, and Timothy S. Simcoe. 2002. "E-Business and Disintegration of the Semiconductor Industry Value Chain." *Industry and Innovation* 9 (3): 155–181.

Madhavan, Jayant, Loredana Afanasiev, Lyublena Antova, and Alon Y. Halevy. 2009. "Harnessing the Deep Web: Present and Future." Paper presented at the CIDR 2009, Fourth Biennial Conference on Innovative Data Systems Research, Asilomar, CA, January 4–7.

Madhavan, Jayant, David Ko, Lucja Kot, Vignesh Ganapathy, Alex Rasmussen, and Alon Y. Halevy. 2008. "Google's Deep Web Crawl." [PVLDB] *Proceedings of the Very Large Database Endowment* 1 (2): 1241–1252.

Magee, Reginald. 2001. "Art Macabre: Resurrectionists and Anatomists." *ANZ Journal of Surgery* 71 (6): 377–380.

Mahler, Julianne, and Priscilla M. Regan. 2003. "Developing Intranets for Agency Management." *Public Performance & Management Review* 26 (4): 422–432.

Mahoney, Julia D. 2000. "The Market for Human Tissue." *Virginia Law Review* 86 (2): 163–223.

Makedon, Fillia, Song Ye, and Yan Zhao. 2003. "On The Design and Implementation of a Web-Based Negotiation System." In *Proceedings of the 9th Panhellenic Conference on Informatics*, ed. I. Pitas and K. Margaritis, 46–57. Thessaloniki: Aristotle University.

Manovich, Lev. 2012. "Trending: The Promises and the Challenges of Big Social Data." In *Debates in the Digital Humanities*, ed. M. K. Gold, 460–475. Minneapolis: University of Minnesota Press.

Maor, Moshe. 2010. "Organizational Reputation and the Duration of Enforcement Decisions: The Case of the U.S. Food and Drug Administration." *Governance: An International Journal of Policy and Administration* 23 (1): 133–159.

Maor, Moshe, and Raanan Sulitzeanu-Kenan. 2013. "The Effect of Salient Reputational Threats on the Pace of FDA Enforcement." *Governance* 26 (1): 31–61.

Marks, Peter, Peter Polak, Scott McCoy, and Dennis Galletta. 2008. "Sharing Knowledge." *Communications of the ACM* 51 (2): 60–65.

Markus, Lynne, and Terry Connolly. 1990. "Why CSCW Applications Fail: Problems in the Adoption of Interdependent Work Tools." In *CSCW 90: Proceedings of the Conference on Computer Supported Cooperative Work*, ed. F. Halasz, 371–380. Los Angeles, CA: ACM Press.

Mayer, R. C., J. H. Davis, and F. D. Schoorman. 1995. "An Integrative Model of Organizational Trust." *Academy of Management Review* 20:709–734.

Mayer-Schönberger, Viktor, and Kenneth Cukier. 2013. *Big Data: A Revolution that Will Transform How We Live, Work, and Think*. Boston, MA: Houghton Mifflin Harcourt.

Mayer-Schönberger, Viktor, and David Lazer. 2007a. "From Electronic Government to Information Government." In *Governance and Information Technology: From Electronic Government to Information Government*, ed. V. Mayer-Schönberger and D. Lazer, 1–14. Cambridge, MA: MIT Press.

Mayer-Schönberger, Viktor, and David Lazer. 2007b. *Governance and Information Technology: From Electronic Government to Information Government*. Cambridge, MA: MIT Press.

McClean, Tom. 2011. "Not with a Bang but a Whimper: The Politics of Accountability and Open Data in the UK." Last modified August 16. http://papers.ssrn.com/sol3/papers.cfm?abstract_id=1899790 (accessed January 21, 2014).

McCubbins, Matthew D., Roger G. Noll, and Barry R. Weingast. 1987. "Administrative Procedures as Instruments of Political Control." *Journal of Law Economics and Organization* 3 (2): 243–277.

McDermott, Patrice. 2010. "Building Open Government." *Government Information Quarterly* 27:401–413.

McLure Wasko, Molly, and Samer Faraj. 2000. "It Is What One Does": Why People Participate and Help Others in Electronic Communities of Practice." *Journal of Strategic Information Systems* 9 (2–3): 155–173.

Meirowitz, Adam, and Joshua A. Tucker. 2004. "Learning from Terrorism Markets." *Perspectives* 2 (2): 331–336.

Millar, Laurence. 2011. "Beth Noveck, Former US Deputy CTO in Interview." Last modified March 18. http://www.futuregov.asia/articles/2011/mar/18/transparency -collaboration-and-participation-inter (accessed March 12, 2014).

Miller, Jason. 2004. "EPA Readying Data Exchange Network." *GCN*, April 2. http:// gcn.com/articles/2004/04/02/epa-readying-data-exchange-network.aspx (accessed March 12, 2014).

Miller, Jason. 2007. "DOD Limits Govworks Buys to $100K." *FCW*, June 7. http://fcw.com/articles/2007/06/07/dod-limits-govworks-buys-to-100k.aspx (accessed March 12, 2014).

Miller, Robert. 2006. "Hurricane Katrina: Communications and Infrastructure Impacts." In *Proceedings of the First Annual Homeland Defense and Homeland Security Conference*, ed. B. B. Tussing, 191–204. Carlisle, PA: U.S. Army War College, Center for Strategic Leadership.

Mitchell, Piers D., Ceridwen Boston, Andrew T. Chamberlain, Simon Chaplin, Vin Chauhan, Jonathan Evans, Louise Fowler, Natasha Powers, Helen Webb, Don Walker, and Annsofie Witkin. 2011. "The Study of Anatomy in England from 1700 to the Early 20th Century." *Journal of Anatomy* 219:91–99.

Mobbs, John D. 1998. "Australia Comes to Its Census: The Public Sector Mapping Agencies and the 1996 Australian Census of Population and Housing." Paper presented at the Federation Internationale des Geometres (FIG) XXIst International Congress of Surveyors: Developing the Profession in a Developing World, Brighton, October 8.

Mobbs, John D. 2001. "CrimTrac: Technology and Detection." Paper presented at the 4th National Outlook Symposium on Crime in Australia, New Crimes or New Responses, Canberra, June 20–21.

Mobbs, John D. 2005. "Working at the Edge of the Data Sharing Envelope." Paper presented at the Safety, Crime and Justice—From Data to Policy Conference, Canberra, June 6–7.

Mobbs, John D. 2012a. First Round of PSMA Questions (correspondence), Australia, May 27.

Mobbs, John D. 2012b. Four Observations and One Question Regarding the Lawrence Report (correspondence), Australia, September 12.

Mobbs, John D. 2012c. PSMA History (correspondence), Australia, August 10.

Moffitt, Susan L. 2010. "Promoting Agency Reputation through Public Advice: Advisory Committee Use in the FDA." *Journal of Politics* 72 (3): 880–893.

Monge, Peter R., Janet Fulk, Michael E. Kalman, Andrew J. Flanagin, Claire Parnassa, and Suzanne Rumsey. 1998. "Production of Collective Action in Alliance-Based Interorganizational Communication and Information Systems." *Organization Science* 9 (3): 411–433.

Moore, John. 2011. "Is Government Ready for the Semantic Web?" *GCN*, March 22. http://gcn.com/Articles/2011/03/21/NIEM-and-Semantic-Web.aspx (accessed January 21, 2014).

Moscoe, Bruce. 2011. Interview with Bruce Moscoe (phone conversation), Phoenix, AZ, August 3.

Moscrop, John James. 2000. *Measuring Jerusalem—The Palestine Exploration Fund and British Interests in the Holy Land.* London: Leicester University Press.

Moynihan, Daniel Patrick. 1999. *Secrecy: The American Experience.* New Haven, CT: Yale University Press.

Moynihan, Donald P. 2009. *The Response to Hurricane Katrina.* Lausanne: International Risk Governance Council (IRGC). http://irgc.org/wp-content/uploads/2012/04/Hurricane_Katrina_full_case_study_web.pdf (accessed November 4, 2013).

Muth, Robert M., and Wesley V. Jamison. 2000. "On the Destiny of Deer Camps and Duck Blinds: The Rise of the Animal Rights Movement and the Future of Wildlife Conservation." *Wildlife Society Bulletin* 28 (4): 841–851.

National Archives and Records Administration (NARA). 2010. "Guidance on Managing Records in Web 2.0/Social Media Platforms." Last modified October 20. http://www.archives.gov/records-mgmt/bulletins/2011/2011-02.html (accessed January 21, 2014).

National Commission on Terrorist Attacks upon the United States. 2004. *The 9/11 Commission Report—Official Government Edition.* Washington, DC: U.S. Government Printing Office.

National Commission on the BP Deepwater Horizon Oil Spill and Offshore Drilling. 2010. "Response/Clean-Up Technology Research & Development and The BP Deepwater Horizon Oil Spill (Staff Working Paper No. 7: Draft)." http://graphics8.nytimes.com/packages/pdf/science/Response.pdf (accessed November 10, 2013).

National Technical Information Service (NTIS). 2014. "Social Security Administration's Death Master File Available through Value-Added Online Products." Washington, DC: National Technical Information Service. http://www.ntis.gov/products/ssa-online.aspx (accessed January 20, 2014).

National Technical Information Service and Social Security Administration (NTIS and SSA). 2013. *Reimbursable Agreement between the U.S. Department of Commerce*

National Technical Information Service (NTIS) and the Social Security Administration (SSA). NTIS-1469. Washington, DC: U.S. Department of Commerce and Social Security Administration (SSA).

Newcomer, Kathryn E., and L. Caudle Sharon. 1991. "Evaluating Public Sector Information Systems: More than Meets the Eye." *Public Administration Review* 51 (5): 377–384.

NIEM Program Management Office. 2007. "Introduction to the National Information Exchange Model (NIEM) Version 0.3." http://www.niem.gov/documentsdb/Documents/Overview/NIEM_Introduction.pdf (accessed November 10, 2013).

Niskanen, William A. 1975. "Bureaucrats and Politicians." *Journal of Law & Economics* 18 (3): 617–643.

Norris, Donald F., and Jae Moon. 2005. "Advancing e-Government at the Grassroots: Tortoise or Hare?" *Public Administration Review* 65 (1): 64-75.

Norris, Pippa. 2001. *Digital Divide: Civic Engagement, Information Poverty, and the Internet Worldwide*. Cambridge: Cambridge University Press.

Nosowitz, Dan. 2011. "Every Six Hours, the NSA Gathers as Much Data as Is Stored in the Entire Library of Congress." *POPSCI*, October 5. http://www.popsci.com/technology/article/2011-05/every-six-hours-nsa-gathers-much-data-stored-entire-library-congress (accessed January 21, 2014).

Noveck, Beth Simone. 2009. *Wiki Government: How Technology Can Make Government Better, Democracy Stronger, and Citizens More Powerful*. Washington, DC: Brookings Institution Press.

Noveck, Beth Simone. 2011. "Testimony of Dr. Beth S. Noveck before the Standing Committee on Access to Information, Privacy and Ethics of the Canadian Parliament." Last modified March 2. http://cairns.typepad.com/blog/2011/03/testimony-before-the-standing-committee-on-access-to-information-privacy-and-ethics-of-the-canadian-.html (accessed January 21, 2014).

Noveck, Beth Simone. 2012. "Demand a More Open Source Government." Last modified September. http://www.ted.com/talks/beth_noveck_demand_a_more_open_source_government.html (accessed January 21, 2014).

OCA. 2010. "Voluntary Codes Guide—What Is a Voluntary Code?" Last modified September 3. http://www.ic.gc.ca/eic/site/oca-bc.nsf/eng/ca00963.html (accessed January 21, 2014).

OECD. 2007. e-Government Studies: Netherlands. Paris: OECD.

Office of Management and Budget (OMB). 2000. *Management of Federal Information Resources, Circular A-130*. Washington, DC: Office of Management and Budget.

Office of Management and Budget (OMB). 2009. "Open Government Directive." Last modified December 8. http://www.whitehouse.gov/open/documents/open -government-directive (accessed January 21, 2014).

Office of Spatial Policy. 2012. "The Australian Government Response to the Report by Dr. Vanessa Lawrence CB on the Investigation into the Spatial Capability of Australia." Last modified April 11. http://www.crcsi.com.au/Resources/ government/The-Australian-Government-response-to-the-report-i (accessed January 21, 2014).

Office of the Attorney General. 1832. "Anatomy Act." Last modified August 1. http://www.irishstatutebook.ie/1832/en/act/pub/0075/print.html (accessed January 21, 2014).

Office of the Under Secretary of Defense for Acquisition Technology and Logistics. 2007. "Report of the Defense Science Board Task Force on Defense Biometrics. 20301–3140." Office of the Under Secretary of Defense for Acquisition Technology and Logistics, Washington, DC.

Olsen, Florence. 2007. "The Environmental Executive." *FCW*, November 19. http:// fcw.com/Articles/2007/11/19/The-environmental-executive.aspx?sc_lang=en&Page =1 (accessed January 21, 2014).

Olson, Mancur. 1971. *The Logic of Collective Action: Public Goods and the Theory of Groups*. 2nd ed. Cambridge, MA: Harvard University Press.

Olson, Mancur. 1982. *The Rise and Decline of Nations—Economic Growth, Stagflation, and Social Rigidities*. New Haven, CT: Yale University Press.

Onishi, Norimitsu, and Martin Fackler. 2011. "In Nuclear Crisis, Crippling Mistrust." *New York Times*, June 13. http://www.nytimes.com/2011/06/13/world/asia/13japan .html?pagewanted=all&_r=0 (accessed November 4, 2013).

Osterloh, Margit, and Bruno S. Frey. 2000. "Motivation, Knowledge Transfer, and Organizational Forms." *Organization Science* 11 (5): 538–550.

Otjacques, Benoît, Patrik Hitzelberger, and Fernand Feltz. 2007. "Interoperability of e-Government Information Systems: Issues of Identification and Data Sharing." *Journal of Management Information Systems* 23 (4): 29–51.

Pálsson, Gísli, and Kristín E. Harðardóttir. 2002. "For Whom the Cell Tolls: Debates about Biomedicine." *Current Anthropology* 43 (2): 271–301.

Panangala, Sidath Viranga, and Don J. Jansen. 2013. *Departments of Defense and Veterans Affairs: Status of the Integrated Electronic Health Record (iEHR) (CRS Report for Congress Prepared for Members and Committees of Congress)*. R42970. Washington, DC: Congressional Research Service.

Papadimitriou, Christos. 2001. "Algorithms, Games, and the Internet." In *Proceedings of the Thirty-Third Annual ACM Symposium on Theory of Computing*, ed. J. S. Vitter, P. Spirakis, and M. Yannakakis, 749–753. Hersonissos: ACM.

Pardo, T. A., and G. K. Tayi. 2007. "Interorganizational Information Integration: A Key Enabler for Digital Government." *Government Information Quarterly* 24 (4): 691–715.

Parry, Bronwyn. 2004. *Trading the Genome: Investigating the Commodification of Bio-Information.* New York: Columbia University Press.

Parycek, Peter, and Michael Sachs. 2010. "Open Government: Information Flow in Web 2.0." *European Journal of ePractice* 9:57–68.

Paull, Dan. 2011. "PSMA Australia's LYNX Infrastructure: Collaborating to deliver capability across governments." Canberra: PSMA Australia Limited. http://www.gsdi.org/gsdiconf/gsdi11/slides/fri/7.4e.pdf (accessed January 20, 2014).

Paull, Dan. 2012. PSMA Shareholder Voting (correspondence), Australia, December 4.

Paull, Dan. 2013. "PSMA Australia's LYNX Infrastructure: Collaborating to Deliver Capability across Governments." Last modified November 3. http://www.gsdi.org/gsdiconf/gsdi11/slides/fri/7.4e.pdf (accessed January 21, 2014).

Paull, Dan, and Dave Lovell. 2010. "Closer Than You Think: The Pioneering Relationship between PSMA Australia and EuroGeographics." In *Proceedings of the FIG Congress 2010: Facing the Challenges—Building the Capacity*, ed. R. Staiger. Sydney: FIG.

Paull, Dan, and Dave Lovell. 2012. "The Pioneering Relationship between PSMA Australia and EuroGeographics: How These Continental Mapping Agencies Are Enabling the Spatial Community." Orono, MA: Global Spatial Data Infrastructure Association. http://www.gsdi.org/gsdiconf/gsdi12/papers/20.pdf (accessed July 29, 2012).

Peled, Alon. 2007. "The Electronic Mountain: A Tale of Two Tels." *American Review of Public Administration* 37 (4): 458–478.

Peled, Alon. 2011. "When Transparency and Collaboration Collide: The USA Open Data Program." *Journal of the American Society for Information Science and Technology* 62 (11): 2085–2094.

Perlroth, Nicole. 2011. "Hackers Breach the Web Site of Stratfor Global Intelligence." *New York Times*, December 25. http://www.nytimes.com/2011/12/26/technology/hackers-breach-the-web-site-of-stratfor-global-intelligence.html?_r=1 (accessed November 2, 2013).

Perri 6, Christine Bellamy, Charles Raab, Adam Warren, and Cate Heeney. 2007. "Institutional Shaping of Interagency Working: Managing Tensions between Collaborative Working and Client Confidentiality." *Journal of Public Administration: Research and Theory* 17 (3): 405–434.

Philipkoski, Kristen. 1999. "Iceland's Genetic Jackpot." *Wired*. Last modified December 10. http://www.wired.com/science/discoveries/news/1999/12/32904 (accessed January 21, 2014).

Phillips, Anne. 2011. "It's My Body and I'll Do What I Like with It." *Political Theory* 39 (6): 724–748.

Picci, Lucio. 2011. *Reputation-Based Governance*. Stanford, CA: Stanford University Press.

Piderit, R., S. Flowerday, and R. Von Solms. 2011. "Enabling Information Sharing by Establishing Trust in Supply Chains: A Case Study in the South African Automotive Industry." *SA Journal of Information Management* 13 (1): 1–8.

Pierre, Jon, ed. 1995. *Bureaucracy in the Modern State: An Introduction to Comparative Public Administration*. Aldershot: Edward Elgar.

Pollock, Rufus, David Newbery, and Lionel Bently. 2008. *Models of Public Sector Information Provision via Trading Funds*. Cambridge: Cambridge University, Department for Business, Enterprise and Regulatory Reform (BERR) and HM Treasury.

Poulsen, Kevin. 2011. "IMF Breached by Sophisticated Hack Attack." *Wired*, June 13. http://www.wired.com/threatlevel/2011/06/imf (accessed January 21, 2014).

Premkumar, G. 2003. "Perspectives of the e-Marketplace by Multiple Stakeholders." *Communications of the ACM* 46 (12): 279–288.

Prins, Corien. 2004. "Access to Public Sector Information." In Need of Constitutional Recognition?" In *Public Sector Information in the Digital Age: Between Markets, Public Management and Citizens' Rights*, ed. G. Aichholzer and H. Burkert, 48–68. Northhampton, MA: Edward Elgar.

Program Manager Information Sharing Environment. 2011. *Information Sharing Environment: Annual Report to Congress*. Washington, DC: Information Sharing Environment (ISE).

PSMA. 2008. PSMA Australia Limited Constitution (Version 1.4), October 14. PSMA Australia Limited.

Public Accounts Committee. 2012. "Implementing the Transparency Agenda." Last modified July 16. http://www.publications.parliament.uk/pa/cm201213/cmselect/cmpubacc/102/10202.htm (accessed March 12, 2014).

Radford, John. 2010. "Case Number 14." Birmingham: Serious Case Reviews (SCR). http://www.lscbbirmingham.org.uk/downloads/Case+14.pdf (accessed July 28, 2012).

Radin, Margaret Jane. 1996. *Contested Commodities*. Cambridge, MA: Harvard University Press.

Rainey, Hal G., Robert W. Backoff, and Charles H. Levine. 1976. "Comparing Public and Private Organizations." *Public Administration Review* 36 (2): 233–244.

Raul, Alan Charles. 2002. *Privacy and the Digital State: Balancing Public Information and Personal Privacy.* Norwell: Kluwer Academic Publisher.

Reddick, C. G. 2005. "Citizen Interaction with e-Government: From the Streets to Servers?" *Government Information Quarterly* 22 (1): 38–57.

Rice, Robert A. 2001. "Noble Goals and Challenging Terrain: Organic and Fair Trade Coffee Movements in the Global Marketplace." *Journal of Agricultural & Environmental Ethics* 14 (1): 39–66.

Riley, Michael, and Sandrine Rastello. 2011. "IMF State-Backed Cyber-Attack Follows Hacks of Lab, G-20." Last modified June 14. http://www.bloomberg.com/news/2011 -06-11/imf-computer-system-infiltrated-by-hackers-said-to-work-for-foreign-state .html (accessed January 21, 2014).

Ritchie, Jean H. 1994. *The Report of the Inquiry into the Care and Treatment of Christopher Clunis.* London: HMSO.

Robbins, Stuart. 2006. *Lessons in Grid Computing: The System Is a Mirror.* Hoboken, NJ: John Wiley.

Roberts, Alasdair. 2004. "ORCON Creep: Information Sharing and the Threat of Government Accountability." *Government Information Quarterly* 21:249–267.

Roberts, Alasdair. 2006a. *Blacked out: Government Secrecy in the Information Age.* Cambridge: Cambridge University Press.

Roberts, Alasdair. 2006b. "The Limits of Control: The Market State, Divided Power, and the Response to 9/11." *International Public Management Journal* 9 (3): 313–332.

Roberts, Alasdair. 2012. "WikiLeaks: The Illusion of Transparency." *International Review of Administrative Sciences* 78 (1): 116–133.

Robinson, David, Harlan Yu, William P. Zeller, and Edward W. Felten. 2009. "Government Data and the Invisible Hand." *Yale Journal of Law and Technology* 11:160–175.

Rocheleau, B., and L. Wu. 2002. "Public versus Private Information Systems: Do They Differ in Important Ways? A Review and Empirical Test." *American Review of Public Administration* 32 (4): 379–397.

Rocheleau, Bruce. 2003. "Politics, Accountability, and Governmental Information Systems." In *Public information Technology: Policy and Management Issues*, ed. G. D. Garson, 20–52. Hershey, PA: Idea Group Publishing.

Rogers Commission. 1986. *Hearings of the Presidential Commission on the Space Shuttle Challenger Accident: February 26, 1986 to May 2, 1986— Report of the Presidential Com-*

mission on the Space Shuttle Challenger Accident—Volume 5. Washington, DC: NASA. http://history.nasa.gov/rogersrep/v5part2.htm (accessed September 8, 2013).

Rosenberg, Lisa. 2013. "A Decidedly Different Obama on Transparency." Last modified January 22. http://sunlightfoundation.com/blog/2013/01/22/a-decidedly -different-obama-on-transparency (accessed January 21, 2014).

Ross, Ian, and Carol Urquhart Ross. 1979. "Body Snatching in Nineteenth Century Britain: From Exhumation to Murder." *British Journal of Law and Society* 6 (1): 108–118.

Rourke, Francis E., and F. Edward. 1961. *Secrecy and Publicity: Dilemmas of Democracy*. Baltimore, MD: Johns Hopkins University Press.

Royal Commission into the New South Wales Police Service (The Wood Royal Commission). 1997. *Final Report: Corruption*. 0731309154. Sydney: The Government of the State of New South Wales.

Russell, Beth. 2012. Museum Modernization (correspondence), Boulder, CO, March 15.

Samuelson, Pamela. 2006. "Enriching Discourse on Public Domains." *Duke Law Journal* 55 (4): 783–834.

Samuelson, Pamela. 2011. "Too Many Copyrights?" *Communications of the ACM* 54 (7): 29–31.

Sandel, Michael. 2012. *What Money Can't Buy—The Moral Limits of Markets*. London: Penguin Books.

Sanders, Troutman. 2009. "FERC and NRC Sign Memorandum of Agreement on Grid Reliability and Nuclear Plants." Last modified September 2. http://www .troutmansandersenergyreport.com/2009/09/ferc-and-nrc-sign-memorandum-of -agreement-on-grid-reliability-and-nuclear-plants (accessed January 21, 2014).

Sarkar, Mitra Barun, Brian Butler, and Charles Steinfield. 1995. "Intermediaries and Cybermediaries: A Continuing Role for Mediating Players in the Electronic Marketplace." *Journal of Computer-Mediated Communication* 1 (3): 1–14.

Sarkesian, Sam C. 1972. "Political Soldiers: Perspectives on Professionalism in the U.S. Military." *Midwest Journal of Political Science* 16 (2): 239–258.

Satz, D. 2010. *Why Some Things Should Not Be For Sale: The Moral Limits of Markets*. Oxford: Oxford University Press.

Saxenian, AnnaLee. 1996. *Regional Advantage: Culture and Competition in Silicon Valley and Route 128*. Cambridge, MA: Harvard University Press.

Schneider, Anne, and Helen Ingram. 1990. "Behavioral Assumptions of Policy Tools." *Journal of Politics* 52 (2): 510–529.

Schoenbrod, David, Richard B. Stewart, and Katrina M. Wyman. 2010. *Breaking the Logjam: Environmental Protection that Will Work*. New Haven, CT: Yale University Press.

Schultze, Charles L. 1977. *The Public Use of Private Interest*. Washington, DC: The Brookings Institution.

Schwindt, Richard, and Aidan R. Vining. 1986. "Proposal for a Future Delivery Market for Transplant Organs." *Journal of Health Politics, Policy and Law* 11 (3): 483–500.

Secretary of State, Attorney General, Secretary of Homeland Security, and Director of Central Intelligence. 2011. *Memorandum of Understanding on the Integration and Use of Screening Information to Protect against Terrorism*. Washington, DC: U.S. Government Printing Office.

Seife, Charles. 2003. "'Terrorism Futures' Could Have a Future, Experts Say." *Science* 301 (5634): 749.

Select Bipartisan Committee to Investigate the Preparation for and Response to Hurricane Katrina. 2006. *A Failure of Initiative*. Washington, DC: U.S. Government Printing Office.

Semantic Web Health Care and Life Sciences (HCLS). 2013. "Semantic Web Health Care and Life Sciences (HCLS) Interest Group." Last modified November 3. http://www.w3.org/2001/sw/hcls (accessed January 21, 2014) .

Serbu, Jared. 2012. "IRS Technology Systems Dramatically Underfunded, Commissioner Says." *Federal News Radio*, April 6. http://www.federalnewsradio.com/?nid=534&sid=2817323 (accessed January 21, 2014).

Shachtman, Noah. 2010. "Exclusive: Google, CIA Invest in 'Future' of Web Monitoring." *Wired*, July 28. http://www.wired.com/dangerroom/2010/07/exclusive-google-cia (accessed January 21, 2014).

Shanahan, Mike. 2012. On Museum Modernization (correspondence), Honolulu, HI, March 14.

Sheumaker, Helen. 2003. "The Commodity of Self: Nineteenth-Century Human Hair Jewelry." In *Commodifying Everything: Relationships of the Market*, ed. S. Strasser, 71–95. New York: Routledge.

Shkabatur, Jennifer. 2012. "Transparency with(out) Accountability: Open Government in the United States." *Yale Law & Policy Review* 31 (1): 66.

Shulman, Stuart W., Lisa A. Thrane, and Mark C. Shelley. 2005. E-Rulemaking. In *Handbook of Public Information Systems*, ed. G. D. Garson, 237–254. Boca Raton, FL: Marcel Dekker.

Silberman, Neil Asher. 1982. *Digging for God and Country—Exploration Archeology, and the Secret Struggle for the Holy Land 1799–1917.* New York: Alfred Knopf.

Simon, Herbert A. 1997. *Administrative Behavior.* 4th ed. New York: The Free Press.

Singer, Natasha. 2012. "You for Sale: Mapping, and Sharing, the Consumer Genome." *New York Times*, June 16. http://www.nytimes.com/2012/06/17/technology/acxiom-the-quiet-giant-of-consumer-database-marketing.html?pagewanted=all (accessed November 2, 2013).

Snellen, Ignace. 2002. "Electronic Governance: Implications for Citizens, Politicians and Public Servants." *International Review of Administrative Sciences* 68 (2): 183–198.

Solove, Daniel J. 2004. *The Digital Person: Technology and Privacy in the Information Age.* New York: New York University Press.

Sowell, Thomas. 1981. *Markets and Minorities.* New York: Basic Books.

Spence, Patric R., Kenneth A. Lachlan, and Donyale R. Griffin. 2007. "Crisis Communication, Race, and Natural Disasters." *Journal of Black Studies* 37:539–555.

Srivastava, Abhishek, Kathryn M. Bartol, and Edwin A. Locke. 2006. "Empowering Leadership in Management Teams: Effects on Knowledge Sharing, Efficacy, and Performance." *Academy of Management Journal* 49 (6): 1239–1251.

Stanley, Ellen. 2004. "School Vouchers: Analysis of the Controversy." Last modified April 29. http://www.newfoundations.com/ConAnalysis/Stanley.html (accessed January 21, 2014).

State of Alaska and USDA Forest Service Alaska Region. 2000. *Memorandum of Understanding between the State of Alaska and USDA Forest Service, Alaska Region on Coastal Zone Management Act and Alaska Coastal Management Program Consistency Reviews.* FS Agreement No. 00MOU-111001-026. Washington, DC: USDA Forest Service.

Stengel, Richard. 1997. "An Overtaxed IRS." *Time*, April 7.

Stern, E., A. Lewinson-Gilboa, and J. Aviram, eds. 1992. *The New Encyclopedia of Archeological Excavations in the Holy Land.* Jerusalem: Israel Exploration Society.

Sternstein, Aliya. 2005. "The Search for 1,000 Points of Light." *FCW*, October 17. http://fcw.com/articles/2005/10/17/the-search-for-1000-points-of-light.aspx?sc_lang=en (accessed January 21, 2014).

Stiglitz, Joseph E. 2001. "On Liberty, the Right to Know, and Public Discourse: The Role of Transparency in Public Life." In *The Rebel Within*, ed. H.-J. Chang, 1–32. London: Anthem.

Stillman, Richard J. 1985. "The Romantic Vision in American Administrative Theory: Retrospectives and Prospectives." *International Journal of Public Administration* 7 (2): 107–148.

Stone, Deborah A. 2002. *Policy Paradox: The Art of Political Decision Making*. New York: W.W. Norton.

Taylor, John. A. 2007. "From Molecules to the Milky Way: Dealing with the Data Deluge." Last modified November 7. http://www.csiro.au/news/ps3ng (accessed January 21, 2014).

The Telegraph. 2009. "Mother and Daughter Who Burned to Death: 'No Excuses' Says Alan Johnson." *The Telegraph*, September 29. http://www.telegraph.co.uk/news/uknews/6241791/Mother-and-daughter-who-burned-to-death-no-excuses-says-Alan -Johnson.html (accessed January 21, 2014).

Tharp, Brent W. 2003. "Preserving Their Form and Features: The Commodification of Coffins in the American Understanding of Death." In *Commodifying Everything: Relationships of the Market*, ed. S. Strasser, 119–141. New York: Routledge.

Thomas, Page A. 1984. "The Success and Failure of Robert Alexander Stewart Macalister." *Biblical Archaeologist* 47 (1): 33–35.

Thomas, Richard, and Mark Walport. 2008. *Data Sharing Review Report*. London: Independent Report. http://amberhawk.typepad.com/files/thomas-walport -datasharingreview2008.pdf (accessed November 10, 2013).

Thormeyer, Rob. 2006. "EPA, Industry Launch Green IT Buying Initiative." *GCN*, May 10. http://gcn.com/articles/2006/05/10/epa-industry-launch-green-it-buying -initiative.aspx (accessed January 21, 2014).

Thurston, Anne Catherine. 2012. "Trustworthy Records and Open Data." *Journal of Community Informatics* 8 (2). http://ci-journal.net/index.php/ciej/article/view/951 (accessed March 11, 2014).

Tocqueville, Alexis de. [1840] 1969. *Democracy in America*. New York: Harper and Row Publishers.

Tomes, Nancy. 2003. "An Undesired Necessity: The Commodification of Medical Services in the Interwar United States." In *Commodifying Everything: Relationships of the Market*, ed. S. Strasser, 97–118. New York: Routledge.

Tomz, Michael. 2001. "How Do Reputations Form? New and Seasoned Borrowers in International Capital Markets." Paper presented at the Annual Meeting of the American Political Science Association, San Francisco, CA, August 20–September 2.

Tschannen-Moran, Megan. 2001. "Collaboration and the Need for Trust." *Journal of Educational Administration* 39 (4): 308–331.

Tufte, Edward R. 1997. *Visual Explanations—Images and Quantities, Evidence and Narrative*. Cheshire, CT: Graphics Press.

UK Comptroller and Auditor General. 2012. "Implementing Transparency: Cross-Government Review." Last modified April 16. http://www.official-documents.gov.uk/document/hc1012/hc18/1833/1833.pdf (accessed January 21, 2014).

U.S. Department of Housing and Urban Development. 2013. "CAIVRS—Credit Alert Interactive Voice Response System." Last modified November 3. http://www.hud.gov/offices/hsg/sfh/sys/caivrs/caivrs.cfm (accessed January 21, 2014).

U.S. Department of Justice—Office of the Inspector General. 2002. *The Immigration and Naturalization Service's Contacts with Two September 11 Terrorists*. Washington, DC: U.S. Government Printing Office.

U.S. General Services Administration. 2006. "The General Services Administration and the Department of Homeland Security Sign a Strategic Sourcing Partnership Memorandum of Understanding (MOU)." Last modified May 17. http://www.gsa.gov/portal/content/102132 (accessed January 21, 2014).

U.S. General Services Administration. 2013. "For Federal Agency Customers—Ordering Form Schedules." Last modified July 25. http://www.gsa.gov/portal/content/197513 (accessed January 20, 2014).

U.S. Geological Survey (USGS) and U.S. Fish and Wildlife Service (USFWS). 1990. *Memorandum of Agreement between the U.S. Geological Survey and the U.S. Fish and Wildlife Service*. Washington, DC: National Academies Press.

U.S. Government Accountability Office. 1991. *Many Federal Agencies Collect and Disseminate Information*. NSIAD-91-173. Washington, DC: U.S. Government Accountability Office.

U.S. Government Accountability Office. 1998. *Observations on FAA's Modernization Program*. GAO/T-RCED/AIMD-98-93. Washington, DC: U.S. Government Accountability Office.

U.S. Government Accountability Office. 2002. *Selected Agencies' Handling of Personal Information*. GAO-02-1058. Washington, DC: U.S. Government Accountability Office.

U.S. Government Accountability Office. 2003a. *Benefits Realized for Selected Health Care Functions*. GAO-04-224. Washington, DC: U.S. Government Accountability Office.

U.S. Government Accountability Office. 2003b. *Homeland Security Efforts to Improve Information Sharing Need to Be Strengthened*. GAO-03-760. Washington, DC: U.S. Government Accountability Office.

U.S. Government Accountability Office. 2003c. *Issues Facing the Army's Future Combat Systems Program*. GAO-03-1010R. Washington, DC: U.S. Government Accountability Office.

U.S. Government Accountability Office. 2003d. *Terrorist Watch Lists Should Be Consolidated to Promote Better Integration and Sharing.* GAO-03-322. Washington, DC: U.S. Government Accountability Office.

U.S. Government Accountability Office. 2004a. *Data Mining: Federal Efforts Cover a Wide Range of Uses.* GAO-04-548. Washington, DC: U.S. Government Accountability Office.

U.S. Government Accountability Office. 2004b. *Major Federal Networks that Support Homeland Security Functions.* GAO-04-375. Washington, DC: U.S. Government Accountability Office.

U.S. Government Accountability Office. 2005a. *21st Century Challenges: Reexamining the Base of the Federal Government.* GAO-05-325SP. Washington, DC: U.S. Government Accountability Office.

U.S. Government Accountability Office. 2005b. *An Update.* GAO-05-207. Washington, DC: U.S. Government Accountability Office.

U.S. Government Accountability Office. 2006a. *The Federal Government Needs to Establish Policies and Processes for Sharing Terrorism-Related and Sensitive but Unclassified Information.* GAO-06-385. Washington, DC: U.S. Government Accountability Office.

U.S. Government Accountability Office. 2006b. *HHS Is Continuing Efforts to Define a National Strategy.* GAO-06-346T. Washington, DC: U.S. Government Accountability Office.

U.S. Government Accountability Office. 2006c. *Utilities Have Made Important Upgrades but Further Improvements to Key System Components May Be Limited by Costs and Other Constraints.* GAO-06-390. Washington, DC: U.S. Government Accountability Office.

U.S. Government Accountability Office. 2006d. *VA and DOD Health Care: Efforts to Provide Seamless Transition of Care for OEF and OIF Servicemembers and Veterans.* GAO-06-794R. Washington, DC: U.S. Government Accountability Office.

U.S. Government Accountability Office. 2007a. *Homeland Security Information Network Needs to Be Better Coordinated with Key State and Local Initiatives.* GAO-07-822T. Washington, DC: U.S. Government Accountability Office.

U.S. Government Accountability Office. 2007b. *Numerous Federal Networks Used to Support Homeland Security Need to Be Better Coordinated with Key State and Local Information-Sharing Initiatives.* GAO-07-455. Washington, DC: U.S. Government Accountability Office.

U.S. Government Accountability Office. 2007c. *An Update.* GAO-07-310. Washington, DC: U.S. Government Accountability Office.

U.S. Government Accountability Office. 2008a. *Demand for the Social Security Administration's Electronic Data Exchanges Is Growing and Presents Future Challenges*. GAO-09-126. Washington, DC: U.S. Government Accountability Office.

U.S. Government Accountability Office. 2008b. *DOD Can Establish More Guidance for Biometrics Collection and Explore Broader Data Sharing*. GAO-09-49. Washington, DC: U.S. Government Accountability Office.

U.S. Government Accountability Office. 2008c. *DOD Needs to Establish Clear Goals and Objectives, Guidance, and a Designated Budget to Manage Its Biometrics Activities*. GAO-08-1065. Washington, DC: U.S. Government Accountability Office.

U.S. Government Accountability Office. 2008d. *Management Improvements Needed on the Department of Homeland Security's Next Generation Information Sharing System*. GAO-09-40. Washington, DC: U.S. Government Accountability Office.

U.S. Government Accountability Office. 2008e. *Significant Challenges Ahead in Developing and Demonstrating Future Combat System's Network and Software*. GAO-08-409. Washington, DC: U.S. Government Accountability Office.

U.S. Government Accountability Office. 2008f. *Testimony before the Senate Committee on Veterans' Affairs—DOD and VA Have Increased Their Sharing of Health Information, but Further Actions Are Needed—Statement of Valerie C. Melvin, Director Human Capital and Management Information Systems Issues*. GAO-08-1158T. Washington, DC: U.S. Government Accountability Office.

U.S. Government Accountability Office. 2009a. *Challenges Remain for VA Sharing of Electronic Health Records with DOD*. GAO-09-427T. Washington, DC: U.S. Government Accountability Office.

U.S. Government Accountability Office. 2009b. *Developing a Collaboration Strategy Is Essential to Fostering Interagency Data and Resource Sharing*. GAO-10-171. Washington, DC: U.S. Government Accountability Office.

U.S. Government Accountability Office. 2009c. *DOD and VA Efforts to Achieve Full Interoperability Are Ongoing; Program Office Management Needs Improvement*. GAO-09-775. Washington, DC: U.S. Government Accountability Office.

U.S. Government Accountability Office. 2009d. *EPA Needs to Coordinate Research Strategy and Clarify Its Authority to Obtain Biomonitoring Data*. GAO-09-353. Washington, DC: U.S. Government Accountability Office.

U.S. Government Accountability Office. 2009e. *Federal Agencies' Experiences Demonstrate Challenges to Successful Implementation*. GAO-09-312T. Washington, DC: U.S. Government Accountability Office.

U.S. Government Accountability Office. 2009f. *Observations on Improving the Toxic Substances Control Act*. GAO-10-292T. Washington, DC: U.S. Government Accountability Office.

U.S. Government Accountability Office. 2009g. *Social Security Administration's Data Exchanges Support Current Programs, but Better Planning Is Needed to Meet Future Demands.* GAO-09-966. Washington, DC: U.S. Government Accountability Office.

U.S. Government Accountability Office. 2009h. *The U.S. Army Corps of Engineers Needs to Improve Its Process for Reviewing Completed Cleanup Remedies to Ensure Continued Protection.* GAO-10-46. Washington, DC: U.S. Government Accountability Office.

U.S. Government Accountability Office. 2009i. *An Update.* GAO-09-271. Washington, DC: U.S. Government Accountability Office.

U.S. Government Accountability Office. 2010a. *Carbon Trading: Current Situation and Oversight Considerations for Policymakers.* GAO-10-851R. Washington, DC: U.S. Government Accountability Office.

U.S. Government Accountability Office. 2010b. *Challenges in Federal Agencies' Use of Web 2.0 Technologies.* GAO-10-872T. Washington, DC: U.S. Government Accountability Office.

U.S. Government Accountability Office. 2010c. *Federal Agencies Have Taken Steps to Improve E-Verify, but Significant Challenges Remain.* GAO-11-146. Washington, DC: U.S. Government Accountability Office.

U.S. Government Accountability Office. 2010d. *Medicare Payments to Federally Qualified Health Centers.* GAO-10-576R. Washington, DC: U.S. Government Accountability Office.

U.S. Government Accountability Office. 2010e. *Nanomaterials Are Widely Used in Commerce, but EPA Faces Challenges in Regulating Risk.* GAO-10-549. Washington, DC: U.S. Government Accountability Office.

U.S. Government Accountability Office. 2010f. *OMB's Dashboard Has Increased Transparency and Oversight, but Improvements Needed.* GAO-10-701. Washington, DC: U.S. Government Accountability Office.

U.S. Government Accountability Office. 2010g. *Undercover Tests Show Five State Programs Are Vulnerable to Fraud and Abuse.* GAO-10-1062. Washington, DC: U.S. Government Accountability Office.

U.S. Government Accountability Office. 2011a. *Agencies Need to Complete Inventories and Plans to Achieve Expected Savings.* GAO-11-565. Washington, DC: U.S. Government Accountability Office.

U.S. Government Accountability Office. 2011b. *Critical Infrastructure Protection: DHS Has Taken Action Designed to Identify and Address Overlaps and Gaps in Critical Infrastructure Security Activities.* GAO-11-537R. Washington, DC: U.S. Government Accountability Office.

U.S. Government Accountability Office. 2011c. *Decennial Census: Census Bureau and Postal Service Should Pursue Opportunities to Further Enhance Collaboration*. GAO-11-874. Washington, DC: U.S. Government Accountability Office.

U.S. Government Accountability Office. 2011d. *Disparate Tax Treatment and Information Gaps Create Uncertainty and Potential Abuse*. GAO-11-750. Washington, DC: U.S. Government Accountability Office.

U.S. Government Accountability Office. 2011e. *DOD Can Better Conform to Standards and Share Biometric Information with Federal Agencies*. GAO-11-276. Washington, DC: U.S. Government Accountability Office.

U.S. Government Accountability Office. 2011f. *Grants.gov: Additional Action Needed to Address Persistent Governance and Funding Challenges*. GAO-11-478. Washington, DC: U.S. Government Accountability Office.

U.S. Government Accountability Office. 2011g. *High Risk: An Update*. GAO-11-278. Washington, DC: U.S. Government Accountability Office.

U.S. Government Accountability Office. 2011h. *Information Sharing Environment: Better Road Map Needed to Guide Implementation and Investments*. GAO-11-455. Washington, DC: U.S. Government Accountability Office.

U.S. Government Accountability Office. 2011i. *Interagency Committee Needs to Better Coordinate Research on Oil Pollution Prevention and Response*. GAO-11-319. Washington, DC: U.S. Government Accountability Office.

U.S. Government Accountability Office. 2011j. *TANF and Child Welfare Programs: Increased Data Sharing Could Improve Access to Benefits and Services*. GAO-12-2. Washington, DC: U.S. Government Accountability Office.

U.S. Government Accountability Office. 2011k. *Taxpayer Privacy: A Guide for Screening and Assessing Proposals to Disclose Confidential Tax Information to Specific Parties for Specific Purposes*. GAO-12-231SP. Washington, DC: U.S. Government Accountability Office.

U.S. Government Accountability Office. 2011l. *To Improve Data and Programs, Agencies Have Taken Steps to Develop a Common Vocabulary*. GAO-12-320T. Washington, DC: U.S. Government Accountability Office.

U.S. Government Accountability Office. 2012a. *Availability and Potential Reliability of Selected Data Elements at Five Agencies—Statement of Anu K. Mittal, Director of Natural Resources and Environment*. GAO-12-691T. Washington, DC: U.S. Government Accountability Office.

U.S. Government Accountability Office. 2012b. *Better Data on Facility Jurisdictions Needed to Enhance Collaboration with State and Local Law Enforcement*. GAO-12-434. Washington, DC: U.S. Government Accountability Office.

U.S. Government Accountability Office. 2012c. *CMS Needs an Approach and a Reliable Cost Estimate for Removing Social Security Numbers from Medicare Cards.* GAO-12-831. Washington, DC: U.S. Government Accountability Office.

U.S. Government Accountability Office. 2012d. *Collecting Data and Sharing Information on Federally Unregulated Gathering Pipelines Could Help Enhance Safety.* GAO-12-388. Washington, DC: U.S. Government Accountability Office.

U.S. Government Accountability Office. 2012e. *DHS Needs to Further Define and Implement Its New Governance Process.* GAO-12-818. Washington, DC: U.S. Government Accountability Office.

U.S. Government Accountability Office. 2012f. *EPA Needs Better Information on New Source Review Permits.* GAO-12-590. Washington, DC: U.S. Government Accountability Office.

U.S. Government Accountability Office. 2012g. *FAA Is Taking Steps to Improve Data, but Challenges for Managing Safety Risks Remain.* GAO-12-660T. Washington, DC: U.S. Government Accountability Office.

U.S. Government Accountability Office. 2012h. FDA Needs to Fully Implement Key Management Practices to Lessen Modernization Risks. GAO-12-346. Washington, DC: U.S. Government Accountability Office.

U.S. Government Accountability Office. 2012i. *Federal Law Should Be Updated to Address Changing Technology Landscape.* GAO-12-961T. Washington, DC: U.S. Government Accountability Office.

U.S. Government Accountability Office. 2012j. *Fragmented Federal Programs that Reduce Mobile Source Emissions Could Be Improved.* GAO-12-261. Washington, DC: U.S. Government Accountability Office.

U.S. Government Accountability Office. 2012k. *Freedom of Information: Additional Actions Can Strengthen Agency Efforts to Improve Management.* GAO-12-828. Washington, DC: U.S. Government Accountability Office.

U.S. Government Accountability Office. 2012l. *Government Is Analyzing Alternatives for Contractor Identification Numbers.* GAO-12-715R. Washington, DC: U.S. Government Accountability Office.

U.S. Government Accountability Office. 2012m. *Improved Guidance and Information Sharing Needed for DOD Project-Level Officials.* GAO-12-401. Washington, DC: U.S. Government Accountability Office.

U.S. Government Accountability Office. 2012n. *Improved Planning and Performance Measures Are Needed to Help Ensure Successful Technology Modernization.* GAO-12-495. Washington, DC: U.S. Government Accountability Office.

U.S. Government Accountability Office. 2012o. *Limited Information on the Use and Effectiveness of Tax Expenditures Could Be Mitigated through Congressional Attention.* GAO-12-262. Washington, DC: U.S. Government Accountability Office.

U.S. Government Accountability Office. 2012p. *Office of Personnel Management Needs to Improve Transparency of Its Pricing and Seek Cost Savings.* GAO-12–197. Washington, DC: U.S. Government Accountability Office.

U.S. Government Accountability Office. 2012q. *Tax Debtors Have Received FHA Mortgage Insurance and First-Time Homebuyer Credits.* GAO-12-592. Washington, DC: U.S. Government Accountability Office.

U.S. Government Accountability Office. 2012r. *VA and DOD Health Care—Department-Level Actions Needed to Assess Collaboration Performance, Address Barriers, and Identify Opportunities.* GAO-12-992. Washington, DC: U.S. Government Accountability Office.

U.S. Government Accountability Office. 2012s. *VA and HUD Are Working to Improve Data on Supportive Housing Program.* GAO-12-726. Washington, DC: U.S. Government Accountability Office.

U.S. Government Accountability Office. 2012t. *Vulnerability to Fraud and Abuse Remains.* GAO-12-697. Washington, DC: U.S. Government Accountability Office.

U.S. Government Accountability Office. 2013a. *Department of Veterans Affairs: Available Data Not Sufficiently Reliable to Describe Use of Consulting Services.* GAO-13-714R. Washington, DC: U.S. Government Accountability Office.

U.S. Government Accountability Office. 2013b. *Export Promotion: Better Information Needed about Federal Resources.* GAO-13-644. Washington, DC: U.S. Government Accountability Office.

U.S. Government Accountability Office. 2013c. *Information Technology: OMB and Agencies Need to More Effectively Implement Major Initiatives to Save Billions of Dollars.* GAO-13-796T. Washington, DC: U.S. Government Accountability Office.

U.S. Government Accountability Office. 2013d. *Social Security Administration—Preliminary Observations on the Death Master File—Statement of Daniel Bertoni, Director Education, Workforce, and Income Security Issues before the Committee on Homeland Security and Governmental Affairs, US Senate.* GAO-13-574T. Washington, DC: U.S. Government Accountability Office.

U.S. Government Accountability Office. 2013e. *Wildland Fire Management: Improvements Needed in Information, Collaboration, and Planning to Enhance Federal Fire Aviation Program Success.* GAO-13-684. Washington, DC: U.S. Government Accountability Office.

U.S. Social Security Administration (SSA). 2009. "Revised CBSV Model Agreement—January 13, 2009." RA-CBSV-09-F. http://www.ssa.gov/cbsv (accessed January 21, 2014).

U.S. Social Security Administration (SSA). 2012. "Data Exchanges." Last modified January 12. http://www.ssa.gov/gix (accessed January 21, 2014).

Van Den Broek, Tijs, Bas Kotterink, Noor Huijboom, Wout Hofman, and Stef Van Grieken. 2011. *Open Data Need a Vision of Smart Government: Roadblocks to a Pan European Market for PSI Reuse.* Netherlands: TNO (Netherlands Organisation for Applied Scientific Research).

Vangen, Siv, and Chris Huxham. 2003. "Nurturing Collaborative Relations." *Journal of Applied Behavioral Science* 39 (1): 5–31.

Vann, Irvin B. 2005. "Electronic Data Sharing in Public Sector Agencies." In *Handbook of Public Information Systems,* ed. G. D. Garson, 143–153. Boca Raton, FL: Marcel Dekker.

Vaughan, Diane. 1996. *The Challenger Launch Decision: Risky Technology, Culture, and Deviance at NASA.* Chicago, IL: University of Chicago Press.

Vickrey, William. 1961. "Counterspeculation, Auctions, and Competitive Sealed Tenders." *Journal of Finance* 16 (1): 8–37.

Wadhwa, Vivek. 2011. "The Death of Open Government." Last modified June 22. http://www.washingtonpost.com/national/on-innovations/the-coming-death-of -open-government/2011/06/21/AGPK3afH_story.html?wpisrc=nl_cuzheads (accessed January 21, 2014).

Washington Post. 2010. "Top Secret America." *Washington Post,* July 20. http:// projects.washingtonpost.com/top-secret-america/articles (accessed January 21, 2014).

Waltzer, Michael. 1983. *Spheres of Justice: A Defense of Pluralism and Equality.* New York: Basic Books.

Waters, Nigel. 2006a. *Government Surveillance in Australia.* Australia: Pacific Privacy Consulting. http://www.pacificprivacy.com.au/Government Surveillance in Australia v6.pdf (accessed November 1, 2013).

Waters, Robin. 2006b. "PSMA Australia—Lessons for Europe?" *GIS Professional,* July/ August. http://docbox.etsi.org/STF/Archive/STF321_TISPAN3_EC_Emergency_Call _Location/Public/Library/Australia/PSMA%20Australia%20-%20lessons%20for%20 Europe.pdf (accessed January 21, 2014).

Weber, Max. 1978. *Economy and Society.* Vol. 2. Ed. G. Roth and C. Wittich. Berkeley: University of California Press.

Weigelt, Matthew. 2011. "Air Force Divisions Pledge to Fight Fraud, Contractor Misconduct." *FCW,* December 16. http://fcw.com/articles/2011/12/16/air-force-mou -procurement-fraud.aspx?sc_lang=en (accessed January 21, 2014).

Weigle, Brett D. 2007. "Prediction Markets Another Tool in the Intelligence Kitbag." MA thesis, U.S. Army War College.

Weiler-Polak, Dana. 2011. "Reports on At-Risk Youth Often Don't Reach Authorities." *Ha'aretz*, December 21. http://www.haaretz.com/print-edition/news/reports-on-at-risk-youth-often-don-t-reach-authorities-1.402635 (accessed January 21, 2014).

Weinberger, David. 2007. *Everything Is Miscellaneous: The Power of the New Digital Disorder*. New York: Times Books.

Wenjing, Liu. 2011. Government Information Sharing: Principles, Practice, and Problems—An International Perspective. *Government Information Quarterly* 28 (3): 363–373.

White, Jay D. 2007. *Managing Information in the Public Sector*. London: M. E. Sharp.

White, Leonard D. 1926. *Introduction to the Study of Public Administration*. New York: The Macmillan Company.

White House—Office of the Press Secretary. 2009. "President Signs Two Executive Orders and Three Memorandums (Press Release)." Last modified January 21. http://www.whitehouse.gov/the-press-office/statement-press-secretary-presidents-signing-two-executive-orders-and-three-memoran (accessed January 21, 2014).

White House. 2010. "Open Government Highlights." Last modified in July. http://www.whitehouse.gov/open/highlights (accessed January 21, 2014).

White House. 2010. *Summary of the White House Review of the December 25 2009 Attempted Terrorist Attack*. Washington, DC: U.S. Government Printing Office.

White House. 2013. "The Obama Administration's Commitment to Open Government: A Status Report." Last modified November 3. http://www.whitehouse.gov/sites/default/files/opengov_report.pdf (accessed January 21, 2014).

Wikipedia. 2013. "Terabyte." Last modified October 31. http://en.wikipedia.org/wiki/Terabyte (accessed January 21, 2014).

Willem, Annick, and Marc Buelens. 2007. "Knowledge Sharing in Public Sector Organizations: The Effect of Organizational Characteristics on Interdepartmental Knowledge Sharing." *Journal of Public Administration: Research and Theory* 17: 581–606.

Wilson, Tom D. 2010. "Information Sharing: An Exploration of the Literature and Some Propositions." *Information Research: An International Electronic Journal* 15 (4). http://www.informationr.net/ir/15-4/paper440.html (accessed January 21, 2014).

Wilson, Woodrow. 1887. "The Study of Administration." *Political Science Quarterly* 2 (2): 202–217.

Wolff, Tobias Barrington. 2002. "The Thirteenth Amendment and Slavery in the Global Economy." *Columbia Law Review* 102 (4): 973–1050.

Wonderlich, John. 2011. "Obama's Open Government Directive, Two Years On." Last modified December 7. http://sunlightfoundation.com/blog/2011/12/07/obamas-open-government-directive-two-years-on (accessed January 21, 2014).

Wood, Susan F., Ruth W. Long, Liz Borkowski, and David Michaels. 2010. *Strengthening Science in Government: Advancing Science in the Public Interest: The Scientists in Government Project*. Washington, DC: The Scientists in Government Project. http://cdm16064.contentdm.oclc.org/cdm/singleitem/collection/p266901coll4/id/2402/rec/8 (accessed October 24, 2013).

World Nuclear Association. 2011. *Fukushima Accident*. London: World Nuclear Association. http://www.world-nuclear.org/info/Safety-and-Security/Safety-of-Plants/Fukushima-Accident (accessed January 21, 2014).

Yackee, Jason Webb, and Susan Webb Yackee. 2006. "A Bias Towards Business? Assessing Interest Group Influence on the US Bureaucracy." *Journal of Politics* 68 (1): 128–139.

Yahoo. 2013. "Fukushima Pipe Leaking Radioactive Water: TEPCO." Last modified September 1. http://sg.news.yahoo.com/fukushima-pipe-leaking-radioactive-water-tepco-045637399.html (accessed January 21, 2014).

Yang, Tung-Mou, and Terrance A. Maxwell. 2011. "Information-sharing in Public Organizations: A Literature Review of Interpersonal, Intra-Organizational and Inter-Organizational Success Factors." *Government Information Quarterly* 28:164–175.

Yu, Harlan, and David Robinson. 2012. "The New Ambiguity of 'Open Government.'" *UCLA Law Review Discourse* 178:178–208.

Yu, Liangzhi. 2006. "Understanding Information Inequality: Making Sense of the Literature of the Information and Digital Divides." *Journal of Librarianship and Information Science* 38 (4): 229–252.

Yu, Shiyang. 2007. "New Model of Enhancing Public Service by Information Sharing: NingBo 81890 Center." *Government Information Quarterly* 24 (4): 709–710.

Yuan, Yu, Janet Fulk, Michelle Shumate, Peter R. Monge, J. Alison Bryant, and Matthew Matsaganis. 2005. "Individual Participation in Organizational Information Commons." *Human Communication Research* 31 (2): 212–240.

Zaheer, A., and B. McEvily. 1998. "Does Trust Matter? Exploring the Effects of Interorganizational and Interpersonal Trust on Performance." *Organization Science* 9:141–158.

Zegart, Amy B. 2004. "Blue Ribbons, Black Boxes: Toward a Better Understanding of Presidential Commissions." *Presidential Studies Quarterly* 34 (2): 366–393.

Zhang, J., and Sharon S. Dawes. 2006. "Expectations and Perceptions of Benefits, Barriers, and Success in Public Sector Knowledge Networks." *Public Performance & Management Review* 29 (4): 433–466.

Zhang, J., Sharon S. Dawes, and J. Sarkis. 2005. "Exploring Stakeholders' Expectations of the Benefits and Barriers of e-Government Knowledge Sharing." *Journal of Enterprise Information Management* 18 (5): 548–567.

Zuiderwijk, Anneke, Marijn Janssen, Sunil Choenni, Ronald Meijer, and Roexsana Sheikh Alibaks. 2012. "Socio-technical Impediments of Open Data." *Journal of E-Government* 10 (2): 156–172.

Zuurmond, A. 1998. "From Bureaucracy to Infocracy: Are Democratic Institutions Lagging Behind?" In *Public Administration in an Information Age: A Handbook*, ed. I. T. M. Snellen and W. B. H. J. van de Donk, 259–272. Amsterdam: IOS Press.

Zyskowski, John. 2009. "Tending the Wiki Garden." *FCW*, January 26. http://fcw.com/Articles/2009/01/26/Tending-the-wiki-garden.aspx (accessed January 21, 2014).

Index

The letter *f* following a page number denotes a figure and *t* denotes a table.

9/11 Commission, 15–16

Abu-Shusheh, 6–7, 126, 191
Accenture, 31, 42, 153
Acxiom Corporation, 26
Administrative Conference of the
    United States, 45
Administrative Office of the U.S. Courts
    (AOUSC), 102, 193
Adultery, 115
Afghanistan, 141
Agencies. *See also specific agency*
  Big Data and, 13, 23–30, 40, 102, 167,
    172
  CEOs and, 18, 32, 88, 90,
    127–128
  CIOs and, 59, 65, 151
  collaboration and, 183, 186–187 (*see
    also* Collaboration)
  computers and, 1–3, 7–8, 23 (*see also*
    Computers)
  cooperation and, 7 (*see also*
    Cooperation)
  guardian syndrome and, 55
  islands of automation and, 31
  meaning of term, 10
  monopolies and, 97–98 (*see also*
    Monopolies)
  open data and, 62–64

  ownership issues and, 22, 69 (*see also*
    Ownership issues)
  selfishness and, 41–46, 52, 55,
    125–126
  transparency and, 32, 58, 61–62,
    69–70, 85, 90, 98, 161, 170, 176
Agnew, Jean-Christophe, 116
Airman Registration and Aircraft
    Registry, 15
Akbulut, Asli Yagmur, 42, 45, 54, 155
Akhavan, P., 32
Akiyama, Nobumasa, 20–21
Alaska, 83–84
Alavi, Maryam, 40
Amazon, 25, 71, 115
American Civil War, 17
American Privacy Act, 84
American Schools of Oriental Research
    (ASOR), 189–190, 193
Anatomy Act, 117
Anatomy Law, 121–122
Anderlik, Mary R., 164
Anderson, Chris, 78
Anderson, Elizabeth, 115, 117, 162, 181
Andrews, Lori, 164
Anteby, Michel, 164
Antitrust laws, 147
Appadurai, Arjun, 107, 142
Apple, 25, 71, 115

Appleyard, Melissa M., 31
Archaeology
  biblical distances and, 5–6
  Bliss and, 2, 5–7, 11, 55, 57, 72, 126,
    179, 189–191
  Byzantine remains and, 6
  Hebron measure and, 5–6
  incentives and, 190
  Jerusalem and, 2, 5–6, 189, 191
  Macalister and, 6–7, 126, 191
  Moabite Stone and, 5
  Mount of Olives and, 6
  relics and, 5
  Southern Shephelah and, 6
  Tel Gezer and, 2, 3f, 6–7, 11, 126, 179,
    189–191
  trust and, 2, 5–6, 190–191
  violence and, 2, 5
  Warren and, 5
Ardichvill, A., 41, 45
Argote, Linda, 40
Arkansas Forestry Commission (AFC),
  83, 193
Armstrong, Pamela K., 55
Ashcroft memorandum, 59
Atta, Mohamed, 15
Austin, Robert D., 58, 60
Australia, 9
  Census of Population and Housing
    and, 86–87
  Commonwealth Attorney-General's
    Department and, 127
  contested commodities and, 115
  CrimTrac and, 127–137, 141,
    183
  data-for-dollars model and, 83
  data trade and, 75, 83, 85–96
  infant malnutrition and, 33
  LYNX system and, 93–94
  New South Wales (NSW), 88, 92, 127,
    137
  Northern Territory (NT), 33, 136
  Parliament and, 87, 129

  Public Sector Information Exchange
    (PSIE) and, 11, 125–137, 141, 154,
    169, 183–184
  Public Sector Mapping Agencies
    (PSMA) and, 85–96, 103, 128, 183
  Queensland, 90
  supply-chain model and, 11, 125–137,
    141, 154, 183
  Victoria, 92, 135
  in vitro fertilization and, 115
Australian Bureau of Statistics (ABS),
  86–90, 95, 193
Australian Census, 86–87
Australia New Zealand Policing
  Advisory Agency (ANZPAA), 136,
  193
Australian Federal Police (AFP), 126,
  193
Australian Land Information Group
  (AUSLIG), 86–89, 95, 193
Australian National Child Offender
  Register (ANCOR), 136–137, 193
Avanade, 25
Aviation Safety Information Analysis
  and Sharing (ASIAS), 31, 193
Ayers, Ian, 27, 78

Backoff, Robert W., 54, 150
Bajaj, A., 153, 157, 185
Balla, Steven J., 186
Bamblett, M., 136
Bandt, William D., 148
Bank of America, 99, 193
Bank Secrecy Act, 78
Bannister, Frank, 58, 61
Bartal, Y., 141
Bartol, Kathryn M., 43
Barton, Mike, 24
Barzelay, Michael, 54
Bass, Gary, 62, 72
Basu, Arnab K., 108, 115
Batcheller, Archer L., 54, 147–148
Bates, Jo, 63

Bath, H., 136
Bauerlein, Valerie, 77
Bawn, Kathleen, 186
Bayh-Dole Act, 173
Beath, Cynthia Mathis, 43
Becker, Gary S., 149
Bekkers, V. J. J. M., 174
Belgium, 175
Bellamy, Christine, 31, 144, 147,
    168
Benbasat, Izak, 54, 186
Bently, Lionel, 173
Bergeron, Heather Ellen, 158
Bernardo, Paul, 33–34
Berners-Lee, Tim, 19, 58, 69–70
Bichard Inquiry, The, 34
Biddick, Michael, 29
Biden, Joe, 58
Big Data
    agencies and, 13, 23–30, 40, 102, 167,
        172
    defined, 23–24
    Google and, 13, 23–28
    ownership advantages and, 24–30
Big science, 30
Bingham, Lisa Blomgren, 68
Binney, William, 27
Biogenetics Project, 164–167
Bio-monitoring, 138–139, 143
Blackley, Michelle, 115
Black markets, 109t, 117–119, 122, 133
Blanco, Kathleen Babineaux, 17
Bliss, Frederick Jones
    archaeology and, 2, 5–7, 11, 55, 57,
        72, 126, 179, 189–191
    Tel Gezer and, 2, 3f, 6–7, 11, 126, 179,
        189–191
Blood
    body part exchanges and, 108–114,
        116–117, 123, 165, 176
    national supply of, 78
    toxicity measurements and, 30
    World War II and, 114

Body part exchanges
    blood and, 108–114, 116–117, 123,
        165, 176
    cadavers and, 105, 116–123, 149,
        164
    contested commodities and, 108–123
    ethics of, 108–123, 142, 149–150, 164
    eyes and, 118
    ova and, 109t, 113f, 114–115, 117
    sperm and, 109t, 113f, 114–116, 123,
        176
    tissues and, 109t, 113f, 117–118, 138
    transplant organs and, 112, 116–117,
        149–150, 157
Body snatching, 117, 119–123
Bollier, David, 106
Bonometti, Robert J., 155
Boston Marathon bombers, 25
Bowman, Diana, 142, 152
Boyd, Danah, 24
Bozeman, Barry, 21–22
Braman, Sandra, 149, 161, 169, 173,
    175, 182, 189
Brand, Stuart, 179
Branscomb, Anne Wells, 147
Braudel, Fernand, 140, 149
Brazil, 9, 85, 184
Brinkmanship, 88
British Broadcasting Commission (BBC),
    35, 62, 193
British Petroleum (BP), 35–36, 193
British Royal Engineers, 5
Bronk, Chris, 146
Brown, Michael, 17–18
Buelens, Marc, 54
Bureau of Land Management (BLM),
    37, 193
Bureau of Ocean Energy Management,
    Regulation and Enforcement
    (BOEMRE), 199n1, 193
Burke, William, 121
Burkert, Herbert, 76
Bush, George W., 43, 48

Business intelligence (BI), 9, 193
  data trade and, 75, 77–78, 80
  Public Sector Information Exchange
    (PSIE) and, 187
Butler, Brian, 155
Byzantine remains, 6

Cadaver exchange
  Anatomy Law of 1832 and, 121–122
  body snatching and, 117, 119–123
  defining personhood and, 105
  ethics and, 105, 110t–111t, 113f, 116,
    118–123, 142, 149, 164
  lessons from, 118–123
  murder and, 117, 119–122
  odor issues and, 120
  pickling and, 120
  Public Sector Information Exchange
    (PSIE) and, 122–123
  supply problem and, 119–120
  transplant organs and, 116–117,
    149
Campbell, Archie, 34
Campos, A., 62, 72
Canada, 9, 33–34, 85, 167, 184
Capaccio, Tony, 51
Caribbean Information Society Portal,
  19
Carr, David F., 35, 39, 51, 187–188
Cate, Fred H., 171
Catholics, 5
CDATA96, 86, 89
Census of Population and Housing
  (Australia), 86–87
Centers for Disease Control and
  Prevention (CDC), 40, 139, 193
Centers for Medicare & Medicaid
  Services (CMS), 2, 33, 78, 80, 82,
  157–158, 194
Central banks, 76–77, 85
Central Intelligence Agency (CIA), 15,
  30, 48, 78, 146, 193
CEO COM Link, 18

Chadwick, Ruth, 165
Challenger Space Shuttle, 13–14
Charalabidis, Yannis, 52, 57–58, 63, 68
Chavez, A., 140
Cheating, 118, 142, 147
Chengalur-Smith, I., 46, 151
Chertoff, Michael, 17
Chief executive officers (CEOs), 18, 32,
  88, 90, 127–128, 193
Chief information officer (CIO), 59, 65,
  151, 193
Chief technology officer (CTO), 60, 194
Child Care and Development Fund
  (CCDF), 37, 193
Child labor, 108, 111t, 115
Chile, 76–77
Chin, Michelle, L., 15
China, 31, 111t
Chow, Chee W., 126
Chu, W., 54
Civil rights, 135, 144, 184
Clarke, Drew, 94
Clarke, Edward H., 141
Clarkson, Gavin, 54, 147–148
Climate change, 33
Clinger-Cohen Act, 97
Coaxing
  existing information sharing
    approaches and, 10, 39–41, 47–52,
    125
  failure of, 48–51
  Public Sector Information Exchange
    (PSIE) and, 125–126
  with standards, 49–50
  with system of systems, 50–51
  via office, 47–49
COBOL (COmmon Business Oriented
  Language), 1–2, 194
Coercion
  existing information sharing
    approaches and, 10, 39–46, 51–52,
    54
  failure of, 44–45

pessimism and, 43
Public Sector Information Exchange
    (PSIE) and, 125, 179–180, 183, 186
tautological nature of, 43–44
United States and, 42, 45
Coglianese, Cary, 61–62
Cohen, Lloyd R., 146
Collaboration, 8
    data trade and, 75–76, 99, 101, 103
    E-Government Act of 2002 and, 151
    existing information sharing
        approaches and, 43–45
    GPRAMA and, 182
    information sharing crisis and, 33
    open data and, 58
    Public Sector Information Exchange
        (PSIE) and, 148, 151, 158, 182–183,
        186–187
    wicked problems and, 33
Columbia Space Shuttle, 14
Combined Online Information System
    (COINS), 62, 194
Commodity Futures Trading
    Commission (CFTC), 35–36, 193
Companies House, 70
Compatibility issues, 7–8, 49, 86, 151,
    156, 168, 182, 186
Comprehensive Environmental
    Response, Compensation, and
    Liability Act (CERCLA), 143–144,
    193
Computers
    Acxiom and, 26
    COBOL and, 1–2
    compatibility issues and, 7–8, 49, 86,
        151, 156
    cost of connecting, 1
    data quality and, 37
    Department of Defense and, 30, 49
    digital traces and, 23
    FEMA and, 36
    integration and, 31–33, 35 (see also
        Integration)

Internal Revenue Service and, 35, 51
interoperability levels and, 49
modernization and, 35, 42, 50, 52,
    112, 151
NSA and, 28
older technologies and, 1
Public Sector Information Exchange
    (PSIE) and, 140–141, 156–157, 168,
    170–171, 174, 185
reputation and, 41
software and, 1–2, 24, 30, 50–51, 62,
    69, 79, 86, 97, 139–141, 154–156,
    171, 187
standalone systems and, 31
Veteran's Administration and, 49
Cone, Edward, 35, 51
Confidentiality, 36, 57, 76, 151
Congressional Research Service (CRS),
    63, 66, 68, 194
Conitzer, Vincent, 141
Connolly, Allison, 157–158
Connolly, Regina, 58, 61
Connolly, Terry, 148
Consent
    contested commodities and,
        114–115
    data trade and, 82, 97–98
    existing information sharing
        approaches and, 10, 39, 41, 45–47,
        51–53, 55
    Public Sector Information Exchange
        (PSIE) and, 125–126, 134, 137,
        165–168, 171, 179–180
Consent Based Social Security Number
    Verification Service (CBSV), 97–98,
    147, 193
Constant, D., 41, 45, 151
Contested commodities
    Australia and, 115
    black markets and, 109t, 117–119
    body parts exchanges and, 108–123
    cadavers and, 105, 110t–111t, 113f,
        116, 118–123, 142, 149, 164

Contested commodities (cont.)
  commoditization and, 105–106,
    112–122, 133–134, 137, 163–167,
    171, 189
  consent and, 114–115
  consumption products and, 110t
  cooperation and, 119
  cresting moment and, 114–115
  CrimTrac and, 133–134
  cryogenics and, 115
  databases and, 107, 112, 133
  deCODE and, 164–167
  ethics and, 105–119, 122–123
  exchange model and, 108–123
  fraud and, 117–119, 133
  genome database and, 164–167, 183,
    189
  governance and, 118
  Health Sector Database Law and,
    164–167, 183, 189
  historical perspective on, 10, 108–123
  Iceland and, 106, 164–167, 183, 189
  incentives and, 105, 108, 109t
  information type and, 112–114
  innovation and, 115
  morality and, 114–115
  NCHRC and, 133–134
  objectifying the self and, 108, 111t,
    112
  ordinary goods and, 105–106
  private sector and, 116
  product labeling and, 116
  public sector data and, 11, 103,
    105–123
  Public Sector Information Exchange
    (PSIE) and, 11, 163–167, 176, 180,
    183, 185, 189
  restricted, 115–117
  sacred, 111t, 112
  technology and, 106, 108, 112, 114–
    115, 119, 121–123
  trust and, 118
  United Kingdom and, 115, 117

  value and, 105–108, 111–114, 118
  waste and, 180
Cook, Meghan E., 153
Cooper, Michael H., 114, 116, 176
Cooperation, 6–7
  contested commodities and, 119
  data trade and, 88–90, 92, 95, 101
  existing information sharing
    approaches and, 44–45, 48
  open data and, 10, 57, 59, 61–62,
    67–68, 70, 73
  Public Sector Information Exchange
    (PSIE) and, 126, 128–129, 135, 175,
    182, 188
Cramton, Peter, 141
Crawford, Kate, 24
Credit Alert Verification Reporting
  System (CAIVRS), 138, 193
Crespi, Gregory S., 112
Cresting moment lesson, 114–115
Crime maps, 60
Criminal Justice System (CJS), 146–147,
  194
CrimTrac
  budget of, 129
  contested commodities and, 133–134
  expansion of, 133
  initial grant of, 141
  integration and, 131
  Mobbs and, 96, 127–131, 133, 135
  National Names Index (NNI) and, 130,
    133
  NCHRC and, 129–135
  ownership issues and, 127–129
  per person fees and, 131
  privacy and, 133–137
  protecting children and, 134–137
  Public Sector Information Exchange
    (PSIE) and, 127–137, 141, 183
  supply-chain model and, 127–137,
    141, 183
CrimTrac Audit Log Integration Facility
  (CALIF), 134, 193

Cross-Agency Priority (CAP) goals, 72, 193

Cruz, Cinthia Betiny, 163, 184, 186

Cryogenics, 115

Cukier, Kenneth, 10
    contested commodities and, 106
    data trade and, 102
    existing information sharing
        approaches and, 40
    information sharing crisis and, 23–27, 29
    open data and, 61, 70
    Public Sector Information Exchange
        (PSIE) and, 147, 167, 169, 172

Culnan, Mary J., 55

Culyer, Anthony J., 114, 116, 176

Customs and Border Protection (CBP), 35, 193

Danko, Stephen, 29

Dartmouth College, 187

Databases. *See also specific agency*
    contested commodities and, 107, 112, 133
    data trade and, 75, 80–83, 87, 101
    deCODE and, 164–167
    DNA, 29, 134–137
    electronic mountains and, 2
    existing information sharing
        approaches and, 46
    Google's indexing of, 188
    governmental, 107, 122, 163
    Iceland's national health, 164–167, 183, 189
    information sharing crisis and, 15, 26, 31, 35
    national security and, 26
    obsolescing, 128–129
    open data and, 62, 72–73
    public, 73, 112
    Public Sector Information Exchange
        (PSIE) and, 122, 128–129, 133, 135–
        136, 139, 141, 151, 154–155, 163–
        167, 171–175, 180, 183, 188–189
    relative sizes of, 26–30
    silo, 15, 141
    terrorism and, 15

Data-for-dollars model, 83

Data.gov, 59–71

DataMarket, 106

Data mining, 77–78, 102

Data quality, 33, 37, 41, 73, 92, 118, 141–142, 163

Datasets
    Big Data and, 22–24 (*see also* Big Data)
    contested commodities and, 106–107
    data trade and, 75, 77, 84, 86–95
    existing information sharing
        approaches and, 40, 45, 52
    information sharing crisis and, 13, 22–24, 30
    open data and, 59, 61–72
    Public Sector Information Exchange
        (PSIE) and, 138, 152, 172, 181, 183

Data trade, 10
    American Privacy Act and, 84
    Australia and, 75, 83, 85–96
    bilateral information sharing
        agreements and, 96–103
    business intelligence (BI) and, 75, 77–78, 80
    central banks and, 76–77, 85
    collaboration and, 75–76, 99, 101, 103
    conditions for free access and, 83–84
    consent and, 82, 97–98
    cooperation and, 88–90, 92, 95, 101
    databases and, 75, 80–83, 87, 101
    Department of Defense (DOD) and, 79, 81, 100, 103
    developing information assets and, 75–78
    duplication and, 92
    efficiency and, 78, 97, 99
    Environmental Protection Agency
        (EPA) and, 79–80, 99

Data trade (cont.)
ethics and, 11, 76
fraud and, 78, 82, 100
Google and, 76–78, 84
Health Sector Database Law and, 164–167, 183, 189
incentives and, 73, 75, 85–96, 98, 102–103
information technology (IT) and, 97
innovation and, 75, 85, 94
integration and, 51, 77, 82–83, 87, 89, 94, 99
Internal Revenue Service (IRS) and, 100
licenses and, 87, 89, 92–95
markets and, 80–83
medical, 75–76
monopolies and, 75, 84, 96–103, 122
morality and, 76
ownership issues and, 78–80, 83, 86, 102
payment mechanisms for, 81–83
privacy and, 76, 84, 102, 134–137
public sector data and, 75, 80–85, 87, 90, 94–96
Securities and Exchange Commission (SEC) and, 99–100
security and, 78, 83, 100, 102
technology and, 77, 79, 84, 86, 98
transparency and, 85, 90, 98
trust and, 75–76, 86, 95, 111t
types of tradable information products and, 80–81
United Kingdom and, 76
United States and, 76–84
unsuitable information types and, 134–137
Veterans Affairs (VA) and, 80, 99
waste and, 10, 75, 96–103
welfare and, 185
Davenport, Thomas H., 39–40, 117
Davis, Shelley, 54

Dawes, Sharon S.
existing information sharing approaches and, 41–42, 45–46, 54
Public Sector Information Exchange (PSIE) and, 149–151, 153, 157, 172, 186
Death Master File (DMF), 29, 80–81, 194
deCODE, 164–167
Deepwater Horizon Oil Drill disaster, 35, 96
Defense Advanced Research Projects Agency (DARPA), 156, 194
Democracy
participatory, 22, 164
Public Sector Information Exchange (PSIE) and, 161–164, 179
reinvigoration of, 179
Denmark, 85
deNovis, 156–159, 165
Department of Commerce (DOC), 37, 79, 144, 194
Department of Defense (DOD), 194
budget of, 29–30
competition for information sharing standards and, 79
cost of information sharing failures and, 33
data trade and, 79, 81, 100, 103
fraud and, 36
Future Combat Systems (FCS) project and, 51
General Services Administration (GSA) and, 100
Government Computer-Based Patient Record (GCPR) and, 49, 194
GovWork and, 81
Hurricane Katrina and, 17–18
IT budget of, 29–30
Joint Strike Fighter and, 51
Office of Personnel Management (OPM) and, 79
open data and, 66
PM-ISE and, 48

Public Sector Information Exchange
(PSIE) and, 144
renewable energy projects and, 36
Specimen Repository for Remain
Identification and, 29
Veterans Affairs (VA) and, 35, 49–50
Department of Education (ED), 78,
194
Department of Energy (DOE), 194
data trade and, 79
existing information sharing
approaches and, 47
information sharing crisis and, 20, 22
Department of Health and Human
Services (HHS), 18, 37, 78, 81, 100,
144, 156–157, 195
Department of Homeland Security
(DHS), 194
data trade and, 79–83, 99–100, 103
E-Verify program and, 81, 83
terrorism and, 16–18, 42, 44–45, 48,
68, 79–83, 99–100, 103, 144
Department of Housing and Urban
Development (HUD), 37, 99, 156,
182, 185, 195
Department of Justice (DOJ), 44, 68, 82,
99, 103, 144, 145t, 194
Department of Motor Vehicles (DMV),
31, 194
Department of Resources, Energy and
Tourism, 94
Department of State (DOS), 78, 82, 100,
144–146, 194
Department of the Interior (DOI), 34,
37, 59, 144, 194
Department of Transportation (DOT),
34, 47, 144, 182, 194
Department of Veteran Affairs (VA), 197
data trade and, 80, 99
Department of Defense (DOD) and,
35, 49–50
Department of Housing and Urban
Development (HUD) and, 99, 185

failure to coax with standards and, 49
Government Computer-Based Patient
Record (GCPR) and, 49
information sharing crisis and, 33,
35–36
open data and, 63
Public Sector Information Exchange
(PSIE) and, 144, 185
renewable energy projects and,
36
De Saulcy, Louis Félicien, 5
Dever, William, 6–7, 126, 191
DeVille de Goyet, Claude, 19
Dexter, Albert S., 54, 186
Digital Cadastral Database (DCDB), 86,
194
Diplopedia, 146
Dirks, K. T., 54, 147
Dixon, Michael, 94, 146
Dizard, Wilson P., 100, 146, 169
DNA databases, 29, 134–137
Documentation, 2, 171
Dodd-Frank Wall Street Reform and
Consumer Protection Act, 46
Douglas, James W., 41, 43
Driver Privacy Protection Act, 76
Driver's licenses, 22, 79
Drucker, Peter Ferdinand, 39
Duchessi, P., 46, 151
Duplication
data trade and, 78, 92
information sharing crisis and, 19, 33,
35–37
open data and, 62
Public Sector Information Exchange
(PSIE) and, 172, 181
Dyer, J. H., 54

Earthquakes, 18–20
Eaton, Kit, 154
eBay, 53, 71, 106, 112, 115, 142
Economist magazine, 68
Edward, F., 41

Efficiency
   data trade and, 78, 97, 99
   duplication and, 19, 33, 35–37, 52, 62,
      92, 172, 181
   exchange model and, 188
   existing information sharing
      approaches and, 43, 51, 54
   governmental, 11, 169
   information sharing crisis and, 11, 18
   Public Sector Information Exchange
      (PSIE) and, 118, 130, 133, 146, 150,
      158, 162–163, 169, 172, 180, 185,
      187–188
   waste and, 180 (see also Waste)
E-government
   democratic ideals and, 163
   developed countries and, 184
   failure of, 188
   information sharing crisis and, 25,
      31
   markets and, 151, 153
   monopolies and, 188
   Public Sector Information Exchange
      (PSIE) and, 141, 143, 151, 153–154,
      163, 170, 176, 184, 188
   public sector IT and, 154
   service quality and, 143, 163, 170,
      176, 184
   U.S. E-Government Act of 2002 and,
      151
   user interfaces and, 141
Electronic Data Gathering, Analysis and
   Retrieval (EDGAR) system, 175, 194
Electronic Health Record (EHR), 35, 194
Electronic mountains
   databases and, 2
   information technology (IT) and, 2,
      8, 11
   Internal Revenue Service (IRS) and,
      1–2, 30
   technology and, 2, 9
   Tel Gezer metaphor and, 2, 3f, 6–7, 11,
      126, 179, 189–191

Elias, Julio Jorge, 149
Ellerman, Denny, 118
Emissions Inventory Exchange Network
   (EIEN), 146, 194
Empire Blue Cross and Blue Shield, 158
Enterprise architecture (EA), 148,
   154–155, 194
Environmental information, 138–144
Environmental Protection Agency
   (EPA), 199n1, 194
   data trade and, 79–80, 99
   Emissions Inventory Exchange
      Network (EIEN) and, 146
   existing information sharing
      approaches and, 42, 46–47
   open data and, 59, 64–66, 68, 71
   Public Sector Information Exchange
      (PSIE) and, 138–139, 144–146, 150,
      182
   safety standards and, 79
   Toxics Release Inventory (TRI) reports
      and, 64
   water safety and, 79–80
Epstein, David, 186
Equal access, 32
Erkkila, Tero, 85
eRulemaking, 59
Estonia, 167
Ethics
   adultery and, 115
   body parts exchanges and, 108–123,
      142, 149–150, 164
   body snatching and, 117, 119–123
   brinkmanship and, 88
   cheating and, 118, 142, 147
   commoditizing cadavers and, 105,
      110t–111t, 113f, 116, 118–123, 142,
      149, 164
   contested commodities and, 105–119,
      122–123
   data trade and, 11, 75–76
   equal access and, 32
   free riding and, 147

genome commoditization and,
  164–167, 183, 189
Health Sector Database Law and,
  164–167, 183, 189
murder and, 34, 117, 119–122
open data and, 60
privacy and, 167–172
product labeling and, 116
Public Sector Information Exchange
  (PSIE) and, 125, 137, 142–143, 161,
  165–168, 176–177, 184
slavery and, 107, 111t, 112–113,
  115–117
transparency and, 32, 58, 61–62,
  69–70, 85, 90, 98, 161, 170, 176
transplant organs and, 112, 116–117,
  149–150, 157
European Commission (EC), 60, 194
European Telecommunications
  Standards, 154
European Union (EU), 9, 194
  data trade and, 85
  existing information sharing
    approaches and, 52, 55
  information sharing crisis and, 31
  Public Sector Information Exchange
    (PSIE) and, 118, 149, 151, 184
Evans, A. M., 62, 72, 183
E-Verify program, 81–83
Ewusi-Mensah, Kweku, 35
Exchange model, 11, 125, 181, 187
  contested commodities and,
    108–123
  efficiency and, 188
  environmental information and,
    138–144
  Public Sector Information Exchange
    (PSIE) and, 138–146
  United States and, 138–146
  U.S. Privacy Act and, 168, 170, 181
Executive Office of the President (EOP),
  43, 194
Eyes, 118

Fackler, Martin, 20
Fader, Sonia, 115–116, 176
Fair trade, 116–117
Falk, Armin, 162
Faraj, Samer, 40, 45, 55
Fathian, M., 32
Fawcett, Stanley E., 33
Federal Aviation Administration (FAA),
  15, 194
  existing information sharing
    approaches and, 51
  information sharing crisis and, 31,
    33, 35
Federal Bureau of Information (FBI),
  194
  Atta and, 15
  data trade and, 82–83
  existing information sharing
    approaches and, 48
  information sharing crisis and, 30, 33
Federal Communications Commission
  (FCC), 71, 194
Federal Emergency Management
  Agency (FEMA), 16–18, 36, 77, 194
Federal Energy Regulatory Commission
  (FERC), 99, 194
Federal Housing Administration (FHA),
  36–37, 194
Federalist 51 (Madison), 138
Feltz, Fernand, 84, 151
Ferrin, D. L., 54, 147
Financial Crimes Enforcement Network
  (FCEN), 99, 194
Finland, 9, 85, 175
Fioretti, Marco, 63
First Genetics, 75
Flanagin, A. J., 43, 75, 147–148
Fletcher, Patricia D., 29–30, 112
Florida Department of Highway Safety
  and Motor Vehicles, 14
Florini, Ann M., 58
Flowerday, S., 54
Foley, John, 30

Food and Drug Administration (FDA),
    35, 139, 142–143, 194
Formerly Used Defense Sites (FUDS),
    143–144, 194
Fountain, Jane E., 33
  data trade and, 99
  existing information sharing
    approaches and, 42–43, 45–46
  open data and, 72
  Public Sector Information Exchange
    (PSIE) and, 141, 147, 149, 151–152,
    158–159, 182–183, 185, 187
Foxworthy, Susanna, 68
Fraud
  agricultural, 78
  black markets and, 109t, 117–119,
    122, 133
  commodities and, 117–119, 133
  credit card, 78
  data trade and, 78, 82, 100, 174–175,
    181
  information sharing crisis and, 33,
    36–37
  labor and, 36, 174
  medical, 2, 82, 158
  Medicare and, 2
  Pell Grants and, 78
  physicians and, 82
  Public Sector Information Exchange
    (PSIE) and, 174–175, 181
  security and, 2, 33, 36–37, 78, 82, 100,
    117–118, 133, 158, 174–175, 181
  unemployment, 174–175
  U.S. Air Force and, 100
  welfare, 36–37
Frederickson, George H., 21–22
Freedom of Information Act (FOIA), 59,
    176, 194
Freedom of information (FOI), 59, 62,
    161, 173, 175–176, 194
Free riding, 147
Frey, Bruno S., 55
Fukushima Nuclear Power Plant, 20–21

Fulk, Janet, 43, 75, 107, 147–148, 188
Full-time equivalent (FTE), 82
Future Combat Systems (FCS), 51, 194
FutureMAP, 177

Gallagher, Michael, 185
Gantz, John, 23–27
Garnett, James L., 16–18
Garson, David, 184, 187, 189
Garvey, Pat, 146
Gates Foundation, 19
Gazis, Denos, 140
Geary, Patrick, 117
Geer, Daniel D., Jr., 141
Gelman, Robert, 29
General Agreement on Tariff Trade, 150
General Services Administration (GSA),
    36, 60, 63, 71, 80–81, 99–100, 195
Gene Trust, The, 75
Genome-commoditization debate,
    164–167, 183, 189
Genomics Collaboration Inc., 75–76
GEODATA, 87
Geographic information system (GIS),
    87, 195
Gerards, Janneke H., 149
Germany, 5, 76
Gertz, Renate, 165
Ghana, 69–70
Gilder, George, 162
Gil-Garcia, J. R., 46, 150–151, 154, 163,
    184, 186
Ginsberg, Wendy R., 63, 66–68
Goldman, Joseph P., 64, 68
Gonen, Mira, 141
Gonen, Rica, 141
Google
  advertising and, 141
  Big Data and, 13, 23–28
  brand name value of, 25
  CIA and, 78
  common standards–based repository
    and, 19

contested commodities and, 114
database indexing and, 188
data trade and, 76–78, 84
NASA and, 76
processing volume of, 27–28
Public Sector Information Exchange
(PSIE) and, 141, 188
Recorded Future and, 78
spell-checking software and, 24
voice recognition software and, 24
Google Analytics, 76–77
Google Deep Web, 188
Google Earth, 84, 114
Google Maps, 66
Governance
contested commodities and, 118
existing information sharing
approaches and, 42
ineffective, 37–38 (see also
Information sharing failures)
Government Accountability Office
(GAO), 2, 8–9, 194
data trade and, 75, 77, 79–83
existing information sharing
approaches and, 43–51
information sharing crisis and, 23,
30–31, 33–37
open data and, 73
Public Sector Information Exchange
(PSIE) and, 97, 99–103, 139,
143–144, 156–158, 168–171, 176,
181, 185–187, 189
Government Computer-based Patient
Record (GCPR), 49, 194
Government Performance and Results
Act Modernization Act (GPRAMA),
42, 72, 151–153, 182, 195
Government-to-government (G2G)
programs, 153, 194
GovWork, 81
Grand Challenge, 19
Grant, Don, 88–89, 93
Great Depression, 21, 59

Greenberg, Andy, 1, 154
Greene, Mary E., 146
Griffin, Donyale R., 16
Gross, Arthur, 35
Groves, Theodore, 141
Grünewald, François, 19
Grupe, Fritz H., 76
Guardian newspaper, 62

Hackers, 154–155
Hair jewelry, 109t, 113
Haiti earthquake, 18–20
Hallote, Rachel, 190
Hamilton, Alexander, 138
Hamilton, Lee H., 15–16, 48
Hara, Noriko, 30, 45
Haram al-Sharif, 5
HarÐardóttir, Kristín E., 164–165,
167
Hare, William, 121
Harper, Jim, 57, 62–63
Harris, Catherine, 25
Hart, Paul, 54, 147, 153
Hattotuwa, Sanjana, 19
Health Insurance Contract Language
(HICL), 157, 195
Health Insurance Portability and
Accountability Act (HIPAA), 50, 117,
195
Hebron measure, 5–6
Heminger, Alan R., 41, 45
Hendler, Clint, 62
Herron, Matt, 179
Hey, Donald, 142
Hickey, Kathleen, 146
Hijmans, Hielke, 150
Hilgartner, Stephen, 41
Hitzelberger, Patrik, 84, 151
Hodge, Graeme, 142, 152
Hoffman-LaRoche, 165, 167
Holden, Stephen H., 29–30, 112
Holder, Eric, 59
Holmes, Martin, 86–87, 94

Holy Land
  Bliss and the, 2, 5–7, 11, 55, 57, 72,
    126, 179, 189–191
  Tel Gezer and the, 2, 3f, 6–7, 11, 126,
    179, 189–191
Homburg, Vincentius, 174
Homeland Security Information System
  (HSIN), 44–45, 195
Homeland Security Operations Center
  (HSOC), 18, 195
Hong Kong, 169
Hoogwout, Marcel, 174
Horner, Christopher, 62
Horowitz, Edward D., 147
House Armed Services Subcommittee on
  Military Personnel, 35
Howard, John, 127
Huber, John D., 186
Huijboom, Noor, 61, 174
Human tissue, 109t, 113f, 117–118, 138
Hunting permits, 22
Hurren, Elizabeth T., 121–122
Hurricane Katrina, 8, 16–18, 96, 101,
  152, 184
Huxham, Chris, 42, 54, 148

Iacono, Suzanne, 41
Iacovou, Charalambos L., 54, 186
Iceland, 9
  contested commodities and, 106
  DataMarket and, 106
  deCODE and, 164–167
  Health Sector Database Law and, 164–
    167, 183, 189
  Public Sector Information Exchange
    (PSIE) and, 164–167, 183, 189
  Supreme Court of, 165
Icelandic Medical Association, 166–167
Immigration and Naturalization Service
  (INS), 15, 195
Incentives, 2
  archaeology and, 190
  Bliss and, 190

  contested commodities and, 105, 108,
    109t
  data trade and, 73, 75, 85–96, 98,
    102–103
  existing information sharing
    approaches and, 10, 39, 43–44, 50,
    52–55
  GPRAMA and, 151
  information sharing crisis and, 15,
    30, 32
  morality and, 55
  NCHRC and, 129–134
  NCIDD program and, 136–137
  open data and, 57, 73
  PSMA and, 89–94
  Public Sector Information Exchange
    (PSIE) and, 8, 125–138, 151, 153,
    156, 159, 166, 168, 171–172, 175,
    179–183, 186, 190–191
  trust and, 7
  withstanding crisis with, 94–95
India, 60, 111t, 184
Information and communication
  technologies (ICTs), 19, 195
Information asymmetry, 146–149
Information Sharing Environment (ISE),
  48, 79, 145t, 195
Information sharing failures
  Challenger disaster and, 13–14
  Columbia disaster and, 14
  data quality and, 37
  data trade and, 99
  Deepwater Horizon Oil Drill disaster
    and, 35
  existing information sharing
    approaches and, 10, 41, 45–52
  exorbitant cost of, 33–38
  fraud and, 36–37 (see also Fraud)
  Fukushima nuclear power plant
    accident and, 20–21
  Haiti earthquake and, 18–20
  Hurricane Katrina and, 16–18
  ineffective governance and, 37–38

lives lost from, 33–35
open data and, 10
private sector and, 30–33
public sector and, 10, 30–33,
115
Public Sector Information Exchange
(PSIE) and, 126, 136, 152, 168–169,
184, 189
September 11, 2001, terrorist attacks
and, 8, 15–16
United States and, 13–18, 34
U.S. Government Accountability
Office (GAO) and, 9
U.S. Office of Management and
Budget (OMB) and, 9
waste and, 35–36 (*see also* Waste)
Information technology (IT), 195
data trade and, 97
electronic mountains and, 2, 8, 11
existing information sharing
approaches and, 42, 44, 49
information sharing crisis and, 29–30,
33
open data and, 59
Public Sector Information Exchange
(PSIE) and, 127–129, 131, 133, 139,
143, 153–158, 163, 168, 179,
182–183, 186–189
Information-type lesson, 112–114
Ingram, Helen, 40–41
Innovation, 7
contested commodities and, 115
data trade and, 75, 85, 94
flexibility and, 31
open data and, 60–61
Peer-to-Patent program and,
188
Public Sector Information Exchange
(PSIE) and, 141, 156, 158–159, 170,
179, 184, 190
technology and, 9, 19, 31, 60–61, 75,
85, 94, 115, 141, 156, 158–159, 170,
179, 184, 190

Insurance
adjudication of claims and, 157
Death Master File (DMF) and, 29
deNovis and, 158
flood, 36
health, 50, 117, 149, 158
HIPAA and, 50, 117
mortgage, 36
Integrated Acquisition System (IAS), 99,
195
integrated Electronic Health Record
(iEHR), 50, 195
Integrated Risk Information System
(IRIS), 139, 144, 195
Integration, 10
CrimTrac and, 131
data trade and, 77, 82–83, 87, 89, 94,
99
e-government and, 31
existing information sharing
approaches and, 41–43, 50–51
FAA and, 31
information sharing crisis and, 14,
31–33, 35–36
modernization and, 35, 42, 50, 52,
112, 151
open data and, 57, 71–72
public interactions and, 31
Public Sector Information Exchange
(PSIE) and, 131, 134, 139–144, 150,
153, 156–157, 163, 168–176, 185,
187
waste and, 36
Intellectual property (IP) rights, 195
copyrights and, 151, 173
data trade and, 86
patents and, 10, 158, 173, 188
Peer-to-Patent program and, 188
Public Sector Information Exchange
(PSIE) and, 128, 150, 161, 172–175
Intelligence Reform and Terrorism
Prevention Act, 48
Intelligent Mail Barcode, 101

Intergovernmental agreement (IGA), 127–128, 195
Internal Revenue Service (IRS), 195
    additional tax laws and, 1
    confidentiality concerns and, 36–37
    cost of information sharing failure and, 33
    data mining and, 78
    data trade and, 100
    electronic mountain of, 1–2, 30
    failed computer system of, 35, 51
    as largest information processing organization in world, 30
    overhaul of Code of, 1
    public sector data and, 112
    Public Sector Information Exchange (PSIE) and, 169–170
    virtual value chain and, 112
    waste and, 35
International Atomic Energy Agency (IAEA), 21, 195
International Carbon Action Partnership, 142
International Monetary Fund (IMF), 154, 195
International Trade Data System, 186–187
International Whaling Convention, 142
Intra-Governmental Payment and Collection (IPAC), 139, 195
Israel, 2, 34, 76
Issa, Darrell, 36
IT Dashboard, 59
Ito, Aki, 77
Iverson, Joel O., 40

Jackelen, George, 147
Jackson, Joab, 146
Jacobs, Jane, 55
Jacobsen, Trond, 54, 147–148
Jafari, M., 32
Jamison, Wesley W., 117
Jansen, Don J., 49

Janssen, Heleen L., 149
Janssen, Katleen, 62
Janssen, Marijn, 52, 57–58, 63
Jarvenpaa, S. L., 41, 55
Jaschik, Scott, 112
Jay, John, 138
Jeffres, L. W., 41, 45
Jenkins, Leesteffy, 142
Jerusalem, 2, 5–6, 189, 191
Jews, 5
Jian, G., 41, 45
Johnson, D. R., 50, 119–122
Johnson, Eric M., 146
Joia, Luiz Antonio, 85
Joint Strike Fighter, 51
Jolly, David, 76
Joskow, Paul L., 118, 142
Jung, Stephen M., 99–100
Jurafsky, Daniel, 157

Kaboolian, Linda, 54
Kaiser, Jocelyn, 167
Kamal, Muhammad Mustafa, 32–33, 43, 147, 186, 188
Kant, Immanuel, 108
Kapucu, Naim, 8, 17
Kash, Wyatt, 29, 78, 183
Kelman, Steven, 45, 182, 185–186
Kieber, Heinrich, 76
Kiesler, S., 41, 45, 151
Kim, Donghwan, 23, 153–154
Kim, Soonhee, 23, 53–54, 153–155
Kim, W. Chan, 55
King, John L., 41
Kolekofski, Keith E., Jr., 41, 45
Koman, Richard, 1
Koppel, Ted, 17–18
Kopytoff, Igor, 106–107
Kostel, Jill A., 142
Kouzmin, Alexander, 16–18
Kraemer, Kenneth L., 41
Kraus, Sarit, 187
Krause, George A., 41, 43

Kreimer, Set, 176
Kugler, Tamar, 147
Kundra, Vivek, 59, 65

Labor, 7, 190
  ANCOR MoU and, 137
  contested commodities and, 108, 111*t*,
    115–116, 120
  E-Verify and, 81, 83
  fraud and, 36, 174
  OPM data monopoly and, 97
  unemployment and, 77, 174
Lachlan, Kenneth A. 16
Lakhani, Karim R., 58, 60
Lam, W., 151, 154, 157, 169, 172
Land Information Centre (LIC), 88, 195
Landler, Mark, 76
Land Registry, 70
Landsbergen, D. B., 42, 149–151,
    153–154, 157, 184
Latvia, 167
Laudon, Kenneth C., 106, 189
Lawrence, Vanessa, 94
Lazer, David, 41, 45, 142, 169, 182
Le Billon, Philippe, 117
Lee, Hyangsoo, 53–54, 155
Leebaert, Derek, 108
Lehmann, Daniel, 141, 187
Leidner, Dorothy E., 40
Lembke, J., 154
Lemonick, Michael D., 164–165, 167
Leonhardt, David, 157
Levees, 16–17
Levine, Charles H., 54, 150
LexisNexis, 102
Li, S., 30
Library of Congress (LOC), 26–28, 195
Licensing, 87, 89, 92–95, 149, 165, 173
Lin, B., 30
Lipowicz, Alice, 97
Littlewood, Nick, 92
Lobbies, 149–150
Locke, Edwin A., 43

Lockheed Martin, 154
Longo, Justin, 63
Los Alamos National Laboratory, 154
Louisiana, 16–18
Lovell, Dave, 92–93
Lovins, Amory, 21
Lukensmeyer, Carolyn J., 64, 68
Luna-Reyes, Luis F., 163, 184, 186
LYNX system, 93–94

Macalister, Robert Alexander Stewart,
    6–7, 126, 191
MacDonald, Sarah, 92
Macher, Jeffrey T., 154
Madhavan, Jayant, 188
Madison, James, 138
Magee, Reginald, 120–122
Mahler, Julianne, 32, 154
Mahoney, Julia D., 118, 180
Makedon, Fillia, 187
"Making Public Data Public" campaign,
    60
Manovich, Lev, 24
Maor, Moshe, 41
Maria, C. B., 41
Markets
  black, 109*t*, 117–119, 122, 133
  body part exchanges and, 108–123
  cadaver exchange and, 105, 110*t*–111*t*,
    113*f*, 116, 118–123, 142, 149, 164
  central banks and, 76–77, 85
  Coase theorem and, 172
  contested commodities and,
    106–123
  data-for-dollars model and, 83
  data trade and, 76, 80–83, 85, 93, 95,
    99
  democracy challenge and, 162–164
  drugs and, 143
  economic meltdown of 2008 and, 46,
    94
  e-government and, 151
  E-Verify and, 81–83

Markets (cont.)
  exchange model and, 11, 125, 145*t*,
    146, 181, 187
  fairs and, 7
  fair trade and, 116–117
  General Agreement on Tariff Trade
    and, 150
  International Trade Data System and,
    186–187
  licensing and, 87, 89, 92–95, 149, 165,
    173
  morality and, 163
  natural tendencies and, 186
  ownership issues and, 172
  payment mechanisms and, 81–83
  prediction, 143
  public-private partnerships and, 76
  Public Sector Information Exchange
    (PSIE) and, 186–187
  royal merchandise and, 7–8, 40
  stock, 25, 90, 149
  supply-chain model and, 11, 125–137,
    154
Marks, Peter, 41
Markus, Lynne, 148
Martin, James H., 157
Marx, Karl, 108
Mauborgne, Renée, 55
Maxwell, Terrance A., 41
Mayer, R. C., 54
Mayer-Schönberger, Viktor, 10
  contested commodities and, 106
  data trade and, 102
  existing information sharing
    approaches and, 40, 45
  information sharing crisis and, 23–27,
    29
  open data and, 61, 70
  Public Sector Information Exchange
    (PSIE) and, 142, 147, 167, 169, 172,
    182
McAuliffe, Christa, 13
McClean, Tom, 62

McCubbins, Matthew D., 186
McDermott, Patrice, 59, 63
McEvily, B., 54
McLure Wasko, Molly, 40, 45, 55
McNamara, Laura A., 146
McPhee, Robert D., 40
Medical issues
  body parts exchanges and,
    108–123
  cryogenics and, 115
  DNA databases and, 29, 134–137
  genome commoditization and,
    164–167, 183, 189
  Health Sector Database Law and,
    164–167
Meirowitz, Adam, 176–177
Memorandum of Understanding (MoU)
  agreements, 9–10, 82, 99–100, 137,
    143, 195
Metadata, 61, 107, 172, 182
Met Office, 70
Mexico, 31, 35, 96, 111*t*
Mill, John Stuart, 108
Millar, Laurance, 58–59
Miller, Jason, 81, 100, 146
Miller, Robert, 16
Minimum Nationwide Person Profile
  (MNPP), 134, 195
Minnowbrook Conference Center of
  Syracuse University, 21–22
Mitchell, Piers D., 119–122
MIT Media Lab, 140
Moabite Stone, 5
Mobbs, John D., 86–90, 95–96,
  127–131, 133, 135
Modernization, 35
  contested commodities and,
    112
  existing information sharing
    approaches and, 42, 50, 52
  Government Performance and Results
    Act Modernization Act (GPRAMA)
    and, 42, 72, 151–153, 182

Public Sector Information Exchange
  (PSIE) and, 151
Moffitt, Susan L., 41
Monge, Peter R., 43, 54, 75, 107,
  147–149
Monopolies
  antitrust laws and, 147
  data trade and, 75, 84, 96–103, 122
  deCODE and, 166
  e-government and, 188
  information sharing crisis and, 22
  Public Sector Information Exchange
    (PSIE) and, 143, 147, 150, 154, 166,
    188
  waste and, 75, 96–103, 122
Monster.com, 97
Montreal Protocol, 142
Moon, Jae, 31
Mooney, Des, 88, 95
Morality
  biotech products and, 164
  body snatching and, 117, 119–123
  consent approach and, 45
  contested commodities and, 114–115
  data trade and, 76
  genome commoditization and, 164–
    167, 183, 189
  Health Sector Database Law and, 164–
    167, 183, 189
  markets and, 163
  murder and, 34, 117, 119–121
  Public Sector Information Exchange
    (PSIE) and, 147, 162–164, 172
  selective incentives and, 55
Morton Thiokol, 13–14
Moscoe, Bruce, 82, 100, 142
Moscrop, John James, 6–7, 126, 191
Mount of Olives, 6
Mowery, David C., 154
Moynihan, Daniel Patrick, 16–18, 58
Murder, 34, 117, 119–121
Muslims, 5
Muth, Robert M., 117

National Aeronautics and Space
  Administration (NASA), 199n1, 195
  Challenger disaster and, 13–14
  Columbia disaster and, 14
  data trade and, 76, 100
  information sharing crisis and, 13–14,
    27–28
  open data and, 66
  volume of data owned by, 27
National Archives and Records
  Administration (NARA), 73, 195
National Association of Clean Water
  Agencies (NACWA), 80, 195
National Automated Fingerprint
  Identification System (NAFIS), 129,
    134, 195
National Bio-surveillance Integration
  Center (NBIC), 144, 195
National Commission on Terrorist
  Attacks, 15
National Criminal History Record
  Checking (NCHRC), 195
  contested commodities and, 133–134
  expansion of, 133
  historical perspective on, 133–134
  incentives and, 129–134
  per person fees and, 131
  selective-incentives solution of,
    129–133
  supply-chain model and, 129–135,
    137
National Criminal Investigation DNA
  Database (NCIDD), 135–137, 195
National Defense Authorization Act, 50
National Drinking Water Advisory
  Council (NDWAC), 80, 195
National Exchange of Policing
  Information (NEPI), 127–128, 137,
    195
National Guard, 17
National Health Service (NHS), 35, 195
National Information Exchange Model
  (NIEM), 145t, 146, 181, 187

National Institutes of Health (NIH), 139, 195
National mapping cadastral agency (NMCA), 86, 92, 94, 195
National Name Index (NNI), 130, 133, 195
National Oceanic and Atmospheric Administration (NOAA), 65–66, 84, 199n1, 195
National Performance Review, 138
National Response Team (NRT), 199n1, 195
National Science and Technology Council (NSTC), 139, 196
National Security Agency (NSA), 196
  electronic communications capture and, 26–28
  huge data volume of, 27–28
  information sharing crisis and, 26–28, 30
  telephone monitoring and, 27
National Technical Information Service (NTIS), 80–81, 196
National Weather System (NWS), 33, 196
Neeman, Zvika, 147
Negotiating software agents, 187
Nelkin, Dorothy, 164
Netherlands, 9, 174–176, 183
Newbery, David, 173
Newcomer, Kathryn H., 39, 155
New Orleans, 16–17
New Source Revenue (NSR), 46, 196
New South Wales (NSW), 88, 92, 127, 137, 196
New Zealand, 9, 69, 136, 169–170
Nextgov.com, 67
Nisan, Noam, 141
Niskanen, William A., 138
No-Fly and Selectee List program, 83
Noll, Roger G., 186
Norris, Donald F., 31
Norris, Pippa, 184

Northern Territory (NT), 33, 136, 196
Nosowitz, Dan, 27
Noveck, Beth Simone, 19, 45, 58, 60–61, 70–71, 188
Nuclear and Industrial Safety Agency (NISA), 20, 195
Nuclear Regulatory Commission (NRC), 99, 195
Nuclear Safety Commission, 20

Obama, Barack, 24, 37, 43, 47, 58–61, 142, 153
Occupational Safety and Health Administration (OSHA), 139, 196
Odenheimer, Alisa, 77
Office of Financial Research (OFR), 46, 196
Office of Management and Budget (OMB), 9, 196
  data trade and, 78
  existing information sharing approaches and, 45
  information sharing crisis and, 29
  open data and, 59, 72–73
  Public Sector Information Exchange (PSIE) and, 138, 151
Office of Personnel Management (OPM), 78–80, 97, 196
Office of Pesticide Programs (OPP), 139, 196
Office of Pollution Prevention and Toxics (OPPT), 139, 196
Office of Research and Development (ORD), 139, 196
Office of the Director of National Intelligence (ODNI), 103, 196
O'Halloran, Sharyn, 186
Oil Spill Recovery Institute (OSRI), 199n1, 196
Olsen, Florence, 79
Olson, Mancur, 53
O'Neill, Molly, 146
Onishi, Norimitsu, 20

Open data (OD), 10, 196
  Ashcroft memorandum and, 59
  collaboration and, 58
  cooperation and, 10, 57, 59, 61–62,
    67–68, 70, 73
  crime maps and, 60
  databases and, 62, 72–73
  data.gov and, 59–71
  defining, 57–58
  Department of Defense (DOD) and,
    66
  as doctrine, 60
  duplication and, 62
  Environmental Protection Agency
    (EPA) and, 59, 64–66, 68, 71
  eRulemaking and, 59
  Freedom of Information and, 62, 161,
    173, 175–176
  incentives and, 57, 73
  information technology (IT) and, 59
  innovation and, 60–61
  integration and, 71–72
  IT Dashboard and, 59
  licenses and, 57
  measuring compliance with, 62–64
  medical issues and, 60
  Obama and, 58–61
  ownership issues and, 69, 173
  passive-aggressive attitudes toward,
    64–68
  politics of, 60
  predictions of agencies' support of,
    61–62
  privacy and, 57
  problem of diffusion and, 72
  problem of inclusion and, 71–72
  Public Sector Information Exchange
    (PSIE) and, 186
  Recovery.gov and, 59
  resistance to, 61–73
  school performance tables and, 60
  transparency and, 58, 61–62,
    69–70
  trust and, 58
  United Kingdom and, 60, 62, 69–70,
    75, 77
  United States and, 58–68, 71–73
  USAspending.gov, 59
  Veterans Affairs (VA) and, 63
Open Government Dashboard, 63
Open Government Directive (OGD), 59,
  64, 196
Open Government Memorandum, 59
Open Government Platform (OGPL),
  60, 196
Open source (OS) software, 50, 58, 60,
  196
Ordinance Survey, 70
Organisation for Economic Co-
  operation and Development
  (OECD), 174–175, 196
O-rings, 13–14
Osterloh, Margit, 55
Otjacques, Benoît, 84, 151
Ottomans, 6
Ova, 109t, 113f, 114–115, 117
Over the counter (OTC) markets, 99,
  196
Ownership issues
  agency fights over, 78–80
  Bayh-Dole Act and, 173
  Big Data and, 24–30
  Coase theorem and, 172
  competitive advantage and,
    24–25
  CrimTrac and, 127–129
  data trade and, 78–80, 83, 86, 102
  deCODE and, 165
  Freedom of Information (FOI) and, 59,
    62, 161, 173, 175–176
  genome commoditization and,
    164–167, 183, 189
  information sharing crisis and, 22
  intellectual property and, 86, 128,
    150, 161, 172–175
  open data and, 69, 173

Ownership issues (cont.)
  Public Sector Information Exchange
    (PSIE) and, 127–129, 161, 165, 172–
    175, 179
  RINIS and, 174
  supply-chain model and, 127–129

Page, V., 41, 45
Palestine Exploration Fund (PEF), 5–7,
  189, 196
Pálsson, Gísli, 164–165, 167
Pan American Health Organization, 19
Panangala, Sidath Viranga, 49
Panel regression analysis, 64
Papadimitriou, Christos, 141
Pardo, T. A., 31, 33, 42, 46, 150–151,
  154, 157, 184
Parry, Bronwyn, 142, 147
Parycek, Peter, 172
Paull, Dan, 92–95
Pavlov, Elan, 141
Peer-to-Patent program, 188
Pentagon, 154
Peripheral Systems, 87–88
Perlrot, Nicole, 154
Perri 6, 151, 169
Philipkoski, Kristen, 164, 167
Phillips, Anne, 108
Picci, Lucio, 118
Piderit, R., 54
Pierre, Jon, 21–22
Pipeline and Hazardous Materials Safety
  Administration (PHMSA), 34, 199n1,
  196
Pizem, Rose, 34
Politics
  e-government and, 25, 31, 141, 143,
    151, 153–154, 163, 170, 176, 184,
    188
  George W. Bush and, 43, 48
  lobbies and, 149–150
  Obama and, 24, 37, 43, 47, 58–61,
    142, 153

  open data and, 60
  privacy and, 11
  Public Sector Information Exchange
    (PSIE) and, 176–177, 179–191
  slow legislation and, 149–150
Politics first approach, 11, 145t, 146,
  174–175, 187
Pollock, Rufus, 173
Pollution, 16, 89, 110t, 118, 139, 142
Population Register Centre, 85
Poulsen, Kevin, 154
Prefontaine, Lise, 45, 149, 172, 186
Premkumar, G., 43, 118, 140–141, 149
Prins, Corien, 55, 84, 147, 151, 162,
  173, 175
Privacy
  absolutist demand for, 184
  American Privacy Act and, 84
  ANCOR and, 137
  Big Data and, 24
  challenges of, 167–172
  citizen rights and, 161, 167–169, 171,
    189
  consent and, 165
  CrimTrac and, 133–137
  Database Law and, 166
  data trade and, 76, 84, 102
  Drivers Privacy Protection Act and, 76
  HIPAA and, 117
  information sharing crisis and, 24,
    30, 32
  medical, 50, 117, 135
  NAFIS and, 129
  NCHRC and, 130, 133–134
  NCIDD and, 135–137
  open data and, 57
  politics and, 11
  protecting children and, 134–137
  Public Sector Information Exchange
    (PSIE) and, 11, 129–130, 133–137,
    150–151, 161, 165–172, 181, 184–
    185, 189
  transparency and, 161

unsuitable information types and,
134–137
U.S. Computer Matching and Privacy
Protection Act and, 170
U.S. Patriot Act and, 184
U.S. Privacy Act and, 168, 170, 181
Private sector data
Big Data and, 13, 23
contested commodities and, 116
databases and, 15 (*see also* Databases)
data growth rate of, 26–27
data trade and, 75–76, 85, 97
existing information sharing
approaches and, 45, 55
four differences of from public sector
data and, 31–33
information sharing failures and,
30–33
processing capabilities of, 27
Public Sector Information Exchange
(PSIE) and, 147, 154–158, 175, 182,
187
reliance on public records and, 29
Problem of diffusion, 72
Problem of inclusion, 71–72
Program Manager of the Information
Sharing Environment (PM-ISE), 48,
196
Protestants, 2
Prusak, Laurance, 39–40
Public Accounts Committee, 70
Public good, 43, 138, 175
Public management information
systems (PMIS), 32, 196
Public relations (PR), 60, 69, 196
Public sector data
Big Data and, 13
citizens' reactionary responses and,
31–32
as contested commodity, 105–123
data trade and, 75, 80–85, 87, 90,
94–96
economic growth and, 9

electronic mountains and, 1
four differences of from private sector
data, 31–33
growth rates of, 26
information-centric, 21–23
information sharing failures and, 10,
33, 38, 52
information technology (IT) and, 112
intensification of collection efforts
and, 30
Internal Revenue Service (IRS) and,
112
islands of automation and, 31
reliability of, 29
Public Sector Information Exchange
(PSIE), 8, 196
Act of, 150–152, 170, 185
advice for technologists and, 187–188
Australia and, 11, 125–137, 141, 154,
169, 183–184
business intelligence (BI) and, 187
cadaver exchange and, 122–123
coaxing and, 125–126
coercion and, 125, 179–180, 183, 186
collaboration and, 148, 151, 158,
182–183, 186–187
commoditization and, 133–134, 137,
163–167, 171, 189
common data definitions and,
156–159
compared to other programs, 144–146
computers and, 140–141, 156–157,
168, 170–171, 174, 185
concept of, 125–126
consent and, 125–126, 134, 137,
165–168, 171, 179–180
contested commodities and, 11,
163–167, 176, 180, 183, 185, 189
cooperation and, 126, 128–129, 135,
175, 182, 188
cost of, 153–154
CrimTrac and, 127–137, 141, 183
data-for-dollars model and, 83

Public Sector Information Exchange
(PSIE) (cont.)
democracy challenge and, 161–164,
179
deNovis and, 156–159, 165
Department of Defense (DOD) and,
144
duplication and, 172, 181
economic foundations of, 146–149
efficiency and, 118, 130, 133, 146,
150, 158, 162–163, 169, 172, 180,
185, 187–188
e-government and, 141, 143, 151,
153–154, 163, 170, 176, 184, 188
environmental information and,
138–144
Environmental Protection Agency
(EPA) and, 138–139, 144–146, 150,
182
ethics and, 125, 137, 142–143, 161,
165–168, 176–177, 184
European Union (EU) and, 149, 151,
184
exchange model and, 11, 125,
138–146, 181, 187
existing legislation and, 151–152
expertise and, 153–154
extending, 183–184
fraud and, 174–175, 181
freedom of information (FOI)
challenge and, 175–176
genome commoditization and,
164–167, 183, 189
Government Performance and Results
Act Modernization Act (GPRAMA)
and, 151–153, 182
as government-to-government (G2G)
program, 153
Iceland and, 164–167, 183, 189
implementation of, 182–184
incentives and, 8, 125–138, 151, 153,
156, 159, 166, 168, 171–172, 175,
179–183, 186, 190–191

information asymmetry and, 146–149
information technology (IT) and,
127–129, 131, 133, 139, 143,
153–158, 163, 168, 179, 182–183,
186–189
initial funding of, 152–153
innovation and, 141, 156, 158–159,
170, 179, 184, 190
integration and, 131, 134, 139,
141–144, 150, 153, 163, 170, 172,
174, 176, 187
intellectual property (IP) challenge
and, 172–175
internal information commons and,
173
Internal Revenue Service (IRS) and,
169–170
legal foundations of, 149–153
lessons for citizens and, 188–189
lobbies and, 149–150
Mobbs and, 96, 127–131, 133, 135
monopolies and, 143, 147, 150, 154,
166, 188
morality and, 147, 162–164, 172
Netherlands and, 174–175, 183
NIEM and, 145t, 146, 181, 187
observations for public sector officials
and, 186–187
open data and, 152
ownership issues and, 127–129, 161,
165, 172–175, 179
politics and, 176–177, 179–191
privacy and, 11, 129–130, 133–137,
150–151, 161, 165–172, 181,
184–185, 189
private sector and, 147, 154–158, 175,
182, 187
promise of, 180–182
protecting children and, 134–137
PSMA and, 128, 133
RINIS project and, 174–176, 183
Securities and Exchange Commission
(SEC) and, 175

security and, 131, 138, 150, 152–154, 163

slow legislation challenges and, 149–150

software and, 154–155, 171, 187

strategy for promoting, 179–191

successful program design and, 155–156

supply-chain model and, 11, 125–137, 154

technology and, 125, 129, 133, 135, 137, 139, 142–146, 150, 153–159, 175, 179, 187–188, 191

terrorism and, 176

transparency and, 161, 170, 176

trust and, 126, 130, 134, 140–141, 147, 151, 168, 171, 181

United Kingdom and, 167, 181–182

United States and, 126, 142, 157, 162, 167, 170, 175, 182–185, 188

unsuitable information types and, 134–137

Veterans Affairs (VA) and, 144, 185

visibility and, 153–154

waste and, 180, 184, 188–189

welfare and, 185

Public Sector Mapping Agencies (PSMA), 196

birth of, 85–89

incentives-driven information sharing solution of, 89–94

lessons from, 95–96

Public Sector Information Exchange (PSIE) and, 128, 183

withstanding crisis and, 94–95

Quakers, 116

Quality assurance (QA), 2, 196

Quebec City, 167

Queensland, 90

Radford, John, 34

Radin, Margaret Jane, 108

Rainey, Hal G., 54, 150

Ram, S., 153, 157, 185

Rastello, Sandrine, 154

Raul, Alan Charles, 149, 151, 172

Recorded Future, 78

Recovery.gov, 59

Red Cross, 17–18

Reddick, C. G., 153

Red October, 18

Reduced Output Spatial Dataset (ROSD), 89, 196

Regan, Priscilla M., 32, 154

Regional Information Sharing System (RISS), 44, 196

Reinsel, David, 23–27

Rental voucher program, 185

Research and development (R&D), 82, 131, 154, 196

Restricted commoditization lesson, 115–117

Resurrectionists, 119

Rice, Robert, 116

Right to information (RTI), 70, 196

Riley, Michael, 154

Risk

CrimTrac and, 133

data trade and, 79, 82, 101

existing information sharing approaches and, 52, 54

information sharing crisis and, 33–34

public sector culture of aversion to, 52

Public Sector Information Exchange (PSIE) and, 133, 139, 161–162, 164, 170–171

Ritchie, Jean H., 34

Robbins, Stuart, 7, 45

Roberts, Aladair, 10, 42, 58, 76

Robinson, David, 61

Rocheleau, B., 32, 42, 150

Rogers commission, 13–14

Roseby, R., 136

Rosenberg, Lisa, 62

Ross, Carol Urquhart, 119–121

Ross, Ian, 119–121
Rothstein, Mark A., 29, 76, 164
Rourke, Francis E., 41
Routing of (Inter)National Information
　Streams (RINIS), 174–175, 183, 196
Royal Australian Engineers (RAE),
　199n1, 196
Royal Australian Survey Corps (RA Svy),
　86, 88, 199n1, 196
Royal merchandise, 7–8, 40
Russell, Beth, 84

Sachs, Michael, 172
Safed, 5
Samuelson, Pamela, 173
Sandel, Michael, 108, 162–163, 177
Sanders, Troutman, 99
Sandholm, Tuomas, 141
Sarkar, Mitra Barun, 155
Sarkis, J., 41, 150, 154, 157
Sarmiento, Juan Pablo, 19
Satz, D., 162
Saunders, Carol, 54, 147, 153
Saxenian, AnnaLee, 31
SCENS, 187
Schneider, Anne, 41
Schoenbrod, David, 151
Schoorman, F. D., 54
Schultze, Charles L., 138
Schwindt, Richard, 116
Science journal, 162
Science-on-Sphere (SOS), 84, 196
Scott, Andrew, 69
Secrecy, 10, 31, 58, 61, 78, 114, 139,
　143
Securities and Exchange Commission
　(SEC), 196
　cost of information sharing failure
　　and, 33
　data trade and, 99–100
　Electronic Data Gathering, Analysis
　　and Retrieval (EDGAR) system and,
　　175

Public Sector Information Exchange
　(PSIE) and, 175
waste and, 35
Security
　classified information and, 10
　confidentiality and, 36, 57, 76, 151
　cost and, 153–154
　database volumes on, 26
　data trade and, 78, 83, 100, 102
　Department of Homeland Security
　　(DHS) and, 16–18, 42, 44–45, 48, 68,
　　79–83, 99–100, 103, 144
　existing information sharing
　　approaches and, 44, 48
　fraud and, 2, 33, 36–37, 78, 82, 100,
　　117–118, 133, 158, 174–175, 181
　hackers and, 154–155
　information sharing crisis and, 15–18,
　　23, 26–28, 30
　National Security Agency (NSA) and,
　　26–28, 30
　Public Sector Information Exchange
　　(PSIE) and, 131, 138, 150, 152–154,
　　163
　secrecy and, 10, 31, 58, 61, 78, 114,
　　139, 143
　unclassified information and, 44,
　　156
　visibility and, 153–154
Seife, Charles, 177
Select Bipartisan Committee to
　Investigate the Preparation for and
　Response to Hurricane Katrina, 18
Selfishness, 41–46, 52, 55, 125–126
September 11, 2001, terrorist attacks, 29
　existing information sharing
　　approaches and, 48
　information sharing failures and, 8,
　　15–16
　open data and, 58
　Public Sector Information Exchange
　　(PSIE) and, 130, 150, 154, 169, 184
Serbu, Jared, 1

Shachtman, Noah, 78
Shanahan, Mike, 84
Sharon, L. Caudle, 39, 155
Shelley, Mark C., 39, 184
Sheumaker, Helen, 176
Shipan, Charles R., 186
Shkabatur, Jennifer, 62
Shoham, Yoav, 141
Shulman, Stuart W., 39, 184
Silberman, Neil Asher, 5
Silicon Valley, 31
Simcoe, Timothy S., 154
Simon, Herbert, 21–22
Singer, Natasha, 26
Slavery, 107, 111*t*, 112–113, 115–117
Small Business Administration (SBA),
    36–37, 196
Smith, Raymond W., 155
Smith, Tiffany, 146
Snellen, Ignace, 174
Social Security Administration (SSA), 1,
    29, 80–82, 98, 185, 197
Social Security Number (SSN), 2, 79, 98,
    197
Software
  adding new, 2
  Army and, 51
  Clinger-Cohen Act and, 97
  complexity of, 51, 62
  computers and, 1–2, 24, 30, 50–51, 62,
      69, 79, 86, 97, 139–141, 154–156,
      171, 187
  data documentation and, 62
  EPA and, 79
  federal developers and, 154
  Internal Revenue Code and, 1
  MIT Media Lab and, 140
  open source (OS), 50, 58, 60
  plethora of different systems of, 30
  program sizes and, 51
  Public Sector Information Exchange
      (PSIE) and, 154–155, 171, 187
  risk-assessment, 79

Social Security Administration and,
    1–2
trading algorithms and, 139–141
UK Treasury and, 62
USAJOBS 3.0, 97
voice recognition, 24
Solid rocket booster (SRB), 13, 197
Solomon Islands, 117
Solove, Daniel J., 29, 39
Southern Shephelah, 6
Spence, Patric R., 16
Sperm, 109*t*, 113*f*, 114–116, 123, 176
Sproull, L., 41, 45, 151
Srivastava, Abhishek, 43
Sensitive But Unclassified (SBU), 44,
    156, 196
Stanley, Ellen, 92, 116
Staples, D. S., 41, 55
Statewide Automated Child Welfare
    Information Systems (SACWIS),
    82–83, 196
Stauffacher, Daniel, 19
Stefansson, Kari, 164
Steinberg, Richard, 141
Steinfield, Charles, 155
Stengel, Richard, 35
Stern, E. A., 64, 68
Sternstein, Aliya, 76
Stewart, Richard B., 151
Stiglitz, Joseph E., 58
Stillman, Richard J., 21–22
Stone, Deborah A., 41
Sulitzeanu-Kenan, R., 41
Superdome, 16
Supply-chain model
  Australia and, 11, 125–137, 141, 154,
      183
  CrimTrac and, 127–137, 141, 183
  NCHRC and, 129–135, 137
  NCIDD and, 135–136
  ownership issues and, 127–129
  Public Sector Information Exchange
      (PSIE) and, 11, 125–137, 154

Supportive Housing, 185
Suspicious activity report (SAR), 99,
    196
Sweden, 70, 85, 175
Switzerland, 76
System for Prediction of Environment
    Emergency Dose Information
    (SPEEDI), 20–21, 197
Szech, Nora, 162

Taiwan, 126
Tayi, G. K., 31, 33, 42, 157
Taylor, John A., 31, 144, 147, 168
Technology
  ANCOR and, 137
  Big Data and, 13, 23–30, 40, 102, 167,
    172
  business intelligence (BI) and, 9
  COBOL and, 1–2
  compatibility issues and, 7–8, 49, 86,
    151, 156
  contested commodities and, 106, 108,
    112, 114–115, 119, 121–123
  data mining, 77–78, 102
  data trade and, 77, 79, 84, 86, 98
  deNovis and, 157–158
  electronic mountains and, 2, 9
  existing information sharing
    approaches and, 41, 47–48, 51–52
  Government Performance and Results
    Act Modernization Act (GPRAMA)
    and, 42, 72, 151–153, 182
  information sharing crisis and, 19–20,
    23, 31–32, 36
  innovation and, 9, 19, 31, 60–61, 75,
    85, 94, 115, 141, 156, 158–159, 170,
    179, 184, 190
  integration and, 10, 31–33 (see also
    Integration)
  IRS and, 112
  medical, 108
  modernization and, 35, 42, 50, 52,
    112, 151

NAFIS and, 129
NCHRC and, 133
NCIDD and, 135, 137
NIEM and, 145t, 146, 181, 187
open data and, 60, 63
Peer-to-Patent program and,
    188
Public Sector Information Exchange
    (PSIE) and, 106, 125, 129, 133, 135,
    137, 139, 142–146, 150, 155–159,
    175, 179, 187–188, 191
RINIS and, 175
software and, 1–2, 24, 30, 50–51, 62,
    69, 79, 86, 97, 139–141, 154–156,
    171, 187
Tel Gezer, 2, 3f, 6–7, 11, 126, 179,
    189–191
Tel (man-made mountain), 1–7, 190
Temple Mount, 5
Temporary Assistance for Needy
    Families (TANF), 82–83, 197
Terrorism
  9/11 Commission and, 15–16
  Atta and, 15
  Big Data analysis and, 25
  Boston Marathon bombing and, 25
  Chertoff and, 17
  Department of Homeland Security
    and, 16–18, 42, 44–45, 48, 68, 79–83,
    99–100, 103, 144
  E-Verify program and, 81, 83
  information sharing failures and, 8,
    15–16, 33
  Intelligence Reform and Terrorism
    Prevention Act and, 48
  National Commission on Terrorist
    Attacks and, 15
  National Security Agency (NSA) and,
    26–28, 30
  No-Fly and Selectee List program and,
    83
  Public Sector Information Exchange
    (PSIE) and, 176

September 11, 2001, attacks and, 8,
    15–16, 29, 48, 58, 130, 150, 154,
    169, 184
  TIPOFF program and, 83
  U.S. Patriot Act and, 184
Terrorist Screening Center (TSC), 83,
    197
Terrorist Threat Integration Center
    (TTIC), 83, 197
Tharp, Brent W., 116, 176
Themistocleous, Marinos, 43, 186
Thomas, Page A., 7
Thomas, Richard, 41
Thornmeyer, Rob, 79
Thrane, Lisa A., 39, 184
Thurston, Anne Catherine, 72
TIPOFF program, 83
Tocqueville, Alexis de, 138
Tokyo Electric Power Company
    (TEPCO), 21, 197
Tomes, Nancy, 116, 176
Tomz, Michael, 54
Toxics Release Inventory (TRI), 64, 197
Toxic Substances Control Act (TSCA),
    138–139, 197
Transparency
  agencies and, 32, 58, 61–62, 69–70,
    85, 90, 98, 161, 170, 176
  data trade and, 85, 90, 98
  environmental issues and, 143–144
  open data and, 58, 61–62, 69–70
  Public Sector Information Exchange
    (PSIE) and, 161, 170, 176
  trust and, 32
Transparency and Digital Engagement,
    69
Transplant organs, 112, 116–117,
    149–150, 157
Transportation Security Agency, 83
Trust
  archaeology and, 2, 5–7, 190–191
  collaboration and, 8 (see also
    Collaboration)
  contested commodities and, 118
  data trade and, 75–76, 86, 95, 111t
  existing information sharing
    approaches and, 41, 47, 54
  information sharing crisis and, 17,
    20, 32
  open data and, 58
  Public Sector Information Exchange
    (PSIE) and, 126, 130, 134, 140–141,
    147, 151, 168, 171, 181
Trust Inc., 75
Tschannen-Moran, Megan, 54
Tsunamis, 20
Tucker, Joshua A., 177
Tufte, Edward R., 13
Tufts Health Plan (THP), 158, 197

UK Treasury, 62
Unclassified information, 44, 156
Unemployment, 77, 174
Unitarians, 5
United Kingdom, 9, 197
  Anatomy Act and, 117
  Brown and, 60
  contested commodities and, 115, 117
  data trade and, 75–77
  open data and, 60, 62, 69–70
  Public Sector Information Exchange
    (PSIE) and, 167, 181–182
United Nations (UN), 19, 106, 154, 197
United States, 9
  American Privacy Act and, 84
  biotech products and, 164
  building single portal interface and,
    31
  central banks and, 76–77
  coercion and, 42, 45
  contested commodities and, 117
  data trade and, 76–84
  Death Master File (DMF) and, 29,
    80–81
  exchange model and, 11, 125,
    138–146, 181, 187

United States (cont.)
  George W. Bush and, 43, 48
  information sharing failures and, 10,
    13–18, 34
  International Trade Data System and,
    186–187
  land management and, 37
  Obama and, 24, 37, 43, 47, 58–61,
    142, 153
  open data and, 58–68, 71–73
  Public Sector Information Exchange
    (PSIE) and, 126, 142, 157, 162, 167,
    170, 175, 182–185, 188
United States Patent and Trademark
  Office (USPTO), 188, 197
Urban, Laura A., 142
Urine, 30
U.S. Air Force, 100
USAJOBS, 97
U.S. Army, 17, 51, 144
USAspending.gov, 59
U.S. Bureau of Reclamation (USBR), 37,
  197
U.S. Census Bureau (Census), 65–66,
  101–102, 156, 193
U.S. Citizenship and Immigration
  Services (USCIS), 15, 197
U.S. Coast Guard, 17
U.S. Commodity Futures Trading
  Commission (CFTC), 35, 193
U.S. Computer Matching and Privacy
  Protection Act, 170
U.S. Congress, 1
  contested commodities and, 107
  data trade and, 76, 80, 82–84, 101
  existing information sharing
    approaches and, 42, 46, 49–50
  information sharing crisis and, 15, 22,
    35–37
  open data and, 63
  Public Sector Information Exchange
    (PSIE) and, 141, 147, 151–152, 162,
    168, 173, 175, 177, 185–186

U.S. Department of Agriculture
  (USDA), 22, 35, 37, 78, 84, 139,
  144, 197
U.S. E-Government Act, 151
U.S. Federal Reserve Bank, 77, 99
U.S. Fish and Wildlife Service (USFWS),
  37, 82, 139, 197
U.S. Forest Service, 83–84
U.S. Geological Survey (USGS), 65–66,
  82, 84, 197
U.S. House Oversight and Government
  Reform Committee, 36
U.S. Marine Corps, 78
U.S. National Park Service (USNPS), 37,
  197
U.S. Navy, 78
U.S. Patriot Act, 184
U.S. Postal Service (USPS), 101–102,
  144, 197
U.S. Privacy Act, 168, 170, 181
U.S. Treasury, 33, 78, 99, 139

Value
  contested commodities and, 105–108,
    111–114, 118
  virtual value chain and, 112
Value-added resellers (VARs), 87, 90,
  92–94, 197
Van, Pham Hoang, 108, 115
Van den Broek, Tijs, 61, 69–70,
  173
Vangen, Siv, 42, 54, 148
Vann, Irvin B., 54, 112, 189
Van Wart, Montgomery, 8, 17
Vassilvitskii, Sergei, 141
Vickrey, William, 141
Victoria, 92, 135
Vining, Aidan R., 116
Virtual value chain, 112
Voice recognition software, 24
Voluntary code (VC), 152, 197
Von Solms, R., 54
Vulkan, Nir, 147

Waffle House Index, 77
Walmart, 26
Walport, Mark, 41
Waltzer, Michael, 108
Warren, Charles, 5
Waste
  bilateral information sharing
    agreements and, 96–103
  contested commodities and, 180
  cost of, 33, 35–36
  data trade and, 10, 75, 96–103
  deNovis and, 158
  duplication and, 19, 33, 35–37, 52, 62,
    92, 172, 181
  existing information sharing
    approaches and, 51
  FAA project and, 51
  hazardous, 150, 156
  integration and, 36
  IRS project and, 51
  NCHRC and, 130
  public administration and, 21
  Public Sector Information Exchange
    (PSIE) and, 180, 184, 188–189
Waters, Robin, 87, 135
Weber, Max, 30
Weigle, Brett D., 177
Weiler-Polak, Dana, 34
Weinberger, David, 142
Weingast, Barry R., 186
Welfare
  data trade and, 82, 185
  fraud and, 36–37
  information sharing crisis and, 30, 34,
    36–37
  Public Sector Information Exchange
    (PSIE) and, 185
Wenjing, Liu, 152, 162, 168, 183
Wentling, T., 41, 45
WestLaw, 102
White, Jay D., 78
White, Leonard D., 21
White, Patrick E., 155

White House Office of Science and
  Technology Policy, 60
Wicked problems, 33
Willem, Annick, 54
Wilson, Woodrow, 21, 41
Wisconsin, 167
Wolff, Tobias Barrington, 115
Wolken, G. J., 42, 150–151, 153–154,
  157, 184
Wonderlich, John, 68
Wood, Susan F., 184
World Bank, 106
World's Oldest Bible, 5
World War I, 114, 197
World War II, 114, 197
Wright, John R., 186
Wu, L., 32
Wyman, Katrina M., 151

Yackee, Jason Webb, 186
Yackee, Susan Webb, 186
Yahoo, 21, 26
Yang, Tong-Mou, 41
Yarkon River, 34
Ye, Song, 187
Yen, David C., 183
Yi, Yumi, 58, 60
Yuan, Yu, 188

Zaheer, A., 54
Zakariya, 190–191
Zegart, Amy B., 186
Zhang, J., 41, 46, 150–151, 154, 157
Zhao, Yan, 187
Zuiderwijk, Anneke, 52, 57–58, 63, 68,
  73
Zuurmond, A., 174
Zyskowski, John, 146